Keynes, Money and the Open Economy

Keynes, Money and the Open Economy

Essays in Honour of Paul Davidson: Volume One

Edited by
Philip Arestis

*Professor of Economics and Head of Department of Economics,
University of East London, UK*

Edward Elgar
Cheltenham, UK • Brookfield, US

Published by
Edward Elgar Publishing Limited
8 Lansdown Place
Cheltenham
Glos GL50 2HU
UK

Edward Elgar Publishing Company
Old Post Road
Brookfield
Vermont 05036
US

A catalogue record for this book is available from the British Library

Library of Congress Cataloging-in-Publication Data
Keynes, money, and the open economy : essays in honour of Paul
    Davidson volume 1 / edited by Philip Arestis.
        "Published to celebrate Paul Davidson's well over four decades of
    devotion to the discipline of economics and to Post Keynesian
    Economics in particular"—Introd.
        Includes bibliographical references and index.
        1. Keynesian economics.   2. Money.   3. Monetary policy.
    4. Davidson, Paul.   I. Davidson, Paul.   II. Arestis, Philip, 1941– .
    HB99.7.K3877   1996
    330.15'6—dc20
                                                                                    96–15345
                                                                                    CIP

ISBN 1 85898 312 6

Printed and bound in Great Britain by
Biddles Limited, Guildford and King's Lynn

Contents

v

Notes on the contributors

Philip Arestis is Professor of Economics and Head of Department of Economics, University of East London. He has also taught at the Universities of Surrey and Cambridge (Department of Extra-Mural Studies) and Greenwich University (where he was Head of Economics Division). He was editor of the *British Review of Economic Issues* and joint editor of the *Thames Papers in Political Economy*, and is joint editor of the recently launched *International Papers in Political Economy*. He has been on the editorial board of a number of journals and is a member of the Council of the Royal Economic Society. His publications include his edited *Post-Keynesian Monetary Economics: New Approaches to Financial Modelling* (Edward Elgar, 1988), his co-authored *Introducing Macroeconomic Modelling: An Econometric Study of the United Kingdom* (Macmillan, 1982), his co-edited *Post-Keynesian Economic Theory: A Challenge to Neo-Classical Economics* (Wheatsheaf, 1984), *A Biographical Dictionary of Dissenting Economists* (Edward Elgar, 1992) and *The Elgar Companion to Radical Political Economy* (Edward Elgar, 1994); also his recent book entitled *The Post-Keynesian Approach to Economics: An Alternative Analysis of Economic Theory and Policy* (Edward Elgar, 1992) and his *Money, Pricing, Distribution and Economic Integration* (Macmillan, 1996). He has published widely in journals and books in post Keynesian economics, macroeconomics, monetary economics and applied econometrics.

Robert A. Blecker is Associate Professor of Economics at American University and a Research Associate of the Economic Policy Institute, both in Washington, DC. He received his BA from Yale University and his MA and PhD from Stanford University. His books include *Beyond the Twin Deficits: A Trade Strategy for the 1990s, US Trade Policy and Global Growth: New Directions in the International Economy* (edited); and *Fundamentals of US Foreign Trade Policy* (co-authored with Stephen D. Cohen and Joel R. Paul). His articles have appeared in the *Cambridge Journal of Economics, Journal of Post Keynesian Economics, International Review of Applied Economics*, and *Weltwirtschaftliches Archiv*. Professor Blecker's research includes work on North American trade liberalization, international capital mobility, the US trade deficit and global imbalances, trade policy in the US steel industry, and the effects of foreign trade on income distribution.

Fernando J. Cardim de Carvalho is Professor of Economics at the Federal University of Rio de Janeiro and has taught economics since 1976. He graduated in 1975, University of Sao Paulo, and completed his PhD in 1986, entitled 'Inflation and Indexation in a Post Keynesian Model of Asset Choice'. In 1981, he attended the First International Summer School, Centro di Studi Economici Avanzati, Trieste (Italy). De Carvalho taught in six other Brazilian universities besides undergraduate courses in Rutgers University (1983 to 1986). He was the President of the National Association of Post Graduate Schools of Economics (ANPEC), 1992–94. In addition to his book *Mr Keynes and the Post Keynesians* (Edward Elgar, 1992) his other works include papers published in the *Journal of Post Keynesian Economics*, *Cambridge Journal of Economics* and *Economies et Societés*, as well as chapters in four books in English and papers in Brazilian journals.

David Colander is the Christian A. Johnson Distinguished Professor of Economics at Middlebury College, Middlebury, Vermont. He has authored, co-authored, or edited 30 books and over 80 articles on a wide range of topics. These include *Principles of Economics* (Richard D. Irwin), *History of Economic Thought* (with Harry Landreth, Houghton Mifflin), *Why Aren't Economists as Important as Garbagemen?* (M.E. Sharpe), and *MAP. A Market Anti-Inflation Plan* (with Abba Lerner, Harcourt Brace Jovanovich). He received his PhD from Columbia University and has taught at Columbia University, Vassar College, and the University of Miami as well as Middlebury. He has also been a consultant to Time-Life Films, a consultant to the US Congress, a Brookings Policy Fellow in Washington DC, and a Visiting Scholar at Nuffield College, Oxford. He has been on the board of numerous economic societies and has been President of the Eastern Economic Association and Vice-President of the History of Economic Thought Society. He is currently on the editorial boards of the *Journal of Economic Methodology* and the *Eastern Economic Journal*, and is on the Board of Advisors of the *Journal of Economic Perspectives*. His latest work focuses on Marshallian general equilibrium, post Walrasian economics, and the methodology appropriate to applied policy economics.

Johan Deprez teaches at California State University, Long Beach, US. He has also taught at Alabama State University, Texas Tech University, the University of Manitoba and the University of Tennessee – Knoxville. He has published on a variety of topics in the Post Keynesian analysis of macroeconomics, monetary economics and international economics. These include 'Rediscovering the Missing Visionary of the Middle Way: A review of Skidelsky on Keynes' (*Journal of Post Keynesian Economics,* Spring 1995); 'The Macrodynamics of Advanced Market Economies: The Post Keynesian Perspective of Alfred Eichner' (*Social Science Quarterly,* September 1991);

'Vertical Integration and the Problem of Fixed Capital' (*Journal of Post Keynesian Economics*, Fall 1990); and 'The User Cost of Fixed Capital in Keynes's Theory of Investment', in P. Davidson (ed.), *Can the Free Market Pick Winners? What Determines Investment* (M.E. Sharpe, 1993). He is currently editing, with John T. Harvey, *Foundations of International Economics: A Post Keynesian Analysis*.

Sheila C. Dow is Reader in the Department of Economics at the University of Stirling where she has been teaching since 1979, with two periods of leave (at the University of Toronto in 1982–83 and the University of Cambridge in 1987). She was educated at the Universities of St Andrews, Manitoba, McMaster and Glasgow. She worked for two years for the Bank of England and for four years for the Department of Finance of the Government of Manitoba, latterly as Senior Economist. Her research interests include post Keynesian economics, monetary theory, history of thought and methodology and regional finance. She is the author of *Money Matters* (with Peter Earl), *Macroeconomic Thought, Financial Markets and Regional Economic Development, Money and the Economic Process* (Edward Elgar, 1993) and *The Methodology of Macroeconomic Thought* (Edward Elgar, 1996), and co-editor of *Money, Method and Keynes: Selected Papers of Victoria Chick* (with Philip Arestis) and *Keynes, Knowledge and Uncertainty* (with John Hillard, Edward Elgar, 1995). In addition she has published a wide range of journal articles and contributions to monographs.

Gary A. Dymski is Associate Professor of Economics at the University of California, Riverside. He has also taught at the University of Southern California. He is on the editorial boards of the *International Review of Applied Economics* and *Geoforum*, and was formerly on the editorial board of the *Review of Radical Political Economics*. He is also a Research Associate of the Economic Policy Institute in Washington, DC. He has co-edited *New Directions in Monetary Macroeconomics. Essays in Honour of Hyman P. Minsky* (University of Michigan Press, 1994) with Robert Pollin, and *Transforming the US Financial System* (M.E. Sharpe, 1993) with Pollin and Gerald Epstein. He has published articles on topics including banking, information and Keynesian uncertainty, race and discrimination in credit markets, the LDC debt crisis, the political economy of finance and urban growth, and the theory of exploitation.

James K. Galbraith is Professor at the Lyndon B. Johnson School of Public Affairs and at the Department of Government, University of Texas at Austin, where he teaches economics and other subjects. He holds degrees from Harvard (AB *magna cum laude*, 1974) and Yale (PhD in Economics, 1981). He studied economics as a Marshall Scholar at King's College, Cambridge in

1974–75, and then served in several positions on the staff of the US Congress, including Executive Director of the Joint Economic Committee in 1981–82. He was a Guest Scholar at the Brookings Institution in 1985. Galbraith is co-author with William Darity Jr of *Macroeconomics*, a new textbook from Houghton Mifflin. He is also the author of *Balancing Acts: Technology, Finance and the American Future* (Basic Books, 1989), and co-author with Robert L. Heilbroner of *The Economic Problem*, a principles text (Prentice-Hall). He contributes frequently to *The American Prospect, Challenge*, the *Texas Observer*, and a variety of professional journals. Galbraith is a Research Associate of the Economic Policy Institute. He is presently Chief Technical Adviser to the State Planning Commission of the P.R. China, on a United Nations project on strengthening macroeconomic institutions and regulation.

G.C. Harcourt is Reader in the History of Economic Theory, University of Cambridge, Fellow, Jesus College, Cambridge and Professor Emeritus, University of Adelaide. He has taught at the Universities of Adelaide, Cambridge and Toronto. He is the author, co-author, editor or co-editor of 16 books; his best known book is *Some Cambridge Controversies in the Theory of Capital* (1972) and he has published five volumes of selected essays, the last one being *Capitalism, Socialism and Post-Keynesianism* (Edward Elgar, 1995). He is the author or co-author of numerous papers in learned journals and edited volumes, including several major survey articles and many intellectual biographies. He has been or is editor or joint editor of several journals, including *Australian Economic Papers* and the *Cambridge Journal of Economics*. He was the economist on the Australian Labor Party's National Committee of Enquiry in 1978–79 and a leader of the anti-Vietnam War movement in South Australia from 1967 to 1975. In June 1994 he was made an Officer in the General Division of the Order of Australia (AO) 'for service to economic theory and to the history of economic thought'.

Peter Howells is Reader in the Department of Economics at the University of East London. He studied at the University of Kent at Canterbury and the LSE. He is the joint author (with Keith Bain) of *An Introduction to Monetary Economics* (1985), *Government and the Economy* (1987), *Understanding Markets* (1988) and *Financial Markets and Institutions* (1994). He has published extensively on endogenous money in *Journal of Post Keynesian Economics* (1992, 1995), *Cyprus Journal of Economics* (1990, 1995) and *Review of Social Economy* (1991). Other papers on aspects of monetary economics have appeared in *Eastern Economic Journal* (1991), *Journal of Economic Issues* (1992) and *Cambridge Journal of Economics* (forthcoming) – all three with Philip Arestis – and in *Weltwirtschaftliches Archiv* (1995).

Claudio Sardoni is Associate Professor of History of Economics at the University of Rome La Sapienza, Italy. His research interests are mainly directed towards classical and Marxian political economy and Keynesian and post Keynesian economics. In particular, he is engaged in the attempt to point out and explore the analytical relations between these two economic traditions. He has published several works in this area. Among his more recent works are: *Marx and Keynes on Economic Recession* (Wheatsheaf and New York University Press, 1987); 'Chapter 18 of the General Theory: Its Methodological Importance' (*Journal of Post Keynesian Economics,* 1990); 'Effective Demand and Income Distribution in the General Theory' (*Journal of Income Distribution,* 1993); 'The General Theory and the Critique of Decreasing Returns' (*Journal of the History of Economic Theory,* 1994); 'Keynes's Vision: Method, Analysis and "Tactics"' (with G.C. Harcourt), in J.B. Davis (ed.), *The State of Interpretation of Keynes* (Kluwer Academic Press, 1994); 'Interpretations of Kalecki', in G.C. Harcourt, A. Roncaglia and R. Rowley (eds), *Income and Employment in Theory and Practice* (Macmillan, 1996).

Malcolm Sawyer is Professor of Economics and Head of the Economics Division at the University of Leeds and formerly Professor of Economics at the University of York. He is the author of several books including *Macroeconomics in Question* (Harvester Wheatsheaf and M.E. Sharpe, 1982), *The Economics of Michal Kalecki* (Macmillan and M.E. Sharpe, 1982, 1985), *The Challenge of Radical Political Economy* (Harvester Wheatsheaf and Barnes and Noble, 1989) and *Unemployment, Imperfect Competition and Macroeconomics* (Edward Elgar, 1995). He is the managing editor of *International Review of Applied Economics*, joint editor of the recently launched *International Papers in Political Economy*, and editor of the series *New Directions in Modern Economics*, published by Edward Elgar. He has recently co-edited *A Biographical Dictionary of Dissenting Economists* (Edward Elgar, 1992) and *The Elgar Companion to Radical Political Economy* (Edward Elgar, 1994). He has published widely in journals and books in the areas of industrial economics, macroeconomics and political economy. His current research interests include the theory of industrial policy and the conceptualization of competition and markets in economic theory, the causes and cures for unemployment, as well as continuing to work on post Keynesian macroeconomics.

Introduction

Philip Arestis

This is the first of two volumes published to celebrate Paul Davidson's well over four decades of devotion to the discipline of economics and to post Keynesian economics in particular. Over this time, Paul Davidson has acquired enormous respect and admiration from colleagues of varied persuasions, as evidenced by the contributions to these two volumes. He is one of the most highly respected proponents of post Keynesian economics.

Paul Davidson's contributions to our discipline are simply vast. They span such a wide range as natural resources, outdoor recreation, public finance, macroeconomic and monetary theory and policy (both domestic and international), income distribution, economic problems of developing economies, history of economic thought and methodology. With Sidney Weintraub he established the *Journal of Post Keynesian Economics* (*JPKE*) and has been its editor ever since its inception in 1978 (co-editor with Weintraub until Sidney's death in 1983). What is particularly interesting about the *JPKE* is that it not only created a platform for 'dissenting economists' but also kept open the lines of communication with the mainstream. All of us who have had some association with the journal know very well and appreciate the enormous amount of time and energy the Davidsons – for we should never forget the heroic efforts of Louise too – have expended for our intellectual development and enjoyment. Paul Davidson has participated in practically every major conference involving Post Keynesian economics, and many others, and has given lectures and seminars to students and colleagues throughout the world. And he has helped a great number of colleagues in their careers, especially the younger members of our profession at that crucial stage of their first published paper, and even before this stage, at the postgraduate level.

Paul Davidson was born on 23 October 1930 in New York and grew up in Brooklyn. His family put a great deal of emphasis on education and they wanted Paul to become a 'professional', preferably a medical doctor. But Paul Davidson ultimately chose economics. He came to economics, however, after he had spent some time in the natural sciences. On graduating in Chemistry and Biology at Brooklyn College, he embarked upon postgraduate work in Biochemistry at the University of Pennsylvania, and even undertook research for a dissertation on DNA. He also taught in the Medical and Dental Schools at the same time. But he soon lost interest and changed gear radically by taking an MBA (his thesis was entitled 'The Statistical Analysis of Economic Time Series'), thereby preparing himself for the world of commerce. It must have been at that time when Paul, a trained biochemist used to experimental decision and statistical inference, realized he could do a better job as an economist. He thus returned to the University of Pennsylvania to do a PhD in Economics under the supervision of Sidney Weintraub. Weintraub's influence on Paul Davidson explains his early interests in Keynes's macroeconomics and in the distribution of income. His dissertation, therefore, focused on a historical exegesis of aggregate income distribution analysis, appropriately entitled 'Theories of Relative Shares', and in 1959 he was awarded the degree of PhD in Economics.

In June 1951 Paul met Louise, and in December 1952 they married. Ever since they have been inseparable – I cannot recall a time when I saw Paul without Louise, or Louise without Paul, at conferences or indeed anywhere else. After teaching economics at Pennsylvania and Rutgers for a short time, he joined the 'real' world as the Assistant Director of the Economics Division for the Continental Oil Company. A year in the corporate sector proved enough for Paul Davidson and he returned to the University of Pennsylvania. In 1966 he moved to Rutgers University, where he stayed for the next 20 years before joining the University of Tennessee in 1986 to take up the Holly Chair of Excellence in Political Economy.

In his critique of mainstream economics he identifies and rejects three axioms of orthodoxy, and uses them as a platform for his own contributions. These are the *axiom of substitutability* (which restores Say's Law and denies the possibility of involuntary unemployment); the *axiom of reals* (which affirms the neutrality of money which is a veil and does not matter; real decisions depend only on relative prices, and income effects are always outweighed by substitution effects); and the *axiom of ergodicity* (which views the future as probabilistic rather than fundamentally uncertain). Paul Davidson argues that it is vital that these axioms be abandoned in order to pave the way to a post Keynesian economics logically consistent with Keynes's analytical framework.

The object of his analysis is a monetary production economy, with money and money contracts at the heart of the system. The money rate of interest is uniquely important in the system precisely because contracts are denominated in money terms; it is this property that can ultimately produce involuntary unemployment. It is, indeed, through the rate of interest that money exerts its impact on the demand for capital goods, thereby controlling capital accumulation. A further crucial consequence of contracts being denominated in money terms is that a close integration of the real and monetary sectors is inevitable, which totally discredits the so-called 'classical dichotomy'. Another feature of Paul Davidson's analysis is that money is endogenously determined in a world of uncertainty, as opposed to risk, and in the modern credit-money banking system. Such a system, he claims, is precisely what Keynes had in mind, and indeed represents the real world. What Davidson terms the 'Keynes School of Political Economy' begins from the premise that monetary and real sectors are closely linked, where the money-wage rate is a fundamental magnitude but with income distribution being of lesser importance by comparison with post Keynesian analysis.

The Keynes School is at the centre of the political spectrum, and as such rejects both marginal productivity theories on the right and surplus approaches on the left. At the methodological level the economy is non-ergodic in real historical time, so that theories and policies based on logical time are disregarded. In this analysis the future is uncertain. It unfolds from decisions made in the present which, although embodying the results of past events, cannot provide probabilistic estimates of what the future might entail. This thesis, along with Sidney Weintraub's aggregate supply function (which involves productivity questions), and the finance motive (which implies a unique demand for money to finance business outlays before they materialize), are the main contributions which make Paul Davidson a post Keynesian. The finance motive enabled him to show that the *IS/LM* framework did not yield a unique equilibrium, since the two relationships are interdependent. More importantly, though, it enabled him to integrate monetary analysis into Keynes's general theory in an original way. The ideas embedded in the developments described here led to his early book with Eugene Smolensky, *Aggregate Supply and Demand Analysis* (Harper and Row, 1964) and to his *magnum opus, Money and the Real World* (Macmillan, 1972).

One aspect of post Keynesian economics which still needs further development is international economics. Here, too, Paul Davidson's contributions have left their mark. In a series of articles and books, he has extended his ideas to the international economic landscape, drawing on his extensive knowledge of, and experience in, international economic relations. The proposal to revise the world's monetary system is his most important contribution in this area. Drawing on Keynes's writings, but substantially extending them, he suggests the creation of an international money clearing unit in a way that puts the onus of balance of payments imbalances on to surplus countries, in a global effective demand framework. These ideas are rooted in his *International Money and the Real World* (Macmillan, 1982) and further elaborated in recent academic articles. It is worth noting at this stage that a certain amount of his work has been put together in two volumes edited by Louise Davidson and published under the titles *Money and Employment, The Collected Writings of Paul Davidson*, Volume 1 (Macmillan, 1990), and *Inflation,*

Open Economies and Resources, The Collected Writings of Paul Davidson, Volume 2 (Macmillan and New York University Press, 1991). His views on post Keynesian macroeconomics have been assembled recently in the book appropriately entitled *Post Keynesian Macroeconomic Theory: A Foundation for Successful Economic Policies for the Twenty-First Century* (Edward Elgar, 1994). In this book Paul Davidson shows how post Keynesian economics, which has evolved from Keynes's 'original logical framework', is the general case applicable to the real world.

In the present two volumes friends of Paul Davidson elaborate upon a number of the issues emanating from his work, which have been briefly touched on or mentioned above. In addition, there is a small number of entries which, although not directly related to Paul Davidson's work, fall, nonetheless, well within his interests as shown in the entries themselves. The current volume begins with an essay on Paul Davidson's views on Keynes and contrasts them with other writers' views. The publication in 1992 of Donald Moggridge's biography of Keynes and Robert Skidelsky's Volume II of Keynes's life seemed an ideal opportunity to compare and contrast the views of these authors on *The General Theory* with those of Paul Davidson. It can also be argued that, given Davidson's emphasis on Keynes's economics, this is the obvious way to begin the proceedings of this volume. The next chapter stays with Keynes's views but this time they are contrasted with those of Einstein, in a piece executed by James Galbraith. The chapter that follows is still concerned with contrasts between Paul Davidson's views and those of other economists. David Colander, however, sets himself a different task. He tries to answer the question of why Paul Davidson has had a hard time communicating his ideas to the mainstream.

Geoff Harcourt and Claudio Sardoni, in their essay entitled '*The General Theory of Employment, Interest and Money*: Three views', find that overall the three views they deal with are pretty much in agreement, though emphasis and details naturally differ. All three authors are sceptical of attempts to fit Keynes's system into a Walrasian framework. Davidson shares Keynes's Marshallian analytical background and his objective of having money there right from the start of the analysis. Skidelsky and Davidson agree on the importance of uncertainty and expectations in Keynes's analysis. Skidelsky in addition stresses the influence of Keynes's own psychological make-up and interest in the psychological factors in original work on the form and approach taken in *The General Theory*. The only serious disagreement concerns the significance of Keynes's decision to leave out the sections on the cooperative, neutral and entrepreneur economies which he initially used to analyse the crucial differences between the classical system and his own new one. He put in their place the analysis of the labour market and took Pigou's 1933 book on the theory of unemployment as the definitive view of the representative classical economist instead. He identified Say's Law as the set of neutral equilibria stretching along the coinciding aggregate demand and supply schedules and argued that competition between entrepreneurs would take the economy to the highest full employment point. Moggridge approves, the others dissent, finding Keynes's argument incoherent at this point. Moggridge accepts Keynes's own account of how *The General Theory* was formed and of what the most important innovations were. All agree that the integration of the multiplier into the new system of thought added an ingredient which had been lacking from the *Treatise on Money* and *Can Lloyd George Do It?*, which made the arguments of the last two incoherent at key points.

In the chapter entitled 'Keynes, Einstein and scientific revolution', James Galbraith reviews the links between Keynes and Einstein, and shows that Keynes was familiar with the basis of relativity theory in the abandonment of Euclid's axiom of parallels, just as he was preparing to write *The General Theory*. Einstein had overthrown Newton's physics, which presupposed an absolute separation of space and time, and which held that the universe was neither more nor less than the sum of its component particles. Both of these views had analogues in classical economics. The analogue of space is the market. The analogue of Newtonian time is money. Just as time is absolutely separated from space, money is absolutely separated from the market. As for reductionism, economists are taught that societies, like Newton's universe, are nothing more than the sum of their individual components. This is the doctrine of microfoundations. The absolute separation of time and space collapsed with special relativity. The newly unified concept, space–time, also destroyed the Euclidean concept of emptiness extending forever in all directions. Space–time is curved. The universe is, then, no longer reducible to its elements; you can no longer get to the whole merely by adding up the parts. Keynes's *General Theory* attacks both Newton's reductionism and his space–time dichotomy, as both were reflected in classical economics. Keynes sought to disestablish the absolute space of classical markets, and to end the separation of markets from the world of money. Keynes characterized his theory as a monetary theory of production. For Keynes, the second classical postulate, the upward-sloping supply curve of labour, was akin to the axiom of parallels in Euclid's geometry. In rejecting it, Keynes effectively threw over the whole idea of a self-contained labour market. In its place, he offered the revolutionary idea that employment was determined by effective monetary demand for output. Involuntary unemployment in the strict sense would now be possible in economies. To complete his theory, Keynes rewrote the theory of interest and money, tying these elements together. The classical dichotomy in economics had been broken. This, along with the deconstruction of labour and capital markets, meant that the reductionist idea of microfoundations had also necessarily to be abandoned.

David Colander, in his contribution entitled '*AS/AD, AE/AP, IS/LM* and *Z*', relates Paul Davidson's *Z* model to the standard mainstream *AS/AD* and *AE/AP, IS/LM* models. In doing so Colander hopes to make Paul Davidson's *Z* model understandable to mainstream economists. The central idea is that Davidson's *Z* model included microfoundations into its core whereas mainstream economics added it in a way that was inconsistent with the Keynesian model and ended up with two inconsistent specifications of aggregate supply. Paul Davidson's *Z* model avoided this inconsistency, but because it looked very neoclassical, incorporating interdependences between aggregate supply and demand along with diminishing marginal returns, mainstream economics did not see the important implications of that *Z* model. David Colander's work has separated out aggregate supply and demand interdependences and issues of diminishing marginal returns, thereby making the inconsistency in the mainstream model clearer. By translating Davidson's *Z* model and the *AE/AP* model into a common model, Colander shows their similarity. *AS/AD* curves are then derived in price/real output space and related to the *IS/LM* models, demonstrating how mainstream macroeconomics confused an aggregate equilibrium curve with an *AD* curve. By respecifying an *AD* curve in price/output space based on first principles, it is shown how Paul Davidson's demand/output curve can be derived from the correctly specified mainstream *AD* curve. This *AD* curve is then combined with a perfectly inelastic *AS* curve, which reflects the interdependence of *AS* and *AD*, thus demonstrating that, correctly specified, the mainstream Keynesian model would arrive at the *Z* model.

Paul Davidson has always emphasized monetary phenomena along with Keynes's views on philosophy. It is, therefore, fitting to continue with Sheila Dow's contribution which touches on both. Her chapter, 'Keynes's philosophy and post Keynesian monetary theory', begins with the observation that the interdependence of Keynes's philosophy and this monetary theory is evident in Paul Davidson's work. This chapter focuses explicitly on the connections between the two, taking Paul Davidson's contributions as a starting-point. The expression of this interdependence in Paul Davidson's work emanates from his emphasis on the central role of money as the denominator of contracts in real economic processes, the roots of Keynes's demand for money in uncertainty and the interrelationships between liquidity preference, production and investment. The close connection between uncertainty and liquidity preference has been drawn out further by the recent interest in the literature of Keynes's philosophy; the current state of thinking is outlined here, focusing on the shift of emphasis from the speculative demand for money to the precautionary demand. This shift, along with a more complex understanding of both the speculative and precautionary demands for money and their relationship to uncertainty, has been helped by a more rigorous analysis of uncertainty itself and its relationship with different degrees of weight. Further recent work has been emphasizing the interrelationship between the supply of credit and liquidity preference, by focusing on banks' own liquidity preference. The connection between these ideas of Keynes's monetary theory and the theory of credit creation as an application of liquidity preference theory has its foundations in Keynes's philosophy in general and this theory of uncertainty in particular. An account is given of how the recent literature on Keynes's philosophy has taken Keynes's theory of uncertainty further, and what implications this has for the theory of credit creation. The focus in the explanation offered is on risk assessment.

Debates within the post Keynesian approach to money, finance and interest rates have been rich and varied. Malcolm Sawyer, in 'Money, finance and interest rates: some post Keynesian reflections', considers some of these debates with special reference to the writings of Kalecki and Keynes. The chapter begins by identifying four themes in post Keynesian macroeconomics, which often serve to distinguish it from the mainstream. The first theme is the question of causality between saving and investment, where the direction runs from the latter to the former. The second theme concerns the relationship between investment expenditure and the creation of money, where the expansion of investment requires finance through the creation of money. The third theme is that money is credit-driven, created in response to the 'needs of trade'. The fourth theme relates to the role of money with particular attention given to the forces determining the rate of interest. There is a 'general background' to the analysis which is that the creation of endogenous money depends on the demand for and supply of bank loans. But whether the money created in this way remains in circulation depends crucially on the demand for money as a stock. Another dimension of the 'general background' is the 'principle of increasing risk' which is seen to apply to all borrowing and lending. Simple ideas have their place in economic analysis, and amongst those the multiplier and endogenous money have a predominant position. It is argued that in effect the two simple ideas that investment stimulates economic activity and saving and that money is largely credit money created by the banking system in response to demands for loans contain valuable insights and are more relevant than their counterparts adhered to by the orthodox approach (saving stimulates investment and money is exogenous and controllable). But the complexities of the real world are such that these ideas have to be modified and placed in the relevant institutional setting.

Fernando Jose Cardim de Carvalho, in the chapter that follows, continues with the issues raised in Malcolm Sawyer's chapter, but he considers 'Paul Davidson's rediscovery of Keynes's finance motive and the liquidity preference versus loanable funds debate'. Among the debates that took place after the publication of *The General Theory*, the exchange between Keynes and Ohlin was certainly one of the most fertile in its implications for the development of Keynes's novel approach to economics. In this debate, Keynes defended his liquidity preference theory of interest rates against Ohlin's neo-Wicksellian loanable funds model, according to which interest rates were determined by the demand for and the supply of credit, themselves determined by desired or planned investment and saving. Keynes reaffirmed his proposition that interest was the reward for accepting illiquid assets and tried to disentangle the roles of money market variables, such as the demand for and supply of money, from those of debt creation and credit. In the first, the finance motive to demand money was introduced, and in the second the relation between short- and long-term finance was clarified, through the distinction between finance and funding. This debate, notwithstanding its importance, was largely forgotten. A few authors, among whom Paul Davidson is one of the most important, were able, by developing Keynes's arguments, to complete a liquidity preference model that became a hallmark of post Keynesian monetary theory. Paul Davidson used the finance motive not only to clarify the connection between money and real transactions, including capital assets, but also to demonstrate Keynes's emphatic statement that monetary and real variables, such as output and investment, could not be analysed separately. The chapter offers a brief review of Keynes's initial arguments, which allows the exploration of Davidson's developments.

Gary Dymski in 'Money as a "time machine" in the new financial world', explores one defining economic feature of money, that is the power it conveys to its holders to transform value across real time in an environment of fundamental uncertainty. The special economic roles of banks and of liquid assets emanate, in part, from their participation in the creation, distribution, and safe storage of the 'time machine' assets of money and credit for households and businesses. This chapter reinterprets these insights in the context of the continuous innovation, deregulation, and globalization that has inundated the financial system since Paul Davidson's *Money in the Real World*. These financial transformations are so profound that they force a reconsideration of the economic roles and social context of money, credit and banks. Financial consolidation, heightened competition, and increasing financial volatility have led to deregulation and the breakdown of segmented banking markets. In conjunction with the information and communication revolutions, they have also led to the emergence of robust primary and secondary direct credit markets, and to the transformation of broker and dealer firms into managers of sophisticated, customer-oriented mutual funds. As a result of these institutional transformations, money as a 'time machine' is no longer available for those with lower incomes and little wealth, who are now often excluded from mainstream financial participation; and the very meaning of money has changed even for those who remain financial citizens in the brave new world of securitization and globalization. The chapter also examines the consequences of this transformation in money and credit for policies aimed at ensuring economic access and at maintaining financial stability. In addition, the implications of this transformation for post Keynesian macroeconomic models are considered, with the conclusion that class divisions now affect not only the division of labour, but access to capital and financial security as well.

Peter Howells, in the chapter, 'Endogenous money and the "state of trade"', argues that what makes the money supply endogenous does not lie critically with the behaviour of the central bank but with the origin of the quantities to which commercial banks passively respond. It is the assertion that the demand for loans (and deposits) originates with other variables in the system, usually summarized in the phrase the 'state of trade', that makes money endogenous. The relevance to the quantity theory is that if the 'state of trade' determines the demand for loans (and the supply of deposits) then the causal order is reversed. It is changes in nominal income that cause money and not the other way round. It may very well be, then, that the obituaries for the quantity theory are premature. Moreover, the state of trade which drives the creation of new deposits through the demand for loans is the same state of trade which drives the demand for money and ensures that the new deposits are willingly held. Money becomes a *result*, and not a *cause* of anything. If the money supply is endogenous, in the sense described here, then the sources of (and antidotes to) inflation are to be found elsewhere, in conflict over shares of output, for example. While the price setting and quantity taking part of the theory is readily accepted, the chapter questions whether the 'state of trade' is an accurate summary of the origin of demand for new loans and deposits in a world where people borrow increasingly for speculative purposes. If it is not, then the supply of new loans (and deposits) can clearly vary from the demand for deposits. Loans can, for example, create 'excess' deposits. The effect of these excess deposits then depends, as it always did in exogenous monetary regimes, on how people respond to the excess.

Johan Deprez, in 'Davidson on the labour market in a money production economy', explores Paul Davidson's views on labour markets. Building on the work of Sidney Weintraub, Paul Davidson situates the labour market explicitly in a monetary context where the wage bargain is made in monetary terms, the demand for labour is derived from the monetary demand that firms face, and the supply of labour is influenced by liquidity preference and other monetary considerations. By implication wage rigidity is an outcome of the way a capitalist economy works by helping to reduce the uncertainty that firms face, as opposed to being a cause of unemployment. This chapter reviews Paul Davidson's work on the labour market, shows how it fits into his body of work as a whole and contrasts it with that of classical economics and with alternative heterodox views. The analysis points to certain ways in which the Davidsonian approach can be strengthened and extended, without losing the central components that Paul Davidson adheres to. This includes a careful distinction between the roles of expectations, forward contracts, and realized sales that results in the formation of the effective demand for labour. The distinctions between equilibrium, disequilibrium and full employment are carefully made, as is the possible distinction between short-period and long-period equilibrium. The avenues by which money and liquidity preference can enter into the labour supply decision are enumerated. The chapter points out how the Davidsonian approach is a general one that can capture a variety of macroeconomic scenarios and can incorporate the classical analysis of the labour market as a special case. The special case assumes away uncertainty, history, money and liquidity preference. If we agree with Davidson that these components are fundamental to a proper understanding of the economy, then the classical special case is irrelevant for analysing the real world.

The remaining parts of this volume are concerned with open economy issues. The first in this regard is my contribution with Malcolm Sawyer where we deal with the topical issue of 'European monetary integration: A post Keynesian critique and some proposals'. The themes of this chapter are that the creation of high levels of economic activity require high levels of effective demand, and that there is a need to create the appropriate institutional arrangements necessary to support high levels of effective demand. The main objections raised against the effectiveness of expansionary demand policies to secure full employment, the existence of non-accelerating inflation rate of unemployment (NAIRU) and the problems of funding of any resulting budget deficits, including the responses of financial markets, are rejected. We suggest that they do not present insurmountable difficulties, although it is argued that high levels of demand would be a necessary but not a sufficient condition for the achievement of high levels of employment and economic activity. The proponents of an independent European system of central banks (IESCB) argue that this institution, assumed to be given the objective of price stability, would not be subject to the short-term pressures of political popularity and expediency which are thought to influence many government decisions on interest rates and monetary policy. The extent to which the creation of an IESCB will affect the levels and distribution of unemployment and economic growth in the European Union (EU) is examined, and the case for an IESCB, with price stability as its sole objective, is rejected on the grounds that it would worsen the performance of the real economy in terms of employment and unemployment, levels of and rates of growth of national output. An alternative mechanism at the European level is thus needed which would be more conducive to the achievement of high levels of employment. The essential features of such an institutional arrangement are sketched under the rubric of a European clearing agency. This alternative is firmly rooted in Keynes's scheme for an international clearing union and in Paul Davidson's work in the area.

The second contribution on the international front is Robert A. Blecker's chapter on 'International trade and the real world'. His essay is in the spirit of Paul Davidson's work on *International Money and the Real World*, but addressed to the more 'microeconomic' side of international trade. In recent years, new theoretical models have shown that free trade is not always the best policy even from a neoclassical perspective. At the same time, traditional concerns about the distributional effects of trade as well as the non-trivial adjustment costs of trade liberalization have been reflected in popular opposition to economic integration schemes. The reaction of mainstream trade economists to this set of challenges has been a curious one, including the assertion that their own theoretical models are unreliable guides to policy and the continued promotion of trade liberalization agreements in spite of mounting evidence of their social costs. This chapter recounts some of the most important instances of this intellectual dissonance, including the models of strategic trade policy, the implications of scale economies for trade, and the distributional and social consequences of trade liberalization. The ways in which orthodox economists have attempted to skew debates over these issues is examined in some detail. An alternative approach to international trade, derived from the post Keynesian and institutionalist traditions, is also discussed. The chapter concludes by suggesting a new form of internationalism, in which more gradual economic integration is accompanied by social and macroeconomic policies designed to offset the potentially harmful consequences of abolishing barriers to international trade and investment. The real reasons behind the current drive toward the formation of trading blocks is also addressed; they have more to do with the strategic imperatives of multinational corporate enterprises than with the real economic interests of ordinary citizens.

A number of colleagues and friends have suggested that a *Festschrift* for Paul Davidson is premature given that he is as productive as ever and no doubt will continue to be so for many years to come. There is a great deal in this reservation. On the other hand, whilst appreciating fully that Paul Davidson's intellectual capital is inexhaustible, celebrating his vast achievements and recognizing the immense debt we owe him for his contributions, his generous help to most of us and his continuous friendship, could take place at any time. Celebrating all these on his 65th birthday seems to be most appropriate. On behalf of all the contributors to the two volumes, I would also wish to express our gratitude to Louise Davidson for her great friendship to all of us and the enormous help she has been giving us not just on matters relating to the *JPKE* but on others as well, not least the most efficient and excellent organization of those extremely stimulating, generous, hugely successful and immensely enjoyable conferences in Tennessee and elsewhere. At a more personal level, I would like to thank her for the help she gave me in preparing the two volumes.

Special thanks must go to the contributors for their willingness to respond to my comments and suggestions with forbearance and good humour. Thanks are also extended to June Daniels and Christine Nisbet of the Department of Economics, University of East London, for their secretarial assistance. Finally, Edward Elgar and his staff, especially Julie Leppard, Jo Perkins and Dymphna Evans, as always have provided excellent support throughout the period it took to prepare both volumes.

1. *The General Theory of Employment, Interest and Money*: Three views

G.C. Harcourt and Claudio Sardoni

In responding to Philip Arestis's request for a contribution to the volume of essays in honour of Paul Davidson, a good friend of G.C.H. of well over 30 years' standing, and of C.S. for 15 years or more, we thought that a 'compare and contrast' essay on interpretations of *The General Theory* would be a peculiarly suitable and appropriate subject. For it would enable us both to outline Paul's own deep and astute interpretation and to compare it with the interpretations in two recent biographies of Keynes – Donald Moggridge's magisterial economist's life (1992) and Volume II of Robert Skidelsky's superb biography (1992), which is centred on the creation, content and criticism of *The General Theory*. Moreover, his original and compelling interpretation has earned the reproach of Don Patinkin because of its post Keynesian characteristics (see Skidelsky, 1992, p. xi), so it seemed a good idea also to compare his arguments and approaches with those of one of America's leading post Keynesian economists.[1]

DAVIDSON'S KEYNESIAN ANTECEDENTS

Ever since G.C.H. has known Paul Davidson – they first met in Bristol in the early 1960s when Davidson gave him Hell all the way through his paper to John Whitaker's seminar – he has always referred G.C.H. (and everyone else) back to the Old Testament (*A Treatise on Money*) and the New Testament (*The General Theory*) for the evidence and authority for his propositions. (The *Tract on Monetary Reform* (1923) also receives honourable mention at times – perhaps it is the central core of the economists' Dead Sea Scrolls?) We doubt if there is anyone else in the profession so adept and thorough at backing up their analytical arguments with telling and clinching quotes from Keynes. Davidson himself was introduced to these great texts by his mentor, the late Sidney Weintraub, who was himself a latter-day St Paul. They both also regarded Marshall as a modern Moses, one who was not only the channel through which the Law was received but also *the* guide to theoretical analysis.[2] In the essay we want to show how this background has shaped Davidson's views of *The General Theory* and of the Keynesian approach to economic theory in general.

DAVIDSON'S INTERPRETATION OF KEYNES – AND AFTER

Davidson developed his ideas over many years in articles and in his *magnum opus, Money and the Real World* (1972, 1978). We have already mentioned how strong an influence Marshall was on Sidney Weintraub and Davidson. It is no accident then that the analytical structure of Davidson's work is usually in terms of supply and demand functions and curves, sometimes Marshall's, sometimes, of course, the aggregate versions of *The General Theory*. So partial is Davidson to supply and demand curves that when he came to analyse the determination of investment in *Money and the Real World* (and in articles leading up to it), he departed from Keynes's emphasis on a comparison between the marginal efficiency of capital and the money rate of interest. He argued instead in terms of stock and flow supply and demand curves, using present value calculations containing the external rate of interest as the discount factor. Furthermore, the analysis takes in Keynes's own (in the *Tract on Monetary Reform*) of spot and future markets (applied there to the analysis of the forward exchanges) in order to determine the short-period flow of expenditure on new capital goods in the economy as a whole. In this way Davidson was able to combine the demand for capital goods in the present situation with the determination of the planned addition to capacity relative to the existing stock of capital goods, taking in both their current costs of production and the cost and availability of finance. This is an integral part of the real world which both Keynes and Davidson analyse so well.

When it comes to considering the money part of the equation, as it were, Davidson is equally illuminating. He has many wise things to say about the inescapable fact of uncertainty giving rise to the need for a liquidity variable with the peculiar and essential properties of money. He has also written on many occasions in scathing tones about the impossibility of finding a place for money in any significant sense other than as a ticket in an Arrow–Debreu general equilibrium system where everything has been coordinated before the 'action' starts. (This is about the only proposition that Paul and Frank Hahn agree on.) Formally, he associates 'a non-neutrality of money analytical system' with Keynes's need to reject the three basic axioms of orthodox neoclassical theory: (1) the axiom of gross substitution ... everything ultimately a substitute for everything else (2) the axiom of reals ... the objectives of agents [ugh!] that determine their actions and plans do not depend on ... nominal magnitudes ... and (3) the axiom of an ergodic economic world ... whereby the future [is] predictable in [a] probability sense. (Davidson, 1990, pp. 333–4)[3]

Because money is there right from the start and because its creation does not create employment, output or income directly, when important decision makers shift their demand for goods to a demand for money, there is a failure in effective demand which the system is *not* equipped automatically to make good either in the short or in the long term.

Even more so, both Davidson and Sidney Weintraub stressed, as Keynes did, the essential role of the wage unit in securing stability in both the general price level *and* the level of activity of the system. This theme runs through their analysis of both unemployment and inflation. Moreover, because the emphasis is on money's role as a store of value, they are both probably, again as Keynes was all his life, in favour of the long-term stability of the general price level (see Brown, 1996). This not only ensures the pre-eminence of money as a store of value, but also helps to minimize the dangers of crisis in a system which is run basically by decision makers trying to make $M' > M$ by the end of the period of production, as Marx stressed in a proposition of which Keynes approved (we are not sure that either Sidney or Paul knew about it!). The point is that the ultimate driving force is a desire to make as large money profits as possible, so that the commodities produced, the labour employed and the accumulation planned are but the means to this end. Not having to worry about a declining long-term value of money is therefore a boon, *ceteris paribus*, though Keynes, from at least the *Tract on Monetary Reform* on, argued passionately that deflation and depression caused greater evils than inflation.

Of course, Davidson does not argue that money wages are necessarily sticky, nor that an assumption of stickiness is essential for Keynes-type results to occur – perish the thought! Nor does he argue that a sticky money wage by itself would ensure an optimum as opposed to, often, a stable systemic outcome. It is rather that he sees very clearly the intricate relationships between the wage unit, on the one hand, and the price level and activity, on the other – and so makes it an essential *policy* variable to be influenced if not controlled. (Both Weintraub and Davidson are rather right-wing when it comes to policy, always preferring a Marshallian–Pigovian carrot and stick approach to directives or controls or administered incomes policies.)

In so far as the wage unit is relevant for the determination of the general price level, Davidson has a soft spot for the fundamental equations of the *Treatise on Money*. With them Keynes advanced one of the earliest analyses of the possibility of cost-push (as well as demand-pull) inflation, an emphasis which Richard Kahn stressed for most of his own working life after the publication of *The General Theory*. But Davidson also clearly expounded the link between the general price level and the demand for money and hence the determination of the rate of interest and its role in turn in determining the level of investment.

Davidson is most subtle in his analysis of the demand for money. Not only is his interpretation of the speculative aspects of the liquidity preference function much in keeping with the original spirit of Keynes's analysis, but also he should receive considerable credit for putting the finance motive, originally introduced by Keynes in 1937, centrally back on the agenda in a series of articles in the 1960s (see Davidson, 1990, Part II). Davidson recognized very clearly that in modern capitalist economies availability of finance (*not* saving) is the ultimate constraint on the rate of accumulation. (This is even true of a situation of full employment, though there, adequate finance has also to be coupled with a release of real resources associated with, say, a rise in the saving ratio.) Not, of course, that the financial constraint will always bite – limp animal spirits may bring investment to an end (or, at least, make it too low a level) before the limits of, for example, bank finance have been reached, especially in a system which includes unused overdraft limits as a feature. But if we may put animal spirits to one side for the moment, the investment market may become congested before investment itself has reached the level which matches full employment saving.

As Bibow (1995) has shown, Davidson overlooked the subtle point that the finance motive only operates in a disequilibrium situation, that it is essentially a disequilibrium phenomenon. But that does not detract from his conceptual insight about the role of finance as the ultimate constraint – an insight which Kalecki also had, so that it is strange that Paul has always been hostile to the latter's contributions. Perhaps there is an ideological and political rather than a purely technical economic reason for this? In any event the factors associated with the finance motive are even more relevant today than when Keynes and then Davidson wrote about them. With the deregulation of so many capital markets, coupled with the great rate of technical advance in the same markets, the resulting imbalance between finance capital and industrial capital has been one of the principal sources of crisis and instability in the world economy. To the analysis of this, Paul Davidson, with his sound grounding in Keynes's writings and his own insights, has made thoughtful and essential contributions (see, for example, Davidson, 1996).

Finally, Davidson has never been especially interested in (perhaps we should say dogmatic about) the exact nature of the microeconomic foundations of the Keynesian system. He has been happy to use markets with Marshallian competitive structures in his models. This reflects Keynes's claim that he took as one of his givens 'the degree of competition' (*The General Theory*, p. 245) and that he did not expect the particular market structures of various industries to make any significant difference to his new and fundamental propositions.[4] In following his lead Davidson is probably reflecting the methodological view that we should try to get by with as simple assumptions as possible in our models in order to make them both tractable and understandable. Nevertheless, a more thorough treatment by Davidson of the nature of the markets in which firms operate would certainly be welcome. An analysis of the actual working of capitalist markets would give Davidson's economics for the real world greater power and conviction. Furthermore, his contribution on this topic would be especially appropriate at a time when most of the so-called New Keynesians argue that 'Keynesian results' can be obtained at the analytical level only by introducing some *ad hoc* hypotheses of imperfect competition.

SKIDELSKY'S POST KEYNESIAN KEYNES

As we mentioned above, Robert Skidelsky was criticized by Don Patinkin for 'having adopted a "post-Keynesian" interpretation of Keynes's economics' (Skidelsky, 1992, p. xi).[5] He was also criticized by Rod O'Donnell for challenging the notion of evolutionary continuity in Keynes's thought from the earliest times to *The General Theory* and beyond. We think Skidelsky is right on both counts. Most of all, Patinkin never properly took on board how very Marshallian in method Keynes was. Skidelsky points out that it was not natural for Keynes to think in a Walrasian general equilibrium manner of everything depending on everything else simultaneously. He was much more accustomed to going around the economy, brilliantly spotlighting each (relevant) part of it in turn. He ignored the rest for the moment – they were at best kept at 'the back of our heads' – while he identified causal relationships – or, if there was mutual determination, he judged whether the two-way influences were of equal importance in both directions, or of overwhelming importance in one. He was, moreover, acutely conscious of the different periods of time associated with nevertheless intertwined processes. Not only was it his own way of seeing processes, it also contrasts starkly with how those he was criticizing saw them. There are obvious examples: investment determining saving as opposed to saving determining investment; the marginal efficiency of capital having to square up against the money rate of interest as opposed to the money rate of interest needing to be consistent with the natural rate of interest; aggregate demand determining output, income and employment as opposed to employment determining output and income; and so on.

No doubt Keynes exaggerated, and Skidelsky highlights this, in order to bring out the contrasts and to try to change *our* ways of looking at things, to get a better feel on processes and to understand better Keynes's 'vision'. But if, as Skidelsky argues (and so does Davidson), Walras's way of doing economics was alien to Keynes, a convinced Marshallian on method, then the method of *The General Theory* does fit correctly under the post Keynesian rubric.

As for Rod O'Donnell's masterly account of Keynes's philosophy and economics (O'Donnell, 1989), if it has one limitation as an account of Keynes's thought processes, it is *too* systematic, explicit and formally logical. It thus leaves too little room for Keynes's leaps of intuition so well documented by Austin Robinson, Skidelsky, Davidson and Moggridge. Moggridge quotes Keynes's letter to O.T. Falk, 19 February 1936: 'The extent to which one sees one's destination before one discovers the route is the most obscure problem of all in the psychology of original work... it is the destination which one sees first [though] a good many of the destinations so seen turn out to be mirages' (Moggridge, 1992, p. 552). Moggridge comments that

> For all his books ... *in every case* Keynes drew up a draft table of contents. He ... thought of the structure of his argument as a whole even before he put pen to paper on any details ... his table of contents [were] sketch maps of how he intuitively thought of the route through the larger problems in book form ... . [For] the complex major works ... the multiplicity of 'maps' illustrates his struggles to find the route and to keep the whole and the parts together. (Ibid., pp. 551–2, emphasis in original.)

Rod O'Donnell is so systematic a thinker himself – to the benefit of us all – that he may not have fully perceived or appreciated how Keynes could have done what he did without following the same systematic path. Skidelsky, though, is more akin to Keynes in his psychological make-up and approach and so has more naturally, and intuitively, appreciated the mode of thought of the complex person whose life and works he has analysed.

Skidelsky puts much emphasis on the psychological nature of Keynes's economics: the central role which Keynes gave to an inescapable uncertain environment within which decisions have to be made, the roles of expectation formation and conventions, the psychologies of the main actors in Keynes's economic dramas – the speculators, investors, rentiers, consumers, money holders, wage earners. He draws subtle portraits of them all; some of the most memorable passages occur, for example, in *The Economic Consequences of the Peace* (1919) as much as in Chapter 12 of *The General Theory*. All this no doubt reflects Keynes's fascination with the Freudian ideas of his day, brought to the UK by some of Keynes's friends, his Moorean philosophical background and his own artistic leanings and understandings. For example,

Skidelsky points out how many ideas and arguments of *The General Theory* were expressed in ordinary language, as much in the drafts as when writing to Lydia. John Coates (1990, 1996) especially has documented this in his studies of Keynes and ordinary language economics.

Skidelsky also brings out Keynes's strong anti-thrift prejudices which he argues were linked to Keynes's many-sided rebellion against Victorian values and morality. This shows itself in his passages on the motives behind the consumption function and in his stress on the residual nature of saving as contrasted with the explicit positive aspects so beloved of the Victorians including Marshall – and Skidelsky's modern Victorian heroine, Margaret Thatcher. All these ideas and attitudes are hard to fit into the formal aspects of neo-Walrasian systems such as Patinkin was accustomed to use, though not, of course, into the all-round thoughts of that passionate socialist, Leon Walras, which are to be found in his later volumes and which are associated with his single-minded commitment to carrying on his father's political and philosophical aims. Certainly Davidson and Skidelsky join company with their emphasis on the overriding influence of uncertainty in the investment and money markets, in the determination of investment and the rate of interest in a monetary production economy. Those themes are reiterated in Davidson's writings, often on his own, but also in significant joint papers with Sidney Weintraub.

We, however, wish to close this section on a note of caution. To lay too much emphasis on psychology could be dangerous, for it could lead to an interpretation of Keynes which relies excessively on methodological individualism. Although, undoubtedly, Keynes speaks of 'psychological laws', it should be emphasized that he almost never refers just to isolated individuals. In general, Keynes speaks of the psychology of specific social groups (speculators, entrepreneurs, wage earners, for example). When we consider issues of social psychology, we must remember that history, institutions and conventions play a crucial role in the determination of attitudes. Similar observations may be made about an explanation of Keynes's anti-thrift attitude which is based only on his rebellion against the attitudes of Victorian England. Although Keynes's position on saving and consumption can be partly explained by his personal rebellion, it is also true that his views essentially derive from his awareness that capitalist economies, with the end of the First World War, entered a new historical phase, in which saving and parsimony no longer played the same central role as before. In particular, for Keynes, it is the almost 'natural' link between saving and investment which disappeared (see, for example, the first pages of *The Economic Consequences of Peace* (1919)). Keynes's theory is well grounded on knowledge not only of the actual working of the economy but also of its historical developments.

MOGGRIDGE'S HISTORICAL KEYNES

Donald Moggridge's account of *The General Theory* is indispensable for the authoritative dating of the development of the system which became *The General Theory*. It is also fascinating for its revelation of Hawtrey's discovery of the multiplier in his comments on the proofs of the *Treatise on Money*, only to reject it out of hand ever after (Moggridge, 1992, p. 535). This throws into relief Keynes's relatively slow appreciation of its meaning – that it was the endogenous process which brought either falls or rises of income to an end – for which he had been searching ever since the banana plantation parable of the *Treatise on Money* and the lack of a clinching argument in *Can Lloyd George Do It?* (1929). He needed to put a precise figure on the change in employment (and output) which could be expected, under precisely defined conditions, from a primary change in employment associated with, say, public works expenditure or an induced rise in private investment expenditure. Associated with this precision would be an account of where the saving came from to match the increased investment. Kahn had provided both in 1931 but Keynes does not appear to have seen the full significance of it all until early 1933 (Moggridge, 1992, p. 563).

Moggridge accepts Keynes's own account (for example, in his letter to Harrod *C.W.*, XIV, 1973, 85–6) of the chronology of discovery and of what the key ingredients of the new system were: the consumption function, the liquidity preference function and the marginal efficiency of capital schedule. He does not put much emphasis on the central importance of uncertainty and expectations though he accepts that the 1937 *Quarterly Journal of Economics* reply to the critics (which does) is a true index of Keynes's assessment of the significance of his new system.

Moggridge also wrote one of the best accounts of the strengths and weaknesses of *IS/LM* as a means of getting a first grip on the new system. It is to be found in the appendix to his book on Keynes (1976) in the *Modern Masters* series. In it he agrees with Davidson that though formally the *IS* and *LM* curves are set out as independent of one another, once actual movements are analysed this assumption is no longer tenable. Hence their limited role is to give us an actual feel for the interrelationships, for existence *including* its fragility, if you like, a 'first glimpse', as Keynes put it, but no more than that, at our own peril. Keynes himself was explicitly aware of this:

> We have now introduced money into our causal nexus for the first time, and we are able to catch a first glimpse of the way in which changes in the quantity of money work their way into the economic system. If, however, we are tempted to assert that money is the drink which stimulates the system to activity, we must remind ourselves that there may be several slips between the cup and the lip. For whilst an increase in the quantity of money may be expected, *cet. par.*, to reduce

the rate of interest, this will not happen if the liquidity-preferences of the public are increasing more than the quantity of money; and whilst a decline in the rate of interest may be expected, *cet. par.*, to increase the volume of investment, this will not happen if the schedule of the marginal efficiency of capital is falling more rapidly than the rate of interest; and whilst an increase in the volume of invest-ment may be expected, *cet. par.*, to increase employment, this may not happen if the propensity to consume is falling off. Finally, if employment increases, prices will rise in a degree partly governed by the shapes of the physical supply func-tions, and partly by the liability of the wage-unit to rise in terms of money. And when output has increased and prices have risen, the effect of this on liquidity-preference will be to increase the quantity of money necessary to maintain a given rate of interest. (*The General Theory*, p. 173)[6]

And, as with Moggridge, so with another famous Fellow of Clare, Brian Reddaway, who, fresh from his supervisions as an undergraduate with Keynes while *The General Theory* was being written, wrote in his splendid review of the book in the *Economic Record* (1936, reprinted in Lekachman, 1964):

Are we then reasoning in a circle? ... no, we are merely faced with the inevitable difficulty of trying to describe a system where the four variables [*I*, *S*, *Y* and *r*] *mutually* determine one another ... our four propositions are represented approxi-mately by

(1) $S = f(Y)$
(2) $I = g(r)$
(3) $I = S$
(4) $M = L_1(Y) + L_2(r)$

... Keynes ... deprecates the spurious air of exactness introduced by too much mathematics ... in his endeavour to describe the system without this sort of shorthand he has tended to obscure the fact that the determination is mutual. (pp. 106–7)

One point where Moggridge is out of step with received opinion is that he does not regret that Keynes scrapped the distinction between the cooperative (and neutral) economy models, on the one hand, and the entrepreneur economy model, on the other, as being the best way of showing the essential difference between the classical system and his own. As we know, these passages, which Moggridge (1992) judges to constitute 'an analytically unsatisfactory distinc-tion' (p. 566), ended up in the laundry basket at Tilton. Keynes's account of Say's Law and his emphasis on the classical postulates in the labour market took their place in the published volume, as did Pigou's *Theory of Unemploy-ment* (1933) as the archetypal representative of the position and propositions of the classical economists.

We have pointed out Davidson's relative lack of interest in the issues raised by different market forms. A similar attitude may be detected in both biographies of Keynes. The issue of the relationship between Keynes and the 'imperfect competition revolution' receives little attention from Moggridge and Skidelsky. 'Imperfect competition' is conspicuous by its absence from the indexes of both their books. Moggridge ignores the issue altogether. Skidelsky does not get beyond stating 'it remains a puzzle that the two escape routes from Marshallian orthodoxy – the one associated with Sraffa and imperfect competition, the other with Keynes and effective demand – never converged in Keynes's lifetime though leading disciples like Kahn and Joan Robinson were heavily involved in both "revolutions"' (Skidelsky, 1992, p. 290). The explanation of Davidson's position, as we have seen, is essentially analytical (his Marshallian–Keynesian view of competition); an explanation, or a justification, of why both the biographers have virtually ignored the problem is harder to find.

From a historical point of view, which of course is central in a biography, the issue of the relationship, or the absence of relationships, between the Keynesian 'revolution' and the other revolution which took place in Cambridge more or less at the same time, whose leaders were all very close friends and colleagues of Keynes, is a fascinating topic. Many questions arise: why did Keynes ignore the contributions on imperfect competition from Kahn, Joan Robinson, and Sraffa? Was this a 'tactical' decision (not to open too many fronts in the struggle against old ideas)?; was Keynes skeptical about the possible macroeconomic implications of the assumption of imperfect competition?; did Kahn or Joan Robinson ever try to involve Keynes in the debate on imperfect competition?; and many more. Given the very high quality of the two biographies, we would have liked to have seen their answers to some of the questions which are raised by the 'puzzle', not least because other scholars in recent days have tackled these themes; see, for example, Darity (1985), Harcourt (1987), Kregel (1985), Marcuzzo (1994), Marris (1991, 1992, 1996), and it would be enlightening to have Moggridge's and Skidelsky's views on and reactions to the issues as well.[7]

SUMMARY AND CONCLUSIONS

To sum up: with one or two exceptions the three views examined are complementary and reinforcing. Most importantly, all are agreed that Keynes's great book does constitute a revolution in 'vision', analysis and method, so that the attempt to derive Keynes-type results *within* the dominant neo-Walrasian framework of modern economic theory (or even the New Keynesian one) is doomed to failure. This has been recognized explicitly and courageously by, for example, Peter Howitt (1996) and, at least implicitly, by Frank Hahn who admits that he has been forced to rely at times on 'plausible' rather than 'clinching' arguments when tackling Lucas and company; see Hahn (1982, p. xi). All this is reassuring, for the three authors concerned – Davidson, Moggridge and Skidelsky – have very different backgrounds and temperaments; yet, after so much of their lifetimes studying the evidence, they *in the main* agree on 'what Keynes really meant'.

NOTES

1. We would like to record here our great sadness that Don Patinkin has died. Though we seldom agreed on economic matters, he was a most admirable and likeable person and a scholar to whom the entire profession is in debt.
2. In the 1950s, and the following decades, Weintraub made important contributions concerning the microeconomic foundations of Keynes's *General Theory*. In particular, Weintraub based Keynes's aggregate demand and supply functions on Marshallian microeconomic foundations, see, for example, Weintraub (1957).
3. Davidson has devoted much effort to his criticism of the axiom of an ergodic world; see, for example, Davidson (1991) .
4. See Shapiro (1996) for a deeply illuminating analysis of this point.
5. Robert's disarming reply – 'If I am guilty of this fallacy, I can say only that this is how Keynes's economics appeared to me, being the person I am' – makes good sense to us and, we imagine, to Paul too. Mark Blaug (1994, p. 1211n) comments on Patinkin's complaint: 'But all that this seems to mean is that Skidelsky treats Keynes as having been obsessed throughout his life by the problem of economic behaviour under uncertainty; if this is a post-Keynesian interpretation, we are all post-Keynesians now'.
6. G.C.H. has always been grateful to his teacher and friend Keith Fearson for pointing out the significance of this passage to him.
7. In his judicial and highly readable review article of the two biographies, Mark Blaug (1994, pp. 1211–12) also regrets the omission.

REFERENCES

References to Keynes's works are from the following edition: *The Collected Writings of John Maynard Keynes*, 29 vols, 1971–79 edited by A. Robinson and D. Moggridge, London: Macmillan for the Royal Economic Society. The listing gives *C.W.*, followed by volume number and date.

Bibow, Jörg (1995), 'Some Reflections on Keynes's Finance Motive for the Demand for Money', *Cambridge Journal of Economics*, **19**, 647–66.
Blaug, Mark (1994), 'Recent Biographies of Keynes', *Journal of Economic Literature*, **32**, 1204–15.
Brown, A.J. (1996), 'The Inflationary Dimension' in Harcourt and Riach (1996).
Coates, John (1990), 'Ordinary Languages Economics. Keynes and the Cambridge Philosophers', unpublished PhD dissertation, Cambridge.
Coates, John (1996), 'Keynes, Vague Concepts and Fuzzy Logic' in Harcourt and Riach (1996).
Darity Jr, W. (1985), 'On Involuntary Unemployment and Increasing Returns', *Journal of Post Keynesian Economics*, **7**, 363–72.

Davidson, Paul (1972), *Money and the Real World*, London: Macmillan, second edition 1978.
Davidson, Paul (1990), *Money and Employment. The Collected Writings of Paul Davidson*, I, edited by Louise Davidson, Basingstoke, Hants: Macmillan.
Davidson, Paul (1991), 'Is Probability Theory Relevant for Uncertainty?', *Journal of Economic Perspectives*, **5**, 129–43.
Davidson, Paul (1996), '*The General Theory* in an Open Economy' in Harcourt and Riach (1996).
Hahn, F.H. (1982), *Money and Inflation*, Oxford: Basil Blackwell.
Harcourt, G.C. (ed.) (1985), *Keynes and his Contemporaries, The Sixth and Centennial Keynes Seminar held at the University of Kent at Canterbury, 1983*, London: Macmillan.
Harcourt, G.C. (1987), 'Theoretical Methods and Unfinished Business' in Reese (1987), 1–22; reprinted in Sardoni (1992).
Harcourt, G.C. and P.A. Riach (eds) (1996), *A 'Second Edition' of The General Theory*, 2 vols., London: Routledge.
Howitt, Peter (1996), 'Expectations and Uncertainty in Contemporary Keynesian Models' in Harcourt and Riach (1996).
Kahn, R.F. (1931), 'The Relation of Home Investment to Unemployment', *Economic Journal*, **41**, 173–98; reprinted in Kahn (1972).
Kahn, R.F. (1972), *Selected Essays on Employment and Growth*, Cambridge: Cambridge University Press.
Keynes, J.M. (1919), *The Economic Consequences of the Peace*, *C.W.*, II (1971).
Keynes, J.M. (1923), *A Tract on Monetary Reform*, *C.W.*, IV (1971).
Keynes, J.M. (1930), *A Treatise on Money*, 2 vols, *C.W.*, V, VI (1971).
Keynes, J.M. (1936), *The General Theory of Employment. Interest and Money*, London: Macmillan, *C.W.*, VII (1973).
Keynes, J.M. (1937), 'The General Theory of Employment', *Quarterly Journal of Economics*, **LI**, 209–23; *C.W.*, XIV (1973), 109–23.
Keynes, J.M. (1937), *The General Theory and After: Part II, Defence and Development*, *C.W.*, XIV (1973).
Keynes, J.M. and H.D. Henderson (1929), *Can Lloyd George Do It?*, *C.W.*, IX, (1972), 86–125.
Kregel, J.A. (1985), 'Harrod and Keynes: Increasing Returns, The Theory of Employment and Dynamic Economics' in Harcourt (1985), pp. 66–88.
Lekachman, Robert (1964), *Keynes' General Theory. Reports of Three Decades*, London: Macmillan; New York: St Martin's Press.
Marcuzzo, Maria Cristina (1994), 'At the Origin of Imperfect Competition: Different Views', in Vaughn (1994), pp. 75–84.
Marris, R.L. (1991), *Reconstructing Keynesian Economics with Imperfect Competition*, Aldershot, Hants: Edward Elgar.
Marris, R.L. (1992), 'R.F. Kahn's Fellowship Dissertation: A Missing Link in the History of Economic Thought', *Economic Journal*, **102**, 1235–43.
Marris, R.L. (1996), 'Yes, Mrs Robinson! *The General Theory* and Imperfect Competition' in Harcourt and Riach (1996).
Moggridge, D.E. (1976), *Keynes*, London: Macmillan.
Moggridge, D.E. (1992), *Maynard Keynes. An Economist's Biography*, London: Routledge.
O'Donnell, R.M. (1989), *Keynes: Philosophy, Economics and Politics*, London: Macmillan.

Pigou, A.C. (1933), *The Theory of Unemployment*, London: Macmillan.

Reddaway, W.B. (1936), 'The General Theory of Employment, Interest and Money', *Economic Record*, **12**, 28–36; reprinted in Lekachman (1964), pp. 99–108.

Reese, D.A. (ed.) (1987), *The Legacy of Keynes*, Nobel Conference, XXII, San Francisco: Harper & Row.

Sardoni, Claudio (ed.) (1992), *On Political Economists and Modern Political Economy. Selected Essays of G.C. Harcourt*, London: Routledge.

Shapiro, Nina (1996), 'Imperfect Competition and Keynes' in Harcourt and Riach (1996).

Skidelsky, Robert (1992), *John Maynard Keynes. Volume Two. The Economist as Saviour*, London: Macmillan.

Vaughn, Karen I. (ed.) (1994), *Perspectives in the History of Economic Thought, Vol. X; Method, Competition, Conflict and Measurement in the Twentieth Century*, Aldershot, Hants: Edward Elgar.

Weintraub, Sidney (1957), 'The Micro-foundations of Aggregate Demand and Supply', *Economic Journal*, **67**, 455–70.

2.   Keynes, Einstein and scientific revolution

James K. Galbraith*

An article honouring Paul Davidson should surely attempt to contribute something in his spirit, and on his themes. This is my proudest effort along such lines, and I offer it here in the hope that it will find favour with readers who have admired and emulated Paul's long efforts to preserve, protect and defend Keynes's theory.

One of the most intriguing and little-noted facts about John Maynard Keynes's (1936) masterwork, *The General Theory of Employment, Interest and Money*, concerns the first three words of its title. These are evidently cribbed from Albert Einstein.[1] Alone that would be only a *curiosum*; but there is more. The parallels between Keynes's economics and relativity theory are deep enough, and evidently intentional enough, to provide a useful framework for thinking about what Keynes meant to do with *his* scientific revolution.

Keynes and Einstein had met. Keynes travelled to Berlin in 1926 to lecture; Einstein attended. Keynes's impressions were not published until 1972 (*C.W.*, X, 382):

> Wordsworth, who had not seen him, wrote of Newton's statue: 'The marble index of a mind for ever Voyaging through strange seas of Thought, alone.' I, who have seen Einstein, have to record something apparently – perhaps not really different – that he is 'a naughty boy', a naughty Jew-boy, covered with ink, pulling a long nose as the world kicks his bottom; a sweet imp, pure and giggling.

A second reference appears in *The New Statesman and Nation* of 21 October 1933. For this issue, Keynes prepared a short commentary to accompany a sketch, by the artist David Low, of Albert Einstein. The playful imagery is now gone; Keynes was by this time becoming a champion of Jewish refugees. Now, to Keynes's eye, Low's drawing evokes an Einstein under attack. Keynes quotes Einstein in the German (*C.W.*, XXVIII, 21):

*This chapter is a revised version of the paper under the same title that was first published in the Winter 1994 issue of *The American Prospect*. It is reprinted here with permission.

14

Assuredly you too, dear reader, made acquaintance as boy or girl with the proud edifice of Euclid's geometry – thus begins the 'Essay on the Special and General Theory of Relativity' – 'Assuredly by force of this bit of your past you would treat with contempt anyone who casts doubts on even the most out of the way fragment of any of its propositions.' It is so indeed. The boys, who cannot grow up to adult human nature, are beating the prophets of the ancient race – Marx, Freud, Einstein... .

The first extant complete table of contents of Keynes's next book, then titled simply *The General Theory of Employment*,[2] was found in a bundle of papers dated December 1933 (*C.W.*, XIII, 421). In the first proofs of that book there is a sentence, deleted from later proofs, that occurs exactly at the point where Keynes declares that the classical theory cannot be applied to the problem of unemployment, and just before this passage:

The classical theorists resemble Euclidean geometers in a non-Euclidean world who, discovering that in experience straight lines apparently parallel often meet, rebuke the lines for not keeping straight – as the only remedy for the unfortunate collisions which are occurring. Yet, in truth, there is no remedy except to throw over the axiom of parallels and to work out a non-Euclidean geometry. Something similar is required in economics.

The deleted sentence reads 'We require, therefore, to work out a more general theory than the classical theory' (*C.W.*, XIV, 366).

Henry David Thoreau[3] writes somewhere that 'some circumstantial evidence is very strong, as when you find a trout in the milk'.

But what, if anything, does it mean?

NEWTON'S PHYSICS AND CLASSICAL ECONOMICS

Albert Einstein came of age in a world where the classical physics of Sir Isaac Newton still reigned. Two features of Newton's world view are pertinent to understanding the classical economics that Keynes meant to attack.

The first is that Newton's physics presupposes an absolute separation of space and time. Space is Euclidean: a three-dimensional void stretching infinitely in all directions. The position of any particle in space can be defined, by means of a system of coordinates, with respect to any observer or any fixed reference point. Motion is the displacement of the particle from one position to another. Velocity is motion, divided by the number of ticks on a clock that it takes for the motion to occur. The clock that is used to measure velocity lies, in a conceptual sense, outside the universe itself. In other words, all observers of an event, provided they were equipped with accurate timepieces, no matter where they might be, would always agree on the exact time that the event occurred. Newton imagined time as an absolutely regular phenomenon that could not depend on the location of the clock or be affected by its movement or any other physical force.

The second feature is reductionism: Newton's universe was neither more nor less than the sum of its component particles. Gravity in Newton's system is the basic force exerted by one massive body on any other. Gravity produces the acceleration of a particle in space, according to the position and mass of all other particles in the universe that exert gravitational force. And, in Newton's view, this interaction of each particle on every other is all there is. Once you knew the position, mass, direction and velocity of every particle in the universe, you would not need to know anything else. Every future event would be fully determined by the laws of motion.

Without going into great detail, it is possible to trace out the role of each of the above features in the classical economics of Keynes's time and in modern neoclassical economics. The analogue of space is the market. Look at any supply and demand diagram. The graph itself is a two-dimensional space. Every point on the graph is a position defined uniquely with respect to the origin. The relationships between variables are presented as forces in this space: in the labour market, demand aligns wages and employment in a downward-sloping relation; supply aligns them along an upward slope. If two curves cross in that space, their point of intersection is an equilibrium position, where the forces balance and the market clears.

The analogue of Newtonian time, in the classical economics, is money. Just as time is absolutely separated from space, money is absolutely separated from the market. Prices and wages may be measured in money terms, but this is only a convenience. The prices that count are relative prices – prices in relation to the prices of other goods. The wages measured in a proper labour market are real wages – an hour's work in terms of the commodities that an hour of work can purchase. Like time, money is an invariable standard. And just as it does not matter whether one measures time in seconds or in hours, or from Andromeda or Cassiopeia, it does not matter whether one measures prices in dollars or dimes, in pesos or yen, or in dollars of 1958 or dollars of 1993. The quantity of money has no effect on the equilibrium of the market; nothing real depends on money in any important way.

The reductionism of Newton's system is equally fundamental to the classical economics – and remains so today. Economists are taught that societies, like Newton's universe, are nothing more than the sum of their individual components. Macroeconomic expressions, though they purport to describe the behaviour of society as a whole, are only a shorthand for the mass of individual human actions. In principle, therefore, the best macroeconomics would be built strictly and rigidly from the theory of individual behaviour, or microfoundations. If there are operational difficulties with this, they must lie mainly in the difficulty of acquiring all the information that is necessary about all the individuals whose preferences and behaviour must be considered. Fundamental difficulties of theory do not arise.

EINSTEIN AND NEWTON'S MECHANICS

By the time Keynes came along, the Newtonian view of the physical universe had crumbled. Einstein's theories of relativity had done it in. The absolute separation of time and space collapsed with Einstein's introduction of a new universal constant, the speed of light. If light travelled through empty space, everywhere and always and irrespective of the direction and velocity of the observer (as Einstein argued and experiments have confirmed) at the same identical speed (186 000 miles per second), then the absolute simultaneity of two or more very distant events could no longer be defined. Clocks in different places will record these events at different times, and none is more correct than any other. Moreover, Einstein showed that space and time were interrelated: time itself advances more slowly near massive bodies than it does in empty space.

Furthermore, this newly unified concept, space–time, also destroyed the Euclidean concept of emptiness extending forever in all directions. Space–time is curved, and Einstein's relativity is the extension of the Riemannian geometry of curved spaces to the physical universe. Near any massive body the shortest distance between two points curves around it (as does the path of a ray of light, a point verified by experiment). For this reason, parallel lines may meet if extended far enough (Keynes's reference to overthrowing Euclid's axiom of parallels is an unmistakable allusion to this feature of Einstein's theory).

But if space–time is curved by the presence of matter, then the shortest distance between two points is no longer defined independently of the distribution of matter in space. And then the system is no longer reducible to its elements; you can no longer get to the whole merely by adding up the parts. The universe is, instead, more easily and more correctly understood by looking at the whole and placing the parts within it. The whole can impose rules on the parts: in a famous phrase 'Space tells matter how to move and matter tells space how to curve' (John Archibald Wheeler, quoted in Davies, 1980, p. 50).

RELATIVITY THEORY AND MONETARY PRODUCTION ECONOMICS

When Keynes wrote his *General Theory*, he had in his gunsights – I shall argue – both Newton's reductionism and his space–time dichotomy, as both were reflected in the classical economics. First, Keynes sought to disestablish the absolute space of classical markets, and to end the separation of markets from the world of money. Keynes characterized his theory as a monetary theory of production, giving lectures on this subject in the fall of 1933 as the *General Theory of Employment* (the preliminary title) was taking shape. Keynes contrasted monetary-production economics with what he called the real-exchange economics of the classical view. In so doing, he broke down the traditional non-monetary concepts of a labour market and a capital market, suffusing both of these subjects with ideas – effective demand and liquidity preference – that cannot be conceived of properly except in monetary terms.

Monetary production is Keynes' space–time: the marriage of conceptual domains previously held to be distinct. In the classical theory of the labour market, for example, Keynes found a first postulate which held that the demand for labour would rise when real wages fell, and vice versa. This was a consequence of the principle of diminishing returns, and an idea that Keynes did not choose (at that time) to dispute. But the idea that demand for labour rises as wages fall cannot, by itself, establish either the actual level of employment or the value of the real wage.

The classicals had closed their model with a second postulate, which held that work time offered would increase when real wages rose. This second postulate was precisely that part of the classical vision that reduced unemployment to a matter of individual decision. If a person was apparently unemployed, it should always be possible for him or her either to find work, or else to eliminate the desire to work and therefore the appearance of unemployment, by sufficiently cutting the wage.

For Keynes, this second postulate, the upward-sloping supply curve of labour, was akin to the axiom of parallels in Euclid's geometry. It should likewise be rejected. In doing so, Keynes threw over not only the supply curve of labour but also the whole idea of a self-contained labour market in the normal supply and demand sense, a construct in which real wages and employment could be modelled together as though one depended directly on the other. In its place, Keynes offered the now familiar, but then revolutionary, idea that employment was determined by effective *monetary* demand for output. Since there was no reason why the total demand for output would necessarily correspond to high or full employment, involuntary unemployment in the strict sense would now be possible in economics.

But what would determine effective demand? Such demand could be divided into two major elements: the consumption demand of households, and the investment demands of business. Here Keynes's reasoning led him to dismantle the second metaphorical, classical, supply and demand market, namely the capital market. In the classical theory, the supply of and demand for capital jointly determined a quantity, namely the total volume of savings and investment, and a price, namely the rate of interest. Investment was demanded by firms, with more being demanded at low interest rates than at high. Savings were supplied by individuals, with more being supplied at high interest than at low. Thus a market for capital determined how much of current output would be consumed, and how much saved and invested. This market, it should be noted, operated wholly apart from the determination of output. Investment and savings did not affect employment and output, but only the division of output between current consumption and capital formation. Here again, Keynes attacked the supply curve. Savings, he proposed, had nothing to do with the interest rate. They were, instead, merely the leftovers after consumption out of income. Investment, he believed, did depend on the interest rate. But a curve of investment demand alone could not determine both the volume of investment and the rate of interest. Keynes now needed an independent theory of the interest rate.

To get an interest rate, Keynes brought in a new market, up to that point largely ignored in economics: the market for debt instruments and, in particular, for money. Interest, he proposed, was not a reward for saving, but the reward for giving up the liquidity, the easy access to immediate purchasing power, that could be had by holding money. The longer the term (the greater the liquidity foregone), the higher the rate of interest. Keynes argued that the interest rate thus reconciled the supply of liquidity (quantity of money) with the demand for it. And in Keynes's new sequence, the interest rate determined in the money market in turn determined the volume of investment. To complete his theory, Keynes tied these elements together. The market for money determined interest. Interest (together with the state of business confidence) determined investment. Investment, alongside consumption, determined effective demand for output. Demand for output determined output and employment. Consumption out of incomes determined savings. Employment determined the real wage.

In this world, a change in monetary policy, such as a cut in interest rates leading to an increase in bank credit, now had fundamental real consequences. The classical dichotomy, in economics as in physics, had been broken. And with the deconstruction of labour and capital markets, the reductionist idea of microfoundations had also necessarily to be abandoned. Workers, Keynes pointed out, bargain for money wages, not real wages. The act of dropping money wages would generate feedbacks through previously unrecognized – monetary – channels in the system. In particular, prices would fall, and real wages (the ratio of wages to prices) would therefore not necessarily change. Falling prices might, however, depress business profit expectations and so cut into demand for investment. This would actually reduce the demand for workers and prevent total employment from rising. The system interacts with itself, and an equilibrium of full employment cannot be achieved within the labour market. Economic space–time is curved.

CONSEQUENCES

In the long run, Keynes did not achieve what he hoped. His parallel to Einstein went unnoticed, apart from one sniffing reference in A.C. Pigou's early review. Lawrence Klein, writing an early interpretation in his 1947 work, *The Keynesian Revolution*, did emphasize Keynes's attacks on microeconomic supply curves. But in the United States the prevailing view became that of Paul Samuelson, who transposed Keynes's unemployment theory into the proposition that wages are 'sticky'. In this interpretation, unemployment occurs simply because labour markets, characterized by supply and demand curves just as in the good old days, do not clear. What Samuelson did – and he is, I think, too good a student of physics not to have known it – was to push the daemon of Keynesian relativity back into its box. And modern American Keynesians, even down to the new Keynesians presently in fashion around Harvard, MIT, Princeton and the Council of Economic Advisers, are Newtonian and Samuelsonian to the core (though with a touch of Von Neumann thrown in nowadays). As such, they have denied themselves the high ground of principle Keynes sought to claim, conceding an enormous advantage to classical free market conservatives on every important policy matter.

Too bad. For one cannot say, as one can with Newtonian physics, that Newtonian economics is good enough for practical situations. The scale of the whole, in the economic case, is not that of the universe or the solar system; it is merely that of the nation state or the global region. Interdependence afflicts us all. The global irrationality of wage cutting, American budget balancing, zero-inflation Federal Reserve targets and Third World austerity programmes is an everyday occurrence. The failure of Keynesian macroeconomics to establish full theoretical independence from the classical labour market and the classical neutrality of money means that we are, in effect, now denied fair discussion of Keynesian solutions to policy problems. The end result is that we cannot cope now, any more than could the classics in their day, with stagnation and involuntary unemployment.

NOTES

1. This point was first made to me in private conversation by Robert Skidelsky. The econo-
    mists Ching-Yao Hsieh and Meng-Hua Ye devote a short chapter in their excellent book
    (1991) to relativity and economics, stating that it would not be an exaggeration to assert
    that Keynes's theory of involuntary unemployment was inspired by Einstein. They do not,
    however, explore the parallelism between space–time and monetary production. Nor does
    Skidelsky, who discusses the Einstein link in his second volume on Keynes (1993). Philip
    Mirowski, whose 1989 book *More Heat Than Light* is a fundamental treatment of the
    relationship between physics and economics, also leaves out the Keynes–Einstein tale.
2. Keynes omitted any comma when expanding this title to include 'Interest and Money'. To
    add a rank speculation to this minor syntactical mystery, might this have been to under-
    score the link to relativity and Einstein?
3. And not Mark Twain as I erroneously wrote in an earlier version of this article.

REFERENCES

References to Keynes's works are from the following edition: *The Collected Writings
of John Maynard Keynes*, 29 vols, 1971–79, edited by A. Robinson and D. Moggridge,
London: Macmillan for the Economic Society. The listing gives *C.W.*, followed by
volume number and date.

Davies, P. (1980), *Other Worlds*, New York: Simon and Schuster.

Hsieh, C.-Y. and M.-H. Ye (1991), *Economics, Philosophy and Physics*, Armonk, NY:
M.E. Sharpe.

Keynes, J.M. (1936), *The General Theory of Employment Interest and Money C.W.*,
VII (1971).

Keynes, J.M. (1933), *Essays in Biography*, *C.W.*, X (1972).

Keynes, J.M. (1937), *The General Theory and After: Part I, Preparation*, *C.W.*, XIII
(1973)

Keynes, J.M. (1937), *The General Theory and After: Part II, Defence and Development*, C.W., XIV (1973).

Keynes, J.M., *Social Political and Literary Writings*, *C.W.*, XXVIII (1982).

Klein L. (1947), *The Keynesian Revolution*, New York: Macmillan.

Mirowski, P. (1989), *More Heat Than Light: Economics as Social Physics, Physics as
Nature's Economics*, Cambridge: Cambridge University Press.

Skidelsky, R. (1993), *John Maynard Keynes: The Economist as Saviour, 1920–1937*,
London: Macmillan.

3. *AS/AD, AE/AP, IS/LM* and *Z*

David Colander

In the movie *Cool Hand Luke* there is a memorable line in which the prison guard tells the hero, who is played by Paul Newman, that 'What we have here is a failure to communicate'. Throughout the film the situation deteriorates further and further until, in the end, the hero is gunned down by intransigent prison guards. Reflecting on Paul Davidson's career, I was reminded of this movie. After all, both Pauls are handsome, suave and debonair, and have a strength of character that is unbreakable. And both suffer from a major failure to communicate.

Just how bad Paul's failure to communicate is can be seen in the following quotation from Robert Solow. Solow states:

> I am very unsympathetic to the school that calls itself Post-Keynesian ... I have never been able to piece together (I must confess that I have never tried very hard) a positive doctrine ... I have read many of Paul Davidson's articles and they often do not make any sense to me. (Klamer, 1984, 137–8)

Solow is not alone in his views; he is simply blunter than most mainstream economists. Because of this failure to communicate, Paul's influence on the mainstream profession has been far less than warranted.

This paper attempts to achieve communication between Paul and the mainstream by simultaneous translation. It is an attempt to relate Paul's canonical model of aggregate equilibrium, the *Z* model, to the standard mainstream *AE/AP*, *IS/LM*, and *AS/AD* models. By doing so I hope to make Paul's *Z* model more understandable to mainstream economists, and perhaps make my work more understandable to Paul and other post Keynesians.

THE *Z* FRAMEWORK

Paul's *Z* model is a summary of his macro views. In this model employment is placed on the horizontal axis; expected sales proceeds (*Z*) and realized demand expenditures (*D*) are placed on the vertical axis. The *Z* curve represents supply forces; it is upward-sloping and bowed upward (due to fixed

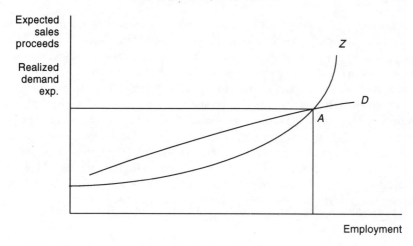

Figure 3.1   The Z framework

money wages and diminishing marginal returns), as in Figure 3.1. The *D* curve represents demand forces; it is also upward-sloping, but is bowed downward (due to differential propensities to spend out of wage and profit income). Thus, the *D* curve intersects the *Z* curve from above, again as in Figure 3.1.

Davidson uses this *Z* model to discuss changes in aggregate employment that will result if there is a difference between expected sales proceeds and realized demand expenditures.[1] The dynamic story (essentially a modified multiplier story) that accompanies the model gives reasons why any difference between *Z* and *D* would cause the economy to gravitate to equilibrium point *A*.

Z AND *AE/AP*

The *Z* model is very similar to the standard *AE/AP* model through which, until recently, most students were introduced to Keynesian economics.[2] The difference is that Davidson's *Z* model directly incorporates microfoundations into the model via the shapes of the curves whereas the mainstream model, because it has many more implicit simplifying assumptions, leaves the microfoundations ambiguous.

One can see the similarities by modifying both models into a common model. To do so, first replace real expenditures with money expenditures on the vertical axis of the *AE/AP* model. Second, transform Davidson's *Z* model's horizontal axis from employment to real output. And third, make the following assumptions: (1) there are diminishing marginal returns; (2) the price level can change but the money wage is constant; and (3) that the marginal propensity to consume decreases as output increases.

These axes transformations and modifications of assumptions give one a modified *AP* curve that has the same general shape as the *Z* curve and a modified *AE* curve that has the same general shape as Davidson's *D* curve. The upward-sloping *AP* curve is bowed upward because diminishing marginal returns cause the price level to rise at an increasing rate as real output increases. The upward-sloping *D* curve is bowed downward because the marginal propensity to consume decreases as real income increases due to differential propensities to spend out of wage and profit income. Thus, in terms of analytics, once one translates the *AE/AP* and *Z* models into a common framework, and modifies assumptions so that they are corresponding, the models become essentially the same.

MICROFOUNDATIONS

If Davidson's *Z* model is simply an elaboration and expansion of the standard *AE/AP* model, wherein lies the problem to communicate? Solow clearly has the ability to follow such an extension. The problem, in my view, lies in the implicit underlying microfoundations that are part of the accompanying dynamic story, but are not specified in the formal model. As I stated above, mainstream economics did not follow Davidson in adding microfoundations directly into the *AP* curve. Instead, when it added a flexible price level, it changed axes and moved to aggregate output and price level space, and used the *AS/AD* model.

This difference is important because in discussing this *AS/AD* model mainstream economists add on to their model various stories of labour market adjustment without carefully specifying how these stories fit into the intuitive logic of the *AE/AP* model. Davidson did not allow such stories to be added on because they conflict with his microfoundations which were built into the specification of his curves. This led mainstream economists to assume that it is Davidson's microfoundations that are at fault, when, in fact, what do not make sense are the mainstream microfoundations (specifically, their labour market adjustment stories when placed in the context of the *AE/AP* model).[3] Unfortunately, Davidson's specification of the *Z* function does not make it clear to most mainstream economists that that is the case. Therein lies the communication problem.

To see where the communication problem developed, and how mainstream economists added microfoundations that do not make sense to the *AE/AP* model, it is helpful to discuss briefly the historical development of the mainstream model.

FROM *AE/AP* TO *IS/LM*

Instead of incorporating microfoundations into the slopes of the *AE* and *AP* curves, as Davidson did, mainstream economists initially expanded Keynesian analysis in another way. They focused on adding the money market into the *AE/AP* model. Thus the textbook presentation of Keynesian economics 'progressed' from the *AE/AP* framework to the *IS/LM* framework. In the 1960s and 1970s this *IS/LM* framework became the one through which mainstream macroeconomists thought about the aggregate economy.

As a tool there is nothing logically wrong with *IS/LM*.[4] However, if the *IS/LM* framework is not used carefully, it presents a serious pitfall in interpreting the intuition behind the model. The reason is that it translates everything into equilibrium space, and incorporates the multiplier into the shape of the *IS* curve. In doing so it hides the dynamics of the multiplier, which involves an interaction between supply and demand – dynamics which were very apparent in the *AE/AP* framework.

It is my suspicion that it was these hidden dynamics that allowed mainstream economists to forget the multiplier process in their intuitive story of labour market adjustment, and to talk about the labour market adjustment as if it occurred independently from the goods market. Those hidden dynamics of the *IS/LM* model are the only way that I can explain the next step in the evolution of the mainstream model – the movement from *IS/LM* to *AS/AD*.

FROM *IS/LM* TO *AS/AD*

In *AS/AD* analysis mainstream economics added an aggregate supply (*AS*) curve to a curve which it derived from the *IS/LM* model and called it an aggregate demand (*AD*) curve. The mainstream *AD* curve was derived from the Keynesian model using the assumption that changes in price level would affect output through some combination of the Pigou effect, Keynes effect, international effect, and intertemporal price level effect. The derivation went as follows (for simplicity, I assume only the Pigou effect is operative): a fall in the price level increases the real money supply, causing the *LM* curve to shift out. The interest rate falls and the economy moves along the *IS* curve, arriving at a higher real output. On a separate graph, plot price level on the vertical axis and real output on the horizontal axis. Place all the combinations of price level and real output points that follow from the above thought experiment on that graph. Doing so gives one a downward-sloping curve that mainstream economics called an aggregate demand curve.

In introductory books students had not yet had *IS/LM* analysis, so this derivation was soon modified to come from the *AE/AP* curves. In the typical introductory textbook presentation a fall in the price level causes the *AE* curve to shift up, increasing real income. Plotting the resulting combination of price levels and real income points on a new graph gives one the down-ward sloping mainstream *AD* curve.

To that so-called aggregate demand curve mainstream economists added an aggregate supply specification which was upward-sloping in the short run and perfectly inelastic in the long run. The explanation of why the short-run *AS* curve slopes upward differs among texts. The most logically consistent explanations use similar reasoning to that given by Davidson in his discus-sion of the microfoundation for the *Z* curve in the short run: diminishing marginal productivity (with fixed nominal wages).[5] In the long-run wages are not fixed and all factors are flexible so the mainstream long-run *AS* curve was perfectly inelastic. If wages are free to fluctuate in the long run, there would be no relative price change, and hence no reason for the *AS* curve to slope upward. The resulting *AS/AD* model has become the central model through which students are now introduced to macroeconomics.

Z, *AE/AP*, AND THE FLAW IN THE *AS/AD* MODEL

Since I have argued that the *AE/AP* model is essentially the same as the *Z* model and that the mainstream *AS/AD* model is derived from the *AE/AP* model, once one makes the appropriate transformations into price level/real output space, there should be a symmetry between *AS/AD* and a correspond-ing set of curves derived from the *Z* model. There is not, and the reason there is not is that there is a serious flaw in the mainstream *AS/AD* model.

This flaw can be seen by considering the derivation in the mainstream *AD* curve. It is a curve derived from models that are supposed to determine equilibrium income – a determination that involves both supply and demand forces. But, for some reason, the combinations of price levels and output levels which are derived from those equilibrium models are called demand curves rather than equilibrium curves.

The flaw in the *AS/AD* model is more than simply a semantic problem. Because the mainstream *AD* curve reflects specific assumptions about both supply and demand, it cannot be meaningfully combined with an *AS* curve. Such an addition overspecifies the model. This overspecification makes it impossible to specify meaningfully the effect of an autonomous shift in the demand curve. To see this, assume the *AS* curve is perfectly inelastic and unchangeable, and that autonomous expenditures increase by 20. How much will the *AD* curve shift out? Using the mainstream curve, the outward shift will not be by 20, but will shift by an amount equal to the multiplier times 20. That multiplier process involves firms increasing output in response to an increase in demand; thus it involves a secondary series of iterative supply responses. But, if the *AS* curve is perfectly inelastic and unchangeable, there can be no supply response. The curves are inconsistent with each other.

Unless the supply curve is perfectly elastic, or is allowed to shift interactively with demand, the mainstream *AS/AD* model has two inconsistent supply specifications. This is true whether it is derived from either the *IS/LM* model or the *AE/AP* model.

The initial reaction of many mainstream economists to having this pointed out to them is: 'So what? That is also the case with the *IS/LM* model'. But there is a major difference: in the *IS/LM* model one is not adding to the analysis an aggregate supply curve as one does in the *AS/AD* model. It is that addition of an *AS* curve that causes the inconsistency.

MY RECONSTRUCTION OF MAINSTREAM *AS/AD* ANALYSIS

I was trained as a mainstream economist and was not introduced to Davidson's Z analysis until I had already been indoctrinated with the mainstream framework. I had skimmed the Z model, but then I saw it as simply a more complete *AE/AP* model. Since I felt the *AE/AP* model was sufficiently complicated for students, I stayed with the *AE/AP* model which was logically consistent. I did not worry about price level; that I added separately.

A Redefined *AD* Curve

In the 1980s my mainstream complacency was broken when I was presented with textbooks that used the *AS/AD* approach. I started to look for a way that I could make sense of this *AS/AD* model. I did so to my satisfaction by redefining the *AD* curve specifically so as to separate out dynamics from statics (Colander, 1995). (I simply followed the definition of the *AD* curve in the standard principles texts. I could do so because these textbook definitions of the *AD* curve did not correspond to the derivations of the *AD* curves in those books.)

The definition I gave the *AD* curve involved specifying it separately from the Keynesian model. To derive it one used a thought experiment that involved holding everything else, including supply, constant, and determining what would happen to the aggregate quantity demanded of real output as the price level changed. In this thought experiment I used the standard classical assumptions – the Pigou effect, etc. – generating a downward-sloping *AD* curve. This redefinition of *AD* allowed me to specify an aggregate demand function as only including the initial effects of any fall in the price level on the quantity of aggregate demand. It did not involve any implicit assumption about supply as did the mainstream *AD* curve. It is, however, related to the mainstream-derived *AD* curve; it simply does not include any multiplied effects of an initial shift. Thus, it is less elastic than the mainstream *AD* curve.

A Simplistic *AS* Curve

Having redefined the *AD* curve so that it made semantic sense, I then had a curve to which an *AS* curve could be added without overspecifying the model. I did this by adding a perfectly inelastic *AS* curve to the model. Thus, for my short-run curve, I used the mainstream long-run specification that the wage and price level would adjust equally. I did so primarily for simplicity of exposition since changing the assumptions will not change the essence of the argument; it just makes the analysis much more complicated. This assumption eliminates the role of diminishing marginal returns and any issue of relative price in the analysis. It also eliminates any distributional effects, leaving one with a highly simplified model with which one can discuss adjustment to equilibrium. These simplifying assumptions focus the analysis on the interdependence between aggregate demand and aggregate supply, and avoid the many complications that can arise when relative price changes are occurring simultaneously.

CLASSICAL AND KEYNESIAN ADJUSTMENT TO EQUILIBRIUM

After making these assumptions one has a model with a perfectly inelastic *AS* curve and a downward-sloping *AD* curve. This model looks identical to the standard mainstream classical model. But there is a fundamental difference between my *AS/AD* model and the mainstream model. In my model the multiplier process – which involves an aggregate interdependence between supply and demand – has not yet been included. Thus, there can be no presumption that the model will lead to an aggregate equilibrium at the intersection of the *AS* and *AD* curves since there can be no presumption that other things remain constant. In the Keynesian model other things definitely do not remain constant.

For the equilibrium to be determined independently of the adjustment process towards that equilibrium, something must fix real output at its initial level. The classical model implicitly assumes that this occurs. That assumption is what allows the price level adjustment time to bring about an equilibrium. Keynesian economics challenged that assumption, but the neo-Keynesians eventually adopted the classical model's assumptions. It assumed that the price level adjusts in a way that producers do not adjust their production; they only adjust their wages and prices. These assumptions are necessary to see that the aggregate supply curve remains constant.

The resulting mainstream neo-Keynesian adjustment story is a very strange story – which has no room for the multiplier or for Keynesian economics. It is a story that requires individuals, faced with excess demand, to assume that the price level will adjust quickly to eliminate the excess demand that they face, not to reduce output. Their willingness to lower their relative price is not at issue. The classical adjustment mechanism requires far more than this willingness. It requires that individuals believe that everyone will adjust their prices instantaneously. This follows because unless everyone lowers their nominal price until aggregate equilibrium is reached, the classical adjustment process will not work completely. That story requires that everyone believes everyone will adjust nominal prices immediately, so that the price level adjusts to bring about equilibrium instantaneously, leaving no chance of any disequilibrium. For most people, this mainstream story is not an acceptable microdynamic foundation; I certainly would not try to sell it to my students.

I think most mainstream economists know that it is not an acceptable story; that is why the above story is not the story that the textbooks tell when they present the analysis. Instead they tell a Keynesian-type dynamic adjustment story even though it is not consistent with their assumption of fixed supply.

The reason they tell a Keynesian story is that the Keynesian model has a much more intuitively reasonable dynamic microfoundation. The Keynesian story is one in which at most output levels aggregate supply is demand-constrained. That means that faced with an increase in demand firms will increase real output, and faced with a decrease in demand firms will decrease output. In the Keynesian model one cannot assume the *AS* curve is stable; it shifts with expectations of demand. Thus, the Keynesian dynamic adjustment story involves a supply response which will bring about a further demand response which ... This is of course the multiplier process. What I am claiming is that the only way of showing the multiplier process in the *AS/AD* model is through interactive shifts of the *AS* and *AD* curves.

Most mainstream economists are uncomfortable with my shifting short-run *AS* curves. This discomfort reflects their tendency to think of the aggregate economy in partial equilibrium terms. In the aggregate, however, stability of aggregate supply (upon which the natural rate assumption is based) is an arbitrary assumption, not a law of nature. It is intuitively much more reasonable to assume the *AS* curve is unstable because aggregate supply depends on expectations of aggregate demand and demand depends on supply. The equilibrium in this model is a type of sunspot model where slight changes in expectations can cause significant changes in the equilibrium level of output.

Since it has the supply curve shifting, this construction undermines the mainstream story of disequilibrium adjustment implicit in the *AS/AD* model. Since the wage–price ratio does not change, firms have no reason to hire more workers because relative costs have not fallen. Unless the mainstream economists add to their story an additional force that will always cause the *AS* curve to shift back to full employment equilibrium, there is no dynamic disequilibrium force pushing the economy back to its initial equilibrium. One such story would involve expectations – for some reason individuals always expect that full employment will be reached and structure their supply decisions accordingly. A second such story would involve price and wage level flexibility. At any level of output lower than full employment, the wage and price level will fall, bringing the Pigou and other effects into play, increasing the quantity of aggregate demand, and shifting the equilibrium level of output – shifting both supply and demand back to the long-run full employment equilibrium. On the surface this story seems much the same as told by the mainstream. But there is a fundamental difference. In this story the Pigou effect must shift both demand and supply back to their equilibrium. It is a story of equilibrium selection in a multiple equilibrium model. In the inconsistent mainstream model the Pigou effect adjustment story is a story of disequilibrium equilibrium adjustment in an equilibrium model. That is why it only need affect demand; supply had remained at its high level.

WHY DID THE MAINSTREAM NOT SEE PAUL'S POINT?

Explained in the above terms, and after initial resistance, I have had reasonable luck in pointing out to mainstream economists the problem in the standard *AS/AD* model. Most with whom I have argued now agree with me that there is a flaw in the textbook model. (But I must admit that few see it as more than simply a pedagogical problem. Still, getting them to see the pedagogical problem is a partial success.) The *Z* model incorporates many of these same insights. Why can mainstream economists follow the above argument, but not accept Paul's *Z* model when it said essentially the same thing?

To see the reason let us return to the *Z* model and Paul's discussion of its microfoundations. In the microfoundations to Davidson's *Z* curve there are two things going on. First there are the diminishing marginal returns, the aspect of the *Z* curve that Davidson emphasizes in his microfoundation discussion. Then, there is the interconnection between *AS* and *AD* (my definition). As I read Paul, he never makes it clear that this interconnection was central to his analysis. Instead, in discussing microfoundations he primarily talks about diminishing marginal returns.

Paul's focus on diminishing marginal returns confuses the matter enormously, and leaves his microfoundations unclear at best, and possibly wrong since so many things are changing. These unclear microfoundations of the Z curve, in my view, go a long way towards explaining why the mainstream did not understand Davidson's point. Had Davidson not included diminishing marginal returns, and had he, instead, focused his microfoundations discussion on the interconnection between *AS* and *AD*, his point that the labour and goods market must be analysed as a composite whole would have been far more understandable. By focusing the microfoundations of the Z curve on diminishing marginal returns, it looked as if Davidson was simply adding a complication, not providing a fundamentally different view of the relevant microfoundations. My alternative specification of the *AS/AD* model was designed to help point it out.

Since mainstream economists did not understand that the microfoundations to the Z curve involved an interdependence of *AS* and *AD*, Davidson's microfoundations to his *D* curve looked very strange. In presenting those microfoundations (Davidson and Smolensky, 1964, pp. 133–4; 155–6) Davidson develops a curve in price level/real output space that he calls a *demand outlay* curve. That demand outlay curve is upward-sloping, not downward-sloping, like the mainstream *AD* curve.

For most mainstream economists Davidson's demand outlay curve is very strange. It is derived from a quite different set of assumptions than mainstream economists use when they think about *AD*. It is not a curve derived from the *IS/LM* model and it does not consider the Pigou and other price level effects on *AD*. Thus, the mainstream could attribute Paul's rejection of their model simply to a rejection of those effects. They did not recognize that although he rejected those effects as quantitatively insignificant, that rejection was not central to his rejection of the mainstream model.[6] The point is that Davidson's *D* curve is a locus of equilibrium points along a shifting *AS* and *AD* curve. It only has meaning given the interconnection between supply and demand. This insight is buried in Davidson's *D* curve. Once one recognizes this insight, it is clear that Davidson's microfoundations to his *D* curve are not inconsistent with my reformulated *AS/AD* analysis. The two curves are shown in Figure 3.2.

The above translations have been sketchy for reasons of limited space. But I believe they have been sufficiently spelled out to convince the reader that a correctly specified mainstream model is not so different from Paul's post Keynesian model. The mainstream economists' difficulty in understanding Paul's criticism of their microfoundations derived from flaws in their microfoundations. These flaws entered because they did not keep clearly in

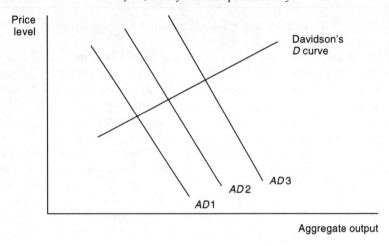

Figure 3.2   Davidson's D *curve and reformulated* AS/AD *analysis*

mind that any curve derived from a model involving the multiplier involved a specification of aggregate supply. Since the multiplier model already includes a specification of aggregate supply it is inappropriate to add an alternative specification of aggregate supply back to the model unless that specification is consistent with the multiplier model specification. The problem of communication arose because Paul's Z formulation did not clearly point out the interconnection, and hence it allowed the mainstream economists to avoid facing up to their problems, implicitly attributing faulty logic to Paul and the post Keynesians.

DAVIDSON'S FATE

Now that I have completed my translations, let me return to the theme with which I started this essay – the comparison of Paul Davidson with Paul Newman's character in *Cool Hand Luke*. I am pleased to end this essay in a quite different way than the movie ended. True, Paul Davidson has not had the influence on the profession that he deserves, but his fate has not been to be chased by the mainstream into a small shack and shot. Instead his fate was to marry a most beautiful and charming wife, to become a connoisseur of fine food and wine; to have great kids; and to have played a major role in influencing many heterodox economists, and even a handful of mainstream economists. Not all that bad an ending, even if the profession never does understand Paul's ideas.

NOTES

1. Given the limited space I have, I will assume the Z model is well known to readers of this book. For those who are unfamiliar with it, see Davidson and Smolensky (1964) and Davidson (1994).
2. Davidson (Davidson and Smolensky, 1964) distinguishes the two by calling the *AE/AP* model a forecasting model and the Z model an equilibrium model. In this paper I do not follow Davidson in making that distinction but, instead, treat both of them as equilibrium models.
3. To say that Davidson's microfoundations point out a problem with mainstream micro-foundations is not to say that his microfoundations are the correct ones, or even perfectly logical, but I will not deal with such issues in this paper.
4. To say that there are no logical problems with *IS/LM* is not to say that it is a useful, or appropriate, framework to capture Keynes's or the classicals' views, or that it corresponds to reality.
5. Some books focus on institutional rigidities of changing prices, but it is difficult to derive a supply curve in competitive markets based on such assumptions; the books that use this approach simply gloss over such inconsistencies.
6. While Davidson's discussion of microfoundations is much more consistent than the main-stream discussion, it also has problems. An important one is the representative agent problem. Paul assumes that one can simply sum up industry curves to arrive at an aggregate curve, but does not discuss the potential, indeed likely, problems of doing so – specifically that in the micro curve the downward slope was based on a change in the relative price, but in the aggregate, relative prices do not change. If wages are not fixed the model falls apart; it is, at best, a microfoundation for a short-run model .

REFERENCES

Colander, D. (1995), 'The Stories We Tell: A Reconsideration of AS/AD Analysis', *Journal of Economic Perspectives*, **9**(3), 169–88.

Davidson, P. (1994), *Post Keynesian Macroeconomic Theory*, Aldershot, Hants: Edward Elgar.

Davidson, P. and E. Smolensky (1964), *Aggregate Supply and Demand Analysis*, New York: Harper & Row.

Klamer, A. (1984), *Conversations with Economists*, Totowa, NJ: Rowman and Allanheld.

4. Keynes's philosophy and post Keynesian monetary theory

Sheila C. Dow

Paul Davidson has been notable, among many things, for being one of the few to keep alive Keynes's monetary theory at the same time as it was being transformed by the neoclassical synthesis. He is also notable for stressing Keynes's philosophical foundations and their implications for his economics at a time when these two aspects of Keynes's work were generally assumed to be separable. This was most evident in his book, *Money and the Real World*, first published in 1972. Paul Davidson has continued over the years to develop these themes in a wide range of publications, bringing them together again in *Post Keynesian Macroeconomic Theory*, published in 1994.

It is the purpose of this contribution to focus on the interdependence between Keynes's monetary theory and his philosophy, taking *Money and the Real World* as the starting-point. A brief account of Paul Davidson's expression of this interdependence is provided in the next section, highlighting the emphasis placed on money's central role in the economic process as the denominator of contracts, the foundations of the demand for money in Keynes's theory of uncertainty, and the interrelationships between liquidity preference and production and investment decisions. Since that book was written, there has been a marked growth in interest in Keynes's philosophy, encouraged by the publication of Keynes's *Collected Writings* (referred to here as *C.W.*). This has led to the emergence of a complex literature elaborating on Keynes's philosophy in general, and on its implications for monetary theory in particular. The focus in this application has tended to be the theory of liquidity preference; an account of this literature is provided in the third section. Detailed analysis of the origins of uncertainty and the basis for differing degrees of uncertainty associated with differing degrees of weight has allowed for a more complex understanding of the speculative and precautionary demands for money, and their relationship with uncertainty.

Paul Davidson has been concerned with the supply of credit in addition to the theory of liquidity preference. Yet there has been a dichotomization within post Keynesian monetary theory between liquidity preference theory and endogenous credit theory, with some suggesting that the two are incompatible. This dichotomization has been challenged by those who have analysed credit creation in terms of banks' liquidity preference, drawing inspiration from Keynes. In so far as the theory of liquidity preference derives from Keynes's theory of uncertainty, so too must this theory of credit creation. The philosophical foundations of this application of liquidity preference theory have not been spelled out before in much detail. An attempt is made in the fourth and fifth sections to remedy this lack, focusing particularly on the question of risk assessment.

PAUL DAVIDSON ON KEYNES'S PHILOSOPHY AND MONETARY THEORY

Paul Davidson made it clear that uncertainty was a central concept for his monetary theory by devoting the second chapter of *Money and The Real World* to 'Uncertainty and the Historical Model'. He refers to Keynes's philosophical work, parallelling that of Knight, as follows: 'Keynes, who had also laboured in the field of probability and non-measurable uncertainty, took up the cudgel and started a revolution in economic thinking' (Davidson, 1972, p. 10). Davidson thereby distanced himself from the neoclassical synthesis account of Keynes, which had confined the significance of uncertainty to the speculative demand for money, and even there represented uncertainty as risk; Davidson was later to publish a symposium in the *Journal of Post Keynesian Economics* in which Hicks (1980–81) expressed his own dissatisfaction with the *IS/LM* apparatus because it had precluded a satisfactory treatment of uncertainty. But more fundamentally Davidson highlights what had been lost in the neoclassical synthesis, i.e. any notion of 'a revolution in economic thinking'. Davidson spells out the crucial distinction between uncertainty and risk, as Keynes had done before, where risk is defined as quantifiable uncertainty. We shall see that it is this distinction which carries through in all our analysis of Keynes's monetary theory and our projections of it into the context of modern monetary theory.

It is important to note that Davidson explicitly derives his theoretical discussion from a vision of the nature of reality; Davidson's approach is thus compatible with the later specifications of critical realism (see Lawson, 1989). It is no accident that 'the real world' features in the title of his book on monetary theory. Davidson argues that uncertainty is the general case in the real world, and risk the particular. In order for uncertainty to be quantified it must be possible for real processes to generate a frequency distribution on the basis of a stable set of structural relationships: there must be, in Keynes's expression, limited independent variety. Keynes went to great lengths to argue that the scope for measuring probability was limited:

> The attention, out of proportion to their real importance, which has been paid...to the limited class of numerical probabilities, seems to be a part explanation of the belief, which it is the principal object of this chapter to prove erroneous, that all probabilities must belong to it. (*C.W.*, VIII, 40)

Davidson uses the terminology of ergodicity to specify the distinction between those processes which yield numerical probabilities and those which do not. In doing so, he extends Keynes's conception to later work on stochastic processes developed by the Moscow School of Probability. Ergodic processes are those which yield averages over time which provide good estimates of space or statistical averages at a point in time, and vice versa; statistical averages then are good predictors. Non-ergodic processes are those where average values vary over time. It follows from Davidson's vision of the economy in terms of processes which unfold irreversibly in historical time that most processes are non-ergodic and thus not amenable to representation as ergodic, stochastic processes. This mirrors Keynes's organicist view of the world (see Carabelli, 1995).

Davidson shows how uncertainty is essential to an understanding of money. First money's role itself is the product of uncertainty. Davidson has demonstrated that contracts, specified in money, are necessary to facilitate the functioning of a capitalist economy. Contracts, where debts are to be discharged in the form of money, introduce a realm of certainty in a generally uncertain environment. This mirrors Keynes's conception of the monetary production economy as a distinctive form of economic organization where money plays an integral part in the planning and organization of production (see Rotheim, 1981). This understanding of money can in turn be contrasted with the separation of money and real activity in mainstream economic theory. Davidson demonstrates the logical problems which arise in mainstream theory when the starting-point is fictional assumptions which preclude unquantifiable uncertainty; the abstraction from money in 'real' models to which money is later appended is one such fiction. But this fiction rules out the very rationale for money's existence (see Davidson, 1977). Subsequent work has developed this view of money as inextricably bound up with the economic process, most notably performing the unit of account function in the specification of debt and labour contracts (see Heinsohn and Steiger, 1987; Wray, 1990).

Davidson further emphasizes that the quantity of money demanded, or the degree of liquidity preference, can only be understood with reference to uncertainty. Here he draws heavily on Keynes's 1937 *Quarterly Journal of Economics* article (*C.W.*, XIV) where Keynes puts even more emphasis on the concept of uncertainty than he had done in *The General Theory*: 'our desire to hold money as a store of wealth is a barometer of the degree of our distrust of our own calculations and conventions concerning the future' (*C.W.*, XIV, 116). This distrust is due to the limited capacity to measure risk, i.e. to uncertainty, which arises when 'there is no scientific basis on which to form any calculable probability whatever. We simply do not know' (*C.W.*, XIV, 114). Liquidity preference thus follows from money's central economic role as the asset whose value is most certain (and thus the asset which denominates contracts and is used in payment). Further, changes in liquidity preference which follow from discrete shifts in confidence in expectations (i.e. in uncertainty) have real consequences for plans to purchase reproducible assets, and thus for income and employment; money is non-neutral in the long run. In chapter 4 of *Money and the Real World*, Davidson accordingly derives the conditions for the stimulation of production of reproducible assets.

In terms of the various sources of liquidity preference, Davidson emphasizes the role of uncertainty as most central to both the speculative and precautionary demands. (Uncertainty is relevant more indirectly to the finance motive through the effect of uncertainty on the investment decision.) For Keynes, the speculative motive was driven by the effort in 'securing profit from knowing better than the market what the future will bring forth' (*C.W.*, VII, 170). Such a conceptualization requires scope for differing sets of expectations about market prices, i.e. uncertainty. The precautionary motive is driven by the need '[t]o provide for contingencies requiring sudden expenditure and for unforeseen opportunities of advantageous purchase' (*C.W.*, VII, 196). Since these purchases could include financial assets as well as reproducible assets, there is a direct link between the speculative motive and the precautionary motive. This link was not apparent in *The General Theory*, and only emerged in Keynes's treatment of the two motives together as the demand for inactive balances in his various 1937 articles on monetary theory.

Davidson had sustained this account of Keynes's theory of liquidity preference as deriving explicitly from his work on probability without the benefit of all Keynes's philosophical papers which were subsequently published in the *Collected Writings* series. But work on these papers, which only began in any depth in the 1980s, has produced a rich literature from which new work has emerged on the content of Keynes's philosophy and the connection between this philosophy and his economics. In the next section we consider the contribution of this literature to our understanding of the theory of liquidity preference.

LIQUIDITY PREFERENCE IN THE KEYNES PHILOSOPHY LITERATURE

Our understanding of the links between Keynes's philosophy and his monetary theory has been enhanced by the recent flowering of scholarship on Keynes's philosophy and its relationship with his economics. The publication of Keynes's *Collected Writings* and the pioneering doctoral work of Carabelli (1988) and O'Donnell (1989) have provided the base material for what is now a large literature on the interdependence between Keynes's philosophy and his economics. The view supported by Davidson as one of a small minority, that Keynes's philosophy underpinned his economics, has now become the conventional wisdom.

The theory of liquidity preference is picked out by O'Donnell and, to a lesser extent by Carabelli, as illustrating this interdependence. O'Donnell (1989, pp. 238–9) focuses attention on the speculative demand for money, since its only possible rationale is 'uncertainty as to the future course of the rate of interest' (*C.W.*, VII, 201). Here O'Donnell is following Keynes's approach of *The General Theory* in lumping the precautionary demand in with the transactions demand for money, and focusing on the speculative demand as being most directly related to uncertainty. O'Donnell (1989, ch. 4) further devotes detailed attention to Keynes's concept of weight, as developed in the *Treatise on Probability*, as determining the degree of confidence held in any probability estimate (i.e. any set of expectations). Weight is derived from the relative amount of relevant evidence brought to bear on the (generally unquantified) estimation of probability. The greater the amount of relevant evidence, the greater the degree of confidence with which expectations may be held as to the relative returns on alternative assets, and thus the less the demand for money which earns no monetary return. This focus on weight highlights an important aspect of Keynes's theory of probability: uncertainty may be a matter of degree. The implication is that speculative demand for money increases with uncertainty. Keynes himself had deflected attention from the question of degree of uncertainty by referring rather to absolute uncertainty in the 1937 *QJE* article: 'We simply do not know' (*C.W.*, XIV, 114).

Money's return is the liquidity premium, which is lower the greater the confidence in expectations as to returns on alternative assets. Abstracting from carrying costs, the returns on alternative financial assets are made up of the expected monetary return plus liquidity (all assets potentially being liquid in some degree). But the expected return is itself uncertain. It must thus be discounted by the degree of belief in the expectation, i.e. in its (generally unquantified) probability (see Runde, 1994). Indeed Keynes had addressed this issue in response to Townshend's attempts to understand Keynes's economics in terms of his theory of probability. Keynes (*C.W.*, XXIX, 293) distinguished between the liquidity premium on money as being associated with weight and the risk premium as being associated with probability. The comparison then is between the greater liquidity attached to money (discounted by weight) and the greater expected return attached to alternative assets (discounted by degree of improbability). New evidence, therefore, which increases confidence in expectations thus reduces money's liquidity relative to the expected return on alternative assets, and may also reduce the discount on the expected return on alternative assets, both encouraging a fall in the demand for money. But, as Runde (1990) pointed out, increased weight may also be associated with reduced probability (albeit held with more confidence) if the new evidence reveals previously unrecognized ignorance. In such a case, the liquidity premium attached to money would have decreased but the expected return on alternative assets, discounted by risk, would also have decreased. The demand for money might then either decrease or increase as a result of the new evidence.

One significant consequence of this work has been not only to treat the speculative demand for money and the precautionary demand together, but to shift attention towards the precautionary demand as the element on which uncertainty has most bearing. While the rationale for speculative demand lies with uncertainty and its consequence in diversity of opinion, the decision on speculative grounds to hold money or not to hold it requires certainty equivalence, i.e. it requires speculators to act as if they were certain. Speculative demand for money rises when speculators act as if they know that the return on alternative assets will be low, i.e. they have confidence in expected return discounted by risk; it is not that money's liquidity premium is high but that the expected return on alternative assets, discounted for risk, is low. As in subjective expected utility theory, speculators are prepared to place bets (see Runde, 1994). Precautionary demand for money arises, however, when the degree of confidence in expectations of returns, discounted for risk, is low; speculators are not prepared to place bets. Money's liquidity premium dominates any expected return discounted for risk. This line of reasoning implies that it is precautionary demand, rather than speculative demand, which is the barometer of the degree of uncertainty (see Chick, 1983).

Yet Winslow (1995) argues that, where uncertainty is a matter of degree, it has direct bearing also on that element of precautionary demand (precautionary demand I) which can be understood as resulting from rational choice; weight is *presumed* to be known, just as probability is presumed to be known under certainty equivalence. But he argues that there is an element of precautionary demand for money (precautionary demand II) which refers rather to situations of absolute uncertainty, where reason cannot be applied. Keynes's theory of probability was an attempt to specify grounds for rational belief.

Thus low weight provides rational grounds for increasing the demand for money according to the precautionary and speculative motives. But Winslow draws attention to Keynes's allowance for the irrational when he specifies the demand for idle balances as 'a barometer of the degree of our distrust of our own calculations and conventions concerning the future' as being based 'partly on reasonable and partly on instinctive grounds' (*C.W.*, XIV, 116). Winslow proceeds to discuss this instinctive element in the demand for money in psychoanalytic terms; he demonstrates that Keynes considered the love of money to be irrational. Since the notion of weight itself requires calculation (which is not necessarily quantifiable), then, he argues, it too comes under the same certainty-equivalence heading as probability and is therefore more properly applied to speculation and to rational precautionary demand than to the absence of speculation entailed in the irrational element of precautionary demand. Precautionary demand arising from absolute uncertainty is then the expression of irrational motives.

But the psychological and the reasonable cannot be so easily dichotomized; they are combined in both the precautionary and speculative motives. Weight is a measure of relevant evidence. Yet the concept of relevance entails knowledge which itself is subject to uncertainty: knowledge as to the causal processes underlying the variable of which expectations are being formed. There is thus the question of relevant evidence with respect to the theory as to these underlying processes, and then relevant evidence with respect to the foundations of this theory, and so on *ad infinitum*. It might be argued that the case of absolute uncertainty corresponds to the case of absolute lack of knowledge, and it is then that instincts take over from reason. But even then, it requires some knowledge to recognize ignorance; absolute uncertainty is not an attainable state, and so weight, and thus relative uncertainty, continue to play a part. The psychological element in the process is not constrained however to cases of high degrees of uncertainty; it enters into the decision (often unconscious) about the degree of confidence to hold in knowledge as to relevance (at whatever level), i.e. how much uncertainty to admit (at whatever level). As Keynes (*C.W.*, VII, 148) pointed out, 'It is reasonable, therefore, to be guided to a considerable degree by the facts about which we feel somewhat confident, even though they may be less decisively relevant to the issue than other facts about which knowledge is vague and scanty'. When asset prices are rising and confidence in expectations is high, those who act may not have more relevant evidence than before; they may simply choose to ignore their ignorance. There is ample evidence, in corporate behaviour for example, of refusal to admit the relevance of new evidence (see Earl, 1984). Thus judgements as to both low and high weight involve a psychological judgement about how much ignorance to recognize and thus how to regard the issue of relevance of evidence. The non-rational thus enters in the very judgement as to the degree of uncertainty. (See Dow, 1995, for a fuller expression of this argument.)

This literature on the implications of Keynes's philosophy for his theory of liquidity preference and how the latter might be developed is still evolving. Meanwhile there has been increasing attention paid within post Keynesian monetary theory to the issue of the centrality or otherwise of Keynes's theory of liquidity preference and its compatibility or otherwise with theories of credit endogeneity. This apparent dichotomy in the monetary theory literature may have served to encourage the focus on the implications of Keynes's philosophy for liquidity preference theory, without considering its applicability to the credit counterpart of money. Yet there is ample scope for such an application by taking again the distinction between risk and uncertainty as our starting-point. It is to this application that we now turn.

KEYNES'S PHILOSOPHY AND THE SUPPLY OF CREDIT

Within post Keynesian monetary theory there has been some divergence of interest between those who have focused on the theory of liquidity preference and those who have focused on endogenous money (see Cottrell, 1994). Thus Kaldor (1982) argued that Keynes had been mistaken to emphasize liquidity preference. Because this theory, he argued, retained too much of orthodox supply and demand analysis, it was easy to incorporate the theory into the *IS/LM* framework and thus make Keynes's theory a special case within the neoclassical synthesis. In any case, if the supply of money is the by-product of credit decisions taken in the private sector relative to an interest rate set by the monetary authorities, then, no matter how valid the theory of liquidity preference in itself, it had no material consequence. It was the investment decision underlying credit demand which should take centre stage.

It has been conventional to identify the focus on money and uncertainty as the American strand of post Keynesianism in which Davidson's leadership has played a pivotal role (see Hamouda and Harcourt, 1988). However, it must be remembered that Davidson and Weintraub (1973) sustained Keynes's vision of a monetary production economy in an analysis which allowed for money supply, as well as money demand, to be endogenously generated by the economic process (although they did retain the monetary authorities' potential capacity to determine the money supply). Central to their analysis is the role of money in an uncertain environment, notably as the denominator of wage contracts. Davidson has continued to retain this conception of money as cause and effect, allowing for the possibility that the banking system under particular institutional arrangements may, 'if willing and able', respond to increases in the demand for credit (see Davidson, 1994, p. 136). Rather than divorcing money and uncertainty from production and investment decisions (and thus the credit market), Davidson has consistently treated them all as fundamentally interrelated.

The endogenous money stream of post Keynesianism has, in contrast, downplayed the direct relationship between money and uncertainty which has been the hallmark of Davidson's interpretation of Keynes. Uncertainty only enters indirectly in so far as it is an element in the determination of investment plans. It is the demand for credit concomitant with these plans which determines the volume of credit the money counterpart of which, it is argued, is willingly held (see for example Moore, 1988).

But there have been many post Keynesians (including Chick, 1983; Kregel, 1984–85; Dow and Dow, 1989; Wray, 1990; Lavoie, 1992; Dow, 1993; Carvalho, 1995; and Arestis and Howells, 1996) who, like Davidson, have explicitly combined liquidity preference theory and endogenous credit theory. The crucial focus, which has generally been absent both from the liquidity preference and endogenous credit streams, is on the decision making of the banks and, in particular, on their liquidity preference. Like Davidson, Chick and Kregel have consistently couched their accounts of liquidity preference theory in terms of uncertainty. In applying liquidity preference theory to banks, therefore, they were demonstrating the applicability of Keynes's philosophy to the theory of credit creation. Latterly, i.e. from the late 1980s, contributions to this literature have been directly addressed to the 'horizontalist' endogenous money position epitomized by Moore's work and made influential by Moore (1988). The focus has been on arguing that banks are not passive in the face of credit demand (as implied by the horizontal money supply curve) but rather make active decisions on the supply of credit according to their state of liquidity preference. Arestis and Howells (1996) in particular argue that the horizontal supply curve is mis-specified; it should be understood as a series of loci of intersection of shifting pairs of curves representing liquidity preference of the non-bank public and the supply of money, derived from the supply of credit.

This focus on banks' liquidity preference is quite consistent with Keynes's own monetary theory (see Dow, forthcoming). Moore (1988) has argued persuasively that Keynes understood the supply of money to be endogenous, in so far as it derives from the supply of credit. It was only for particular purposes in *The General Theory* that he took the money supply as given. But, rather than considering the supply of credit to be determined by the demand of the non-bank public (as in the horizontalist theory), Keynes saw it as determined by the banking system, by which he meant the private sector banking system in conjunction with the monetary authorities. Scope is thus provided for the banks themselves to influence the volume of credit. Indeed, Carvalho (1995, p. 18) points out that the theory of liquidity preference was introduced by Keynes as a way of explaining the portfolio behaviour of the banks at the start of the First World War, given the uncertainty of the time, which thwarted the efforts of the Bank of England to sustain asset prices. Further, Keynes discussed interest rate determination in terms of the banks' liquidity preference: '[T]he rate of interest [is] determined by the interplay of the terms on which the public desires to become more or less liquid and those on which the banking system is ready to become more or less liquid' (*C.W.*, XIV, 219). Liquidity preference for banks, just as for non-banks, is grounded in uncertainty, and thereby in Keynes's philosophy. The same considerations of probability estimation under uncertainty with respect to expected returns on assets, and the degree of relevant evidence which may be brought to bear, also apply to banks. Banks' liquidity preference too is vulnerable to discrete shifts with changing evidence, changing confidence with which that evidence is assessed and changing conceptions of relevance. There is a clear connection then between banks' liquidity preference and credit creation. Taking account of banks' liquidity preference has the direct implication that, far from dichotomizing the theories of liquidity preference and endogenous money, the two are closely interrelated and thus potentially enrich each other.

Further, by considering liquidity preference with respect to banks rather than households, important new directions of theory development are suggested. First, the expression of liquidity preference for banks has implications for the size of their portfolios as much as their composition; for banks, the decision to lend is a decision simultaneously to shift the balance of assets towards illiquidity and to expand the portfolio. Thus the manifestation of a fall in banks' liquidity preference is an increase in advances which involves the creation of a new debt (as opposed to the purchase of existing securities which does not). Furthermore, banks can also express their liquidity preference on the liability side of their balance sheets in terms of the structure of funding they choose; a bank with low liquidity preference might thus choose to compete for new sight deposits rather than borrow at term from the interbank market. Therefore, a fall in liquidity preference would be associated with an expansion in bank portfolios together with a shift towards a (*ceteris paribus*) less liquid asset structure and liability structure.

This conception of liquidity preference has particular consequences for banks, given their capacity to create credit. Nevertheless the theory of liquidity preference could usefully be extended similarly to both sides of household and firms' balance sheets, and to their size as well as their composition (see Dow and Dow, 1989; Dow, 1993, pp. 165–8). The argument for doing so is given increased force by the changing pattern of household and company finance. Now the prevalent pattern is for both households and firms to be both borrowers and lenders; both are actively concerned with the size as well as the composition of their balance sheets. Thus, when liquidity preference falls, households and firms are more willing to expand their portfolios by incurring debt in order to buy consumer durables and capital goods, respectively. Alternatively, when liquidity preference rises because of increased uncertainty, the refusal to place bets takes the form of an unwillingness to incur more debt to finance illiquid assets. The volume of credit is thus determined by the demand for credit on the part of households and firms (which in turn is influenced by liquidity preference) and the willingness of the banks to supply it (which in turn is influenced by their liquidity preference), together with the influence of the monetary authorities on the financial environment within which these judgements are made.

The second area of enquiry suggested by consideration of banks' liquidity preference takes us back even more directly to Keynes's philosophy. Banks are conventionally depicted as determining their willingness to supply credit to particular customers, or classes of customers, on the basis of risk assessment. The endogenous money literature slides over issues raised by risk assessment by presuming banks to be willing to meet the demand for credit expressed by creditworthy customers (see Moore, 1988, p. 24). A theory of endogenous money has also been developed in the new Keynesian literature (see for example Stiglitz and Weiss, 1981) which raises the issue of risk assessment, but does so in conventional mainstream terms, i.e. by presuming economic processes to be ergodic. In other words, the default risk attached to a prospective loan is presumed to be knowable. (It is a further crucial assumption, for explaining credit rationing, that risk is known by the borrower, but is not known by the lender.) In contrast, Keynes's philosophy would suggest that risk in general is not known, but is a matter of uncertainty. This is as true for the borrower as it is for the lender.

Yet the fact remains that loans are demanded and supplied, and thus risk assessments are made, in spite of this uncertainty. The case of extreme uncertainty in which 'we simply do not know' can only apply to (some) cases of refusal to ask for loans, or to supply them. Yet cases where loan demand is met cannot be characterized by certainty. We need to draw here on the analysis of degrees of uncertainty. We explore this development and its implications for risk assessment in the next section.

KEYNES'S PHILOSOPHY AND RISK ASSESSMENT

It is hard to imagine a debt situation which would approximate to the ergodic. Even debt issued to finance financial transactions is subject to uncertainty even when apparently completely hedged: then there is default risk attached to other financial institutions to consider. As far as corporate borrowing to finance capital projects is concerned, each project is a crucial experiment, not amenable to capture in frequency distributions, as Shackle (1972) has argued. But this uncertainty is compounded by uncertainty over cash flow, as Minsky (1982) has analysed in detail. Further, the knowledge set available to borrowers and lenders is different, both in terms of direct knowledge and of indirect knowledge with respect to the structural relationships governing the borrower's capacity to service the debt. It is not the new Keynesian case where borrowers potentially have full knowledge and lenders have none; it is that they have different knowledge, and necessarily incomplete knowledge.

Risk assessment as far as bank credit is concerned is an assessment of default risk. This poses different forms of risk for borrowers and lenders, a phenomenon raised by Keynes and developed most notably by Minsky (1975). Considering risk assessment in terms of the Keynes philosophy literature, it involves establishing rational grounds for belief in the proposition that a borrower will or will not default. Rational grounds for belief require the marshalling of evidence of various kinds relevant to the state of knowledge as to the structural relationships underlying the borrower's financial position. The degree of probability attached to the proposition will be higher the more the relevant evidence supports the proposition. The weight attached to that probability will be higher the greater the volume of relevant evidence. Where confidence in risk assessment is inadequate, the loan will not be sought and/or will not be granted, and both parties will fall back on attempting to maintain liquidity. Loan requests may of course not be sought and/or not be granted because of a confident assessment of undue risk. Refusal of loan requests due to absolute uncertainty rather corresponds to the element of precautionary demand which operates in the absence of rational grounds, while refusal due to high perceived risk corresponds to that element of precautionary demand based on reason, and to speculative demand.

Generally the *complete* absence of reason associated with precautionary demand in times of absolute uncertainty is unlikely to have significant application to banks. The procedures of risk assessment internal to banks require loan officers to form an assessment of a loan application. Even if the loan officer 'simply does not know', some formal rationale must be expressed (if only for internal bank purposes) for the decision. There is in other words a requirement to ignore ignorance and express some (albeit qualitative) judgement as to risk. Even more so, credit rating agencies are required to make quantitative risk assessments of potential borrowers. This means that estimates of risk are being expressed and quantified regardless of degree of uncertainty. Still degree of uncertainty has a significant role to play in credit creation. In particular there is scope for changing degrees of uncertainty to be expressed as changing estimates of risk.

As Minsky (1975) has shown, changing perceptions of borrowers' and lenders' risk shift the credit demand and supply curves, altering interest charges and the volume of credit. Changes may occur because new evidence arises which suggests that risk has actually changed, or because this evidence changes the degree of confidence with which the assessment is viewed. In other words, risk assessment under uncertainty is of two orders: estimate of probability of default (i.e. default risk) and estimate of confidence attached to the risk estimate (based on weight of evidence). But it is important how far risk assessors recognize the scope of weight. Non-rationality enters in the (usually subconscious) decision as to how far to recognize low weight, or uncertainty. Keynes discussed how assessments are made in the (perceived) absence of weighty evidence. The gap is filled by group or societal conventions, including infectiously high or low animal spirits. In other words, low weight according to one view of what is relevant does not always cause high liquidity preference if weight appears high from another view of relevance. Indeed it is only with the aid of such considerations that we can understand credit market behaviour which sometimes appears to go against available evidence of undue risk. The reaction time of the banks to Mexico's default and also to the emergence of bad domestic debt in the 1980s (far less to prior evidence that these developments were likely) seemed remarkably slow. The role of conventional judgements about market direction is strong in the financial sector, so that credit may be granted with confidence as to low default risk simply because this confidence is shared throughout the sector. Similarly, borrowers may seek credit when the available evidence might suggest an excessive borrowers' risk because animal spirits are running high.

We need therefore to go beyond the two-tier approach to knowledge (with respect to probability and weight) and consider additional elements (see Dow, 1995). The notion of relevant evidence presumes certain knowledge of the underlying structure, i.e. of relevance, when in fact that knowledge too is subject to uncertainty of varying degrees. Indeed, logically we could engage in an infinite regress with respect to uncertainty about uncertainty about uncertainty. But Keynes's theory was designed to establish grounds for rational belief as a basis for action, and infinite regress with respect to uncertainty would remove all basis for action. In practice, therefore, actions are taken as if we had good knowledge of underlying structures. But this line of reasoning implies also that confidence in risk assessment may founder not only because of inadequate evidence (low weight) but also because, in response to some stimulus, *recognition* of uncertainty with respect to underlying structures increases. The onset of awareness of bad debts experienced recently by many banking systems could be one such trigger. The withdrawal from the credit market may thus be understood as much as a recognition of lack of knowledge as a collapse in conventional confidence on the one hand, or rational judgement on the other.

CONCLUSION

It has been the purpose of this essay to focus on the interdependence of Keynes's philosophy for his monetary theory, both with respect to liquidity preference and with respect to the provision of credit. Both are discussed in terms of their common origins in the theory of probability. Recent developments in the theory of probability inspired by Keynes were considered. First, the development of the sources of differing degrees of uncertainty was discussed and its implications for a shift in emphasis between the precautionary and speculative demands for money explained. Second, the theory was applied to the issue of risk assessment in the credit market. The possibility was explored of applying ideas about uncertainty with respect to the foundations of weight to the issue of changing estimates of borrowers' and lenders' risk.

It is remarkable to realize that the Keynes philosophy literature is scarcely ten years old. Yet its impact on our understanding of the underpinnings of Keynes's economics has been enormous. By drawing on this literature, we can see more clearly the interconnectedness between liquidity preference and credit creation. Yet much is still to be done. First, the question of the philosophical foundations for credit market analysis deserves much more detailed attention. Second, considerable efforts need to be devoted to continuing to build up a post Keynesian theory of money and credit which takes account of changing patterns of financial behaviour and of financial institutions. The most significant departure is the change in household and company portfolio behaviour which has made both sectors significant borrowers and lenders. By considering liquidity preference in the context of bank portfolios, i.e. by applying the theory to the size as well as composition of these portfolios, we may be able to derive useful ideas for adapting liquidity preference theory to apply to other sectors.

REFERENCES

References to Keynes's works are from the following edition: *The Collected Writings of John Maynard Keynes*, 29 vols, 1971–79, edited by A. Robinson and D. Moggridge, London: Macmillan for the Royal Economic Society. The listing gives *C.W.*, followed by volume number and date.

Arestis, P. and P. Howells (1996), 'Theoretical Reflections on Endogenous Money', *Cambridge Journal of Economics*.

Carabelli, A. (1988), *Keynes's Method,* London: Macmillan.
Carabelli, A. (1995), 'Uncertainty and Measurement in Keynes: Probability and Organicness' in S.C. Dow and J. Hillard (eds), *Keynes, Knowledge and Uncertainty,* Aldershot, Hants: Edward Elgar.
Carvalho, F.J.C. de (1995), 'Post-Keynesian Developments of Liquidity Preference Theory' in P. Wells (ed.), *Post-Keynesian Economic Theory,* Boston, Mass.: Kluwer.
Chick, V. (1983), *Macroeconomics After Keynes: A Reconsideration of the General Theory,* Oxford: Philip Allan.
Cottrell, A. (1994), 'Post Keynesian Monetary Economics', *Cambridge Journal of Economics,* **18**(6), 587–606.
Davidson, P. (1972), *Money and the Real World,* London: Macmillan. References in the text are to the second, 1978, edition.
Davidson, P. (1977), 'Money and General Equilibrium', *Économie Appliquée,* **30**(2), 541–63.
Davidson, P. (1982–83), 'Rational Expectations: A Fallacious Foundation for Studying Crucial Decision-Making Processes', *Journal of Post Keynesian Economics,* **5**(2), 182–98.
Davidson, P. (1994), *Post Keynesian Macroeconomic Theory. A Foundation for Successful Economic Policies for the Twenty-First Century,* Aldershot, Hants: Edward Elgar.
Davidson, P. (1995), 'Uncertainty in Economics', in S.C. Dow and J. Hillard (eds), *Keynes, Knowledge and Uncertainty,* Aldershot, Hants: Edward Elgar.
Davidson, P. and S. Weintraub (1973), 'Money as Cause and Effect', *Economic Journal* **83**(332), 1117–32.
Dow, A.C. and S.C. Dow (1989), 'Endogenous Credit Creation and Idle Balances', in J. Pheby (ed.), *New Directions in Post-Keynesian Economics,* Aldershot, Hants: Edward Elgar.
Dow, S.C. (1993), *Money and the Economic Process,* Aldershot, Hants: Edward Elgar.
Dow, S.C. (1995), 'Uncertainty about Uncertainty', in S.C. Dow and J. Hillard (eds), *Keynes, Knowledge and Uncertainty,* Aldershot, Hants: Edward Elgar.
Dow, S.C. (forthcoming), 'Keynes and Endogenous Money' in G.C. Harcourt and P. Riach (eds), *A Second Edition of the General Theory,* London: Routledge.
Earl, P.E. (1984), *The Corporate Imagination. How Big Companies Make Mistakes,* Brighton, Sussex: Wheatsheaf.
Hamouda, O. and G.C. Harcourt (1988), 'Post-Keynesianism: From Criticism to Coherence?', *Bulletin of Economic Research,* **40** (January).
Heinsohn, G. and O. Steiger (1987), 'Marx and Keynes: Private Property and Money', *Économies et Sociétés,* **18**, *Monnaie et Production,* 1, 37–72.
Hicks, J.R. (1980–81), 'IS–LM: An Explanation', *Journal of Post Keynesian Economics,* **3** (Winter), 139–54.
Kaldor, N. (1982), *The Scourge of Monetarism,* Oxford: Oxford University Press.
Keynes, J.M. (1921), *A Treatise on Probability, C.W.,* VIII (1973).
Keynes, J.M. (1936), *The General Theory of Employment, Interest and Money, C.W.,* VII (1973).
Keynes, J.M. (1937), *The General Theory and After: Defence and Development, C.W.,* XIV (1973), 109–23.
Keynes, J.M. (1979), *The General Theory and After: A Supplement, C.W.,* XXIX.
Kregel, J. (1984–85), 'Constraints on the Expansion of Output and Employment: Real or Monetary?', *Journal of Post Keynesian Economics,* **7**(2),139–52.

Lavoie, M. (1992), *Foundations of Post-Keynesian Economic Analysis,* Aldershot, Hants: Edward Elgar.

Lawson, T. (1989), 'Abstractions, Tendencies and Stylised Facts', *Cambridge Journal of Economics*, **13**, 59–78.

Minsky, H.P. (1975), *John Maynard Keynes*, London: Macmillan.

Minsky, H.P. (1982), *Inflation, Recession and Economic Policy*, Brighton, Sussex: Wheatsheaf.

Moore, B. (1988), *Horizontalists and Verticalists*, Cambridge: Cambridge University Press.

O'Donnell, R.M. (1989), *Keynes: Philosophy, Economics and Politics*, London: Macmillan

Rotheim, R.J. (1981), 'Keynes' Monetary Theory of Value (1933)', *Journal of Post Keynesian Economics*, **3** (Summer), 568–85.

Runde, J. (1990), 'Keynesian Uncertainty and the Weight of Arguments', *Economics and Philosophy*, **6**, 275–92.

Runde, J. (1994), 'Keynesian Uncertainty and Liquidity Preference', *Cambridge Journal of Economics*, **18**(2), 129–45.

Shackle, G.L.S. (1972), *Epistemics and Economics*, Cambridge: Cambridge University Press.

Stiglitz, J. and A. Weiss (1981), 'Credit Rationing in Markets with Imperfect Information', *American Economic Review*, **71**, 393–410.

Winslow, T. (1995), 'Uncertainty and Liquidity-Preference', in S.C. Dow and J. Hillard (eds), *Keynes, Knowledge and Uncertainty*, Aldershot, Hants: Edward Elgar.

Wray, L.R. (1990), *Money and Credit in Capitalist Economies: The Endogenous Money Approach*, Aldershot, Hants: Edward Elgar.

5. Money, finance and interest rates: some post Keynesian reflections

Malcolm Sawyer*

Paul Davidson has made many contributions in the area of money and finance, and I would highlight here his rediscovery of Keynes's finance motive (Davidson, 1965; Keynes, 1937b), his emphasis on the peculiar nature and properties of money (Davidson, 1972) and the incompatibility of general equilibrium set in an ergodic world with the existence of money, seen as necessary in a non-ergodic uncertain world (Davidson, 1977). In this chapter, our focus is on the relationship between the planned expansion of expenditure and the financial system which can be related to the finance motive.

In the area of macroeconomic analysis, there would seem to be (at least) four specific propositions which serve to delineate the post Keynesian approach from others. These are:

1. In the relationship between savings and investment (one of equality *ex post* in the simple case of a closed private economy) the direction of causation runs from investment to savings.
2. (At least in an industrialized economy) money is credit money largely (or wholly) created within the private sector in response to 'the needs of trade'.
3. The expansion of investment (and expenditure in general) requires financing through the creation of money. This third point links (1) and (2) together and the real and monetary sectors of the economy (Davidson, 1965).
4. Since savings and investment are brought into equality through variations in the level of economic activity, the rate of interest does not perform that role but rather can be seen as a monetary phenomenon. This was clearly stated by both of the founding fathers of post Keynesian economics (Kalecki and Keynes). 'The rate of interest cannot be determined by the demand for and supply of capital because investment automatically brings into existence an equal amount of savings. Thus,

*The author is grateful to Philip Arestis for comments on a first draft.

investment "finances itself" whatever the level of the rate of interest. The rate of interest is, therefore, the result of the interplay of other factors' (Kalecki, 1954, p. 73). And, 'the rate of interest at any time, being the reward for parting with liquidity, is a measure of the unwillingness of those who possess money to part with their liquid control over it. The rate of interest is ... the "price", which equilibrates the desire to hold wealth in the form of cash with the available quantity of cash ...' (Keynes, 1936, p. 167).

It is argued here that whilst these four propositions are more relevant to the real world than the corresponding propositions which would be associated with the neoclassical orthodoxy,[1] nevertheless they have to be qualified in various ways. Indeed, it would sometimes seem that some post Keynesians adopt the extreme versions of these four propositions in order to avoid any hint of being associated with the corresponding orthodox proposition. Thus, for example, the extreme position on (2) would be the 'horizontalist' view of Moore (1988) and others which seeks to deny any sense in which the stock of money may limit economic activity (in nominal terms).

The purpose of this chapter is to consider some debates within the post Keynesian approach on these issues, with special reference to the writings of Kalecki and Keynes. The chapter has three main sections with interrelated themes. The first main section considers the question of causality between savings and investment; the second discusses the relationship between investment expenditure and the creation of money. The third section further elaborates the role of money with particular attention to the rate of interest. It should be noted that the discussion in this chapter is framed in terms of a closed economy without a government other than as a possible provider of money. This is done to aid exposition and to focus on some key issues which are not directly affected by consideration of an open economy and of budget deficits.[2]

The general background to our discussion is that the creation of credit money depends on the demand for and supply of (net) bank loans. Whether the money thereby created remains in existence depends on the demand for money as a stock. Credit money can be destroyed as well as created and if there is not a demand to hold the money brought into existence an option available to those in debt to banks is to repay loans, thereby destroying some money. However in a world of uncertainty and adjustment costs, the stock demand for money is not straightforward: all we mean here by demand for money is a willingness at any moment in time to hold a particular amount of money, even if there is an intention shortly to change the amount held (e.g. awaiting an opportune moment to pay off a debt).[3] Most financial flows are in effect recycling funds from savers (surplus units) to investors (deficit units), but some from banks to the non-bank sector will involve the creation of money.[4] The 'principle of increasing risk' would seem to apply to all borrowing and lending whether it is 'old' money or 'new' money, though our focus here will be on 'new' money (of course, in practice 'new' and 'old' cannot be distinguished).

CAUSALITY BETWEEN SAVINGS AND INVESTMENT

It is argued here that there is no simple causal linkage between savings and investment and that two different approaches to the question of causality should be distinguished. The first approach arises from a thought experiment of the form: compare two otherwise identical time periods (or sets of time periods) where the only difference is the intended level of investment (or of savings): the difference in the intended level then *causes* something or other to happen. This approach arises from (though is not limited to) comparative static exercises and in that respect uses the concept of logical time (Robinson, 1974). The second approach relates to a historical process whereby investment expenditure at one time influences future savings which in turn influence investment expenditure in the subsequent time period. Further, in some cases savings and investment decisions are taken by the same economic agent (usually the enterprise) whilst in other cases those decisions are separated. In the first approach, it is possible to answer the question on the causality involved whereas in the second approach it is not.

The simple circular flow of income representation of Keynesian economics suggests a separation between those who make savings decisions and those who make investment decisions, and then it is possible to ask causal questions on the relationship between savings and investment and also on the mechanisms for bringing them into equality. When much of savings is undertaken by the same individuals who are making investment decisions, answering the causal question is much more difficult, especially when it is recognized that there are mutual influences at work.

The creation of money through loans clearly permits investment expenditure to proceed ahead of the corresponding savings being generated (with actual investment leading to actual savings). There are two differing views in Kalecki's work on the nature of the causal links between investment and savings.[5] The first is that the causal link runs from investment to savings. However, the causal link is based on a thought experiment: suppose that planned investment expenditure rises, then what happens? The general view on the direction of causation is well summarized by Kalecki in his review of Keynes (1936) when he wrote that

For the time being we must stress that, following the previous reasoning, saving does not determine investment but, on the contrary, it is precisely investment which creates savings. The equilibrium between the demand for capital and the supply of capital always exists, whatever the rate of interest, because investment always forces savings of the same amount. (Kalecki, 1990, p. 228)

Kalecki's focus was on investment rather than on savings, and he said little about intended savings (as compared with actual savings). However, in an article published in 1934 but only recently available in English (Kalecki, 1934)[6] he compared 'three systems' which differ in respect of whether 'the principle of preservation of purchasing power rules' and the manner in which the central bank operates. Of interest here is system III (which Kalecki regarded as closer to reality than the other two) in which the above-mentioned principle does not apply and in which the central bank creates money as required. In this system, Kalecki analysed the effects of increased savings whereby the economy 'moves to a new quasi-equilibrium which is characterized by a lower aggregate employment and output' (p. 218).

The second view on the question of causality comes from Kalecki's analysis of the trade cycle. Since the trade cycle is seen as a continuous process through time with no beginning and no end, it is impossible to talk of causation in the sense of an initial cause. It is also the case that the analysis of the trade cycle could be viewed as firmly based in historical time (in the sense of recognizing that time is irreversible). There is a well-known two-way relationship between profits and investment in the analysis of Kalecki and others (notably Joan Robinson): at the level of the enterprise, profits influence investment decisions, whilst at the aggregate level investment expenditure generates profits. Since profits and savings are closely linked in Kalecki's work, there is also a two-way relationship between savings and investment. In some versions of his trade cycle analysis, Kalecki included a 're-investment' factor in the investment equation which reflects the degree to which savings in one period influence investment in a subsequent period (at the level of the enterprise).[7] The firm's financial resources are based on its current savings and additional savings generate some additional investment but on a less than one-for-one basis. 'The inflow of new gross savings ... push forward the barriers set to investment plans by the limited accessibility of the capital market and "increasing risk" (Kalecki, 1991, p. 164).

The question of causality becomes more complex in the approach of authors such as Eichner (1976), Harcourt and Kenyon (1976) where pricing decisions are modelled as seeking to ensure sufficient profits (and hence savings in the form of internal finance) to finance the planned investment expenditure.[8] It could be said that the plans for investment precede decisions on pricing and the generation of savings, though to the extent to which investment is internally financed the act of savings precedes in time the act of investment.

This discussion suggests that the question of causality between savings and investment cannot be answered by saying that one causes the other, but rather that there is a complex interrelationship between them.

INVESTMENT AND THE CREATION OF MONEY

It is clear that any expenditure in a monetary economy has to be financed in some way whether by the use of existing money or through the extension of credit (including the creation of credit money). Similarly, any excess of investment over the level of savings has to be financed by some form of 'new' money. This money may be released from idle balances or created through the banking system.

Kalecki (1933, 1990) (especially 1990, pp. 94–6) drew the distinction between 'unattached' deposits ('deposits without a specific designation'), investment reserves ('funds used for the immediate financing of the production of capital goods') and money in circulation. The financing of investment may occur through the shifting of money from 'unattached' deposits to investment reserves through borrowing by the intending investors. But

> in reality, the increased demand for investment reserves and money in circulation is met not only by a change of unattached deposits to deposits of specific designation but also by an expansion of the credit operations of banks, i.e. by credit inflation in the strict sense, when the assets and liabilities of banks increase. In other words, the increase of credits is matched on the side of assets by an increase in investment reserves, and on the side of liabilities by an increase of money in circulation. (Kalecki, 1990, p. 95)

Both Kalecki and Keynes were clear on the potentially crucial role played by the banks in the expansion of the level of economic activity. One of Kalecki's statements is:

> [T]he possibility of stimulating the business upswing is based on the assumption that the banking system, especially the central bank, will be able to expand credits without such a considerable increase in the rate of interest. If the banking system reacted so inflexibly to every increase in the demand for credit, then no boom would be possible on account of a new invention, nor any automatic upswing in the business cycle. ... Investments would cease to be the channel through which additional purchasing power, unquestionably the *primus movens* of the business upswing, flows into the economy. (Kalecki, 1990, p. 489)

Keynes wrote in similar terms: for example

the banks hold the key position in the transition from a lower to a higher scale of activity. If they refuse to relax (i.e. to provide additional finance), the growing congestion of the short-term loan market or the new issue market, as the case may be, will inhibit the improvement, no matter how thrifty the public purpose to be out of their future income. On the other hand, there will always be exactly enough ex-post saving to take up the ex-post investment and so release the finance which the latter had been previously employing. The investment market can become congested through shortage of cash. It can never become congested through shortage of saving. This is the most fundamental of my conclusions within this field. (Keynes, 1937b, pp. 668–9)

But Keynes also introduced the role of liquidity preference into the credit creation process:

It follows that, if liquidity-preferences of the public (as distinct from the entre-preneurial investors) and of the banks are unchanged, an excess in the finance required by current ex-ante output (it is not necessary to write 'investment', since the same is true of *any* output which has to be planned ahead) over the finance released by current ex-post output will lead to a rise in the rate of interest; and a decrease to a fall. I should not have previously overlooked this point, since it is the coping-stone of the liquidity theory of the rate of interest. (Keynes 1937b, p. 667)

Once it is acknowledged that any increase in investment will usually require to some degree creation of money, then not only is the multiplier process much more complex than suggested in the textbooks[9] but has to be contingent on the further reactions of numerous individuals. The particularly significant reactions can be listed:

1. the willingness of banks to grant loans and thereby create money;
2. as savings occur (as a result of the investment expenditure) the use to which those savings are put, and specifically the extent to which those savings are used, directly or indirectly, to repay loans and thereby extinguish part of the money stock;
3. when savings are 'forced', the reactions of those who save more than they would wish (and presumably have consumed less);
4. the responses of those in receipt of the money created, e.g. whether it is used to buy goods and services, to acquire financial assets or to pay off loans (and thereby extinguish money);[10]
5. the interaction between the demand for money increased by the level of economic activity and the stock of money.

Thus there can be many differing responses of the economy to an increase in expenditure financed by an expansion of credit money, depending on how each of the five reactions just listed turn out. Each of the reactions is likely to depend on the institutional arrangements as well as expectations, precluding any universally valid multiplier analysis.

Moore (1988) claims that the traditional Keynesian concept of the multiplier is 'fundamentally flawed' on the following basis:

> The multiplier relationship provides $\Delta Y = \Delta I/(1 - b)$ where Y refers to output, I to investment and b the marginal propensity to consume, whereas with a constant (or random) velocity of circulation $\Delta Y = V.\Delta M$ where V is the velocity of circulation, and since money is created to finance the investment $\Delta M = \Delta I$ consistency between the two equations appears to require $V = 1/(1 - b)$. (p. 312)

Cottrell (1994a) provides a critique of this analysis: our position is similar to his though we summarize it in a slightly different way, and place emphasis on two perspectives on the status of the multiplier formula.

The multiplier process should be seen as a thought experiment to illustrate some interesting points, rather than as a process which will be fully seen in the real world. In contrast, Moore (1994) argues that 'in a nonergodic world it is impossible even to conceive of any stable macroeconomic equilibrium configuration towards which the system· is tending. Ergo, there can be no Keynesian income multiplier' (p. 127). The multiplier process is worked out for a specified difference in investment and propensity to save, and could be said to belong to an ergodic world. But it is possible to conceive of an equilibrium towards which the economy is moving (as indeed large numbers of economists have done) but where that equilibrium is never attained due to other changes occurring.

The reconciliation between the two formulae given above depends on the status given to them, and here I look at two different perspectives. First, the multiplier relationship (cf. Chick, 1983, ch. 14) can be viewed as an identity in the period when the change in investment occurs with the marginal propensity to consume defined as the actual propensity with no implication that it is the households' desired propensity. If the velocity of circulation equation is similarly treated, but with the velocity of circulation treated as a constant, then it would indeed be the case that the multiplier equation 'is dead', for the story here is that the determining equation is the velocity of circulation one (since it is assumed that people's desires about the velocity of circulation are 'respected'). The velocity of circulation equation is an equilibrium one whilst the multiplier equation is an identity (with an adjustable marginal propensity to consume). But this clearly happens by assumption of a constant velocity of circulation. If instead V is allowed to vary and we write $\Delta Y = V.\Delta M + \Delta V.M$, then little can be said without further assumptions about what happens immediately following an increase in investment (financed by an increase in loans and thereby the stock of money).

It is assumed by Moore that the money created by banks in response to the demand by enterprises for loans to finance investment is maintained in existence. This means not only that banks are willing to accept the increased volume of total loans outstanding but more significantly that individuals are willing to hold the money even when they have outstanding loans. Clearly one option (much touted by Kaldor and Trevithick, 1981) is that some loans are repaid, thereby reducing the stock of money. Treating the velocity of circulation as a constant would seem to imply that the increased stock of money is willingly held (as transactions demand) by the non-bank private sector. Hence, in the short period, the equations could either read $\Delta Y = \Delta I/(1 - b)$ and $\Delta Y = V.\Delta M + \Delta V.M$ with $\Delta M = \Delta I$ or $\Delta Y = \Delta I/(1 - b)$ and $\Delta Y = V.\Delta M$ but with $\Delta M \neq \Delta I$ and hence there is no problem of reconciliation.

The second perspective is to treat the two equations as equilibrium conditions with b and V treated as the desired marginal propensity to consume and velocity of circulation. Money will be created and destroyed *en route* to equilibrium, and the reconciliation then requires that $\Delta M = \Delta I/V.(1 - b)$ where ΔM now refers to the difference between the initial stock of money and the final stock in the new equilibrium.

It should be stressed that this is a limited thought experiment with a number of implicit *ceteris paribus* assumptions. Notable amongst these are the assumption that the rate of interest is held constant and that banks and others permit the stock of money to adjust without any impact on the rate of interest. Clearly, variations in the rate of interest would further complicate the story by influencing investment behaviour, the holding of money and the creation of loans.

ENDOGENOUS MONEY AND THE RATE OF INTEREST

The post Keynesian analysis of endogenous money is often presented as the horizontalist case (to use Moore's terminology) whereby loans (and thereby money) are available to an unlimited degree at the prevailing interest rate on loans: 'The credit money stock is credit-driven and demand determined. Both the base and the money stock are endogenous. The money supply function is horizontal in interest-money space. The supply and demand for credit money are interdependent, and interest rates [sic] are exogenous' (Moore, 1989, p. 66). The interest rate on loans is seen as a mark-up over the central bank minimum lending rate though it is recognized that different classes of borrowers will be charged different rates of interest depending on perceived riskiness.

I would argue that the horizontalist analysis is a closer approximation to the realities of the current stage of banking in many industrialized monetary economies than the other extreme position of the verticalist analysis. The horizontalist position does reflect the credit nature of money, the difficulties of control by the central authorities and the way in which money expands to meet 'the needs of trade'. It is clearly useful for expositional purposes and does enable some key insights on, for example, the role of monetary expansion in the inflationary process to be presented in a relatively simple way without detailed consideration of the complexities of the monetary and credit system. From the oft-quoted situation that most firms have agreed overdraft facilities substantially in excess of their current overdrafts, it can be readily inferred that for most firms at most times their borrowing can be increased to finance higher levels of expenditure, if they so wished.[11]

I would argue that there are some misconceptions in this portrayal of the money and banking systems. First, to say that the interest rate on loans is a mark-up on the discount rate (or any other interest rate related to the cost of funds to the bank) should not be taken to mean either that a uniform price on loans is charged to customers nor that the mark-up is constant. By comparison with the debates over mark-up pricing, it can be recognized that costs are the starting-point for the setting of prices, but subject to a variety of modifications (e.g. the mark-up may vary with the degree of monopoly, or with the state of demand).

Second, the observation that banks 'are price setters and quantity takers in their retail loan and deposit markets' (Moore, 1994, p. 123) does not establish that the supply of loans or the supply of money curves are horizontal in any meaningful sense.[12] It could be similarly observed that the publisher of the book in which this chapter is included has set the price and is willing to supply whatever is demanded at that price, and hence the supply curve for this book is horizontal. But the publisher will have made calculations on what demand they believe will be forthcoming at the price set: different levels of expected demand would have led to different levels of prices. In the case of books, since unit costs do not increase with output, the publisher will be delighted to supply more than had been anticipated at the prevailing price. In this example, it could be concluded that the supply curve for a book was downward-sloping though once the price has been set, any quantity will be supplied, giving the appearance of a horizontal supply curve.[13] Whilst it may be the case that over a considerable range banks would set the same price for different levels of (expected) demand (and in that sense offer a horizontal supply curve) it cannot be inferred from the observation that banks are price setters and quantity takers.[14]

Third, the observations that the central bank declares the discount rate and that banks are usually seen to respond to the discount rate in the setting of their own interest rates (on loans, deposits etc.) tell us little about the determinants of the discount rate. One extreme response would be that the central bank is merely a conduit for the forces which influence the discount rate: in the absence of an auctioneer, someone has to set the price. The constitutional position of the central bank (or equivalent) varies between countries with different degrees of so-called independence and with different objectives set by legislation or custom. But there remains the obvious point that the decisions of the central bank will be influenced by policy objectives and by the perceived interests of the financial community.

Fourth, it can be noted that the liquidity preferences of the banks are ignored in this story. In particular, there is no reaction from the banks when the use of overdraft facilities is increased or reaction to variations in the loan to reserve (or similar) ratios.

The distinction between credit (in this context specifically net bank loans granted over some specified period of time) and money tends to become blurred in this analysis.[15] Clearly, when bank loans are created there is a direct addition to the stock of money, and there is that linkage between loans and money. Whilst on the supply side there may be some further links, it is clear that on the demand side there is (almost) a complete separation. The demand for (net) loans is related to desires to increase expenditure in some form (and the holding of the money created by the loans prior to spending may be seen in terms of the finance motive for holding money (Keynes, 1937a)). The demand for money is a stock demand related to transaction and other motives. On the supply side, banks may be supplying as much money as they wish to do so (e.g. are fully 'loaned up') and are then reluctant to extend further loans. Thus at the extremes the supply of loans and the supply of money are closely linked (i.e. either when both loans and money are readily supplied by the banks at the prevailing structure of interest rates or when the banks are unwilling to supply further loans or money) but that does not necessarily extend to intermediate positions. It could be further argued that the 'principle of increasing risk' (Kalecki, 1937) is a major factor influencing the supply of loans in the sense that after some point any individual firm (or indeed household) can only take out further loans at a higher (and perhaps prohibitive) price. But 'liquidity preference' (Keynes, 1936) is more a factor determining the supply of money in the sense that the banks' portfolio positions (including deposits, total loans and reserves) are influenced by attitudes towards liquidity position.

It is rather paradoxical that the horizontalist analysis has been widely adopted within post Keynesian circles, for the notion that there is an infinitely elastic supply of loans at the prevailing rate of interest conflicts with much other post Keynesian thinking. It clearly conflicts with Kalecki's 'principle of increasing risk' and with any notion of credit rationing arising from uncertainty and moral hazard. The construction of the supply of loans curve is problematic when enterprises with different risk ratings face different interest rates unless all enterprises face an unlimited borrowing capacity at the rate of interest which they are charged (for then the supply of loans can be drawn as infinitely elastic at the base loan rate with the risk premia built in). But it is difficult to believe that different enterprises will not face different risk ratings and that the rating of an individual enterprise does not change with the volume of loans. If the loan opportunity curve facing an enterprise is at all upward-sloping (which may include a very steep portion where the enterprise is credit-rationed) then the aggregate supply of loans curve will be dependent on the distribution of loans across enterprises.

The neoclassical assumption of price taking applied to the financial markets is then that enterprises can borrow or lend as much as they wish at the prevailing rate of interest (cf. Modigliani and Miller, 1958). In contrast, post Keynesian analysis has rightly stressed the role of retained profits for the financing of investment (partly on the basis of the lower cost of internal finance over external finance) and the limits which enterprises face in raising external finance (e.g. Kalecki, 1937, 1943). The writings of Kalecki can be seen as making three points in this regard.

First, in his discussion of the 'principle of increasing risk' (Kalecki, 1937 and 1939), he argued that the assumption that 'the rate of risk is independent of the amount invested ... has to be dropped ... in order to obtain a realistic solution of the problem of limited investment. It is reasonable to assume that marginal risk increases with the amount invested'. Further, if 'the entrepreneur is not cautious enough in his investment activity, it is the creditor who imposes on his calculation the burden of increasing risk, charging the successive portions of credits above a certain amount with a rising rate of interest' (Kalecki, 1990, p. 288). The principle of increasing risk is based on the simple proposition that banks or other capital market institutions are more reluctant to lend to an entrepreneur whose debt is large relative to own resources because of the increased risk that profits in any given year will be insufficient to service the loan, an increased risk of bankruptcy and of default on the loan. This may be reflected in higher interest charges to an entrepreneur with a higher ratio of debt to own wealth, which in turn heightens the bankruptcy risk (from higher interest charges). This may form an absolute on a firm's ability to borrow (where the limit is related to the profitability and own wealth of the firm).

Second, the availability of funds rather than diseconomies of scale in production or management or limitations of the size of the market is the limiting factor on the size of a firm. 'The size of a firm thus appears to be circumscribed by the amount of its entrepreneurial capital both through its influence on the capacity to borrow capital and through its effect on the degree of risk' (Kalecki, 1971, p. 106).

Third,

investment decisions are closely related to 'internal' accumulation of capital, i.e. to the gross savings of firms. There will be a tendency to use these savings for investment, and, in addition, investment may be financed by new outside funds on the strength of the accumulation of entrepreneurial capital. The gross savings of firms thus extend the boundaries set to investment plans by the limited capital market and the factor of 'increasing risk' (Kalecki, 1971, p. 111).

This and the previous point also relate back to the earlier discussion on causality between investment and savings and illustrate that in Kalecki's approach savings do have some influence on investment as well as vice versa.

Two particular points of relevance to this chapter emerge from these quotes from Kalecki. First, there is not only some influence of savings on investment but the nature of that influence depends on who makes those savings. Savings made out of profits, appearing as internal finance, tend to encourage investment for well-known reasons. But savings made from non-profit income have to be recycled through the financial markets to reach the enterprises and as such are subject to the 'principle of increasing risk'.

Second, the 'principle of increasing risk' applies to all forms of finance whether supplied through the banking system or not. Indeed, Kalecki specifically considered whether the analysis applied to the case of joint stock companies and the issue of equity and concluded that it did. But the strong implication is that the analysis does apply to the banking system and hence to the financing of investment through the granting of loans and thereby the creation of money. The literature on credit rationing (Stiglitz and Weiss, 1981 for example) should be seen as quite consistent with a post Keynesian perspective and to some degree Kalecki's 'principle of increasing risk' can be seen as a precursor to that literature.

Whilst the horizonalist position may provide a useful approximation for much of the operation of a monetary economy, it should not be taken as the universal case. If it were, then it would mean jettisoning two insights gained from Kalecki and Keynes, namely the 'principle of increasing risk' and the notion of liquidity preference.[16] It is then argued that at some specific points the further expansion of economic activity may be limited by the constraints on the granting of further loans which come from some combination of the 'principle of increasing risk' impinging on enterprises and 'liquidity preference' restraining banks' lending.

The sharpest contrast between the endogenous money supply approach (particularly in its horizontalist guise) and the approaches of Kalecki and Keynes is perhaps that which relates to the determination of the general level of interest rates.[17] It can first be noted that it becomes inappropriate to talk any longer of *the* rate of interest even as a theoretical construct. The extreme version of the endogenous money supply views the structure of interest rates as built upon the central bank discount rate (or the equivalent) which is treated as predetermined:

> The corollary to the theory of radical endogeneity of the money stock is the idea that the rate of interest is exogenous, in the sense that it is set by decision of the central bank. Of course, this is strictly true only for the central bank's own discount rate, which leaves the term- and risk-structure of rates in relation to the discount rate still to be determined. But in some versions of the endogenous money theory the latter relativities are conceived as fairly straightforward cases of Kaleckian mark-up pricing. (Cottrell, 1994b, pp. 598–9)

However for both Kalecki and Keynes the level of interest rates is built on the demand for and supply of money. They both viewed the rate of interest as set by the interaction of the demand for and supply of money. For Keynes (1936) the stock of money is taken as determined by the central bank and the demand for money depends on, *inter alia*, liquidity preference: 'an individual's liquidity-preference is given by a schedule of the amounts of his resources, valued in terms of money or of wage-units, which he will wish to retain in the form of money in different sets of circumstances' (Keynes, 1936, p. 166). The rate of interest is then set by the interaction between the stock of money and the demand for money.

Kalecki (1954) concluded

> that the velocity of circulation V is an increasing function of the short-term rate of interest ρ or: $T/M = V(\rho)$. It follows directly from this equation that given the function V the short-term rate of interest, ρ, is determined by the [nominal] value of transactions, T, and the supply of money, M, which, in turn is determined by banking policy. (p. 74)

The long-term rate of interest is linked with the short-term rate of interest based on substitution between the corresponding financial assets but that is not of direct concern here.

Kalecki's discussion of the equality of transactions demand for money with the stock of money is characteristically laconic, but can be elaborated as follows. The banks can vary their portfolios of assets and liabilities and in doing so would influence the structure and general level of interest rates and the stock of money. However, the level of interest rates and the (nominal) level of economic activity also influence the non-bank sector's willingness to hold money. Further, the 'banking policy' will influence the supply of money. Kalecki does not explicitly mention the central bank discount rate (though I would read banking policy etc. as including the setting of that discount rate).

This approach can to some degree be seen as formalized in Tobin (1969) where he presents what he described as a general equilibrium approach. It reflects the idea that the stock of money and relative interest rates arise from the interaction between the behaviour of banks and of the non-banking private sector. The stock of money is then only what it is (at least in equilibrium) because the non-banking private sector willingly holds the money and the banks willingly accept the deposits. However, as an approach, Tobin's model has a number of shortcomings. First, it does not incorporate the dynamic element associated with the increase in the demand for loans associated with plans for increased expenditure. Second, it treats the amount of base money and the central bank discount rate as exogenous. In the long run base money and the discount rate dominate the determination of the money supply so that it becomes determined by exogenous (to the private sector) factors.

This discussion would appear consonant with the views expressed by Wray when he writes that

> the theory of interest rates which comes out of the endogenous money approach is neither a mark-up theory nor a theory of the demand and supply of hoards. The interest rate is largely determined by the willingness of banks and other financial institutions to allow their balance sheets to expand. ... The central bank discount policy is also important, but this policy is constrained by the ability of banks to adjust to higher interest rates in the case of tight money policy, and by bank willingness to lower interest rates in the case of loose money policy. (Wray, 1990, p. 188)

Macroeconomic analysis has often been conducted in terms of 'the' rate of interest, and for some purposes that may be sufficient. But the influence of the assumption of a single interest rate (and hence of a single interest-bearing financial asset) on some of the discussion in the area of money is malign. The recognition of different interest rates may help to reconcile some of the approaches mentioned above. The central bank discount rate can be seen as the interest rate on which others are based, but it should not be treated as exogenous. For not only is that discount rate likely to be used as an instrument of government policy to influence the structures of interest rates and thereby the exchange rate and the level of economic activity, but it may also be used to maintain the financial system itself. But we may proceed on the basis of the banking system treating the discount rate as given (that is we assume that there is no attempt by the banking system to set their interest rates with a view to influencing the discount rate). With a particular discount rate, the influence of the factors noted by Kalecki and by Keynes can be seen to come into play through the following routes. The rate of interest on deposits is set so that the public are willing to hold those deposits and cash: this merely extends the equation from Kalecki given above. Liquidity preference considerations govern two sets of decisions. The balance between holding financial assets with a fixed price relative to money and which can be readily transformed into money (or believed by the holders to have that property) and other financial and non-financial assets could be seen as influenced by liquidity preference considerations. This can be described as the balance between broad money and other assets. The other route by which liquidity preference has an influence would clearly be the willingness of banks to extend loans.

It is rather unlikely that a general theory of money and rates of interest can be formulated since not only does consideration have to be given to the specific institutional arrangements under which money is created or, to use the terminology of Chick (1986), which stage the financial system has reached, but also to the interest rate policy adopted by the central bank. It can readily be acknowledged that the policy targets of central banks (whether of their choosing or imposed by government) in the setting of the discount rate vary over time and place, and have appeared to include the level of the exchange rate, the level of domestic economic activity or the level of the stock of money (or its rate of increase). It may be appropriate to treat the discount rate as exogenously given for some analysis, but the more general case would be to view the discount rate in terms of an endogenous relationship with other macroeconomic variables, represented as a reaction function (for the central bank).

CONCLUSIONS

Simple ideas have their place in economic analysis, and amongst those we would place the multiplier and endogenous money. We have in this chapter argued that in effect these two simple ideas (that investment stimulates economic activity and savings and that money is largely credit money created by the banking system in response to demands for loans) contain valuable insights and are more relevant than their counterparts adhered to by the orthodox approach (savings stimulates investment and money is exogenous and controllable). But the complexities of the real world are such that these ideas have to be modified and placed in the relevant institutional setting.

NOTES

1. The corresponding propositions of orthodoxy are taken to be

    (i)   causation runs from savings to investment with savings viewed as the constraining factor on economic growth;

    (ii) money can be modelled as exogenously determined and controllable by the central bank (or equivalent);

    (iii) little thought is paid to how investment (or indeed any expansion of expenditure) is financed;

(iv)   the rate of interest is set on a loanable funds basis, governed by thrift and productivity, bringing savings and investment into equality, and hence can be seen as a real phenomenon (though this conflicts with i above).

2. This means that the net outflow of domestic currency resulting from external financing is omitted from consideration.
3. For an extensive discussion on the demand for endogenous money see Howells (1995b).
4. Banks are here simply defined as those financial institutions (or parts thereof) whose liabilities are generally accepted as a medium of exchange.
5. For discussion on the causal links between investment and savings see, for example, Asimakopulos (1983), Kregel (1995).
6. See Chapple (1995) for a discussion of this contribution by Kalecki and the question of whether it can be viewed as anticipating Keynes's contribution.
7. See Sawyer (1996) for discussion of Kalecki's work on the trade cycle and of the re-investment factor.
8. For further discussion see Sawyer (1995, chs 8 to 10).
9. Lipsey and Chrystal (1995, pp. 560–62) discuss the multiplier without any mention of how the increases in expenditure are financed and define the multiplier as 'the change in equilibrium national income that occurs in response to a change in autonomous expenditure' (p. 561).
10. Arestis and Howells (1996) in their section entitled 'The demand for endogenous money' and Howells (1995b) in a section entitled 'Relative interest rates' discuss this aspect in some detail.
11. This rather overstates the case since with uncertain flows of revenue and expenditure, enterprises would wish on average to operate with some safety margin of unutilized credit facilities.
12. See Howells (1995a) for extensive discussion on the confusions often arising between the supply of loans (or credit) and the supply of money.
13. In practice the story is much more complex, especially in the case of books, where production is undertaken in batches and supplied from stock.
14. There are, of course, additional complications arising from variations in the credit ratings of bank customers.
15. We find statements such as 'because bank loans create bank deposits, the supply of credit money is driven by the demand for bank credit' (Moore, 1994, p. 122) rather confusing in this regard.
16. Those insights may, of course, be wrong or insubstantial. I am asserting here that these insights are useful not because Kalecki and Keynes said so but because they do reflect what I perceive as attributes of the industrial monetary economy.
17. In *The General Theory*, Keynes assumed an exogenous money stock determined by the central bank. But in earlier and later work, he worked with a money supply which was endogenous. Discussion as to why Keynes adopted the tactic of an exogenous money supply would take us too far afield in this chapter.

REFERENCES

Arestis, P. and P. Howells (1996), 'Theoretical Reflections on Endogenous Money', *Cambridge Journal of Economics,* **20**, forthcoming

Asimakopulos, A. (1983), 'Kalecki and Keynes on Finance, Investment and Saving', *Cambridge Journal of Economics,* **7**.

Chapple, S. (1995), 'The Kaleckian Origins of the Keynesian Model', *Oxford Economic Papers*, **47**, 525–38

Chick, V. (1983), *Macroeconomics after Keynes*, Oxford: Philip Allan.

Chick, V. (1986), 'The Evolution of the Banking System and the Theory of Saving,

Investment and Interest', *Économies et Sociétés*, série MP, no.3, reprinted in P. Arestis and S. Dow (eds), *On Money, Method and Keynes: Selected Essays*, London: Macmillan.

Cottrell, A. (1994a), 'Endogenous Money and the Multiplier', *Journal of Post Keynesian Economics*, **17**, 111–20.

Cottrell, A. (1994b), 'Post-Keynesian Monetary Economics', *Cambridge Journal of Economics*, **18**.

Davidson, P. (1965), 'Keynes's Finance Motive', *Oxford Economic Papers*, **17**, reprinted as chapter 1 in Davidson (1990).

Davidson, P. (1972), 'Money and the Real World', *Economic Journal*, **82**, reprinted as chapter 7 in Davidson (1990).

Davidson, P. (1977), 'Money and General Equilibrium', *Économie Appliquée*, **4**, reprinted as chapter 12 in Davidson (1990).

Davidson, P. (1978), 'Why Money Matters: Lessons from a Half-Century of Monetary Theory', *Journal of Post Keynesian Economics*, **1**, reprinted as chapter 13 in Davidson (1990).

Davidson, P. (1982), *International Money and the Real World*, London: Macmillan.

Davidson, P. (1986), 'Finance, Funding, Saving and Investment', *Journal of Post Keynesian Economics*, **9**, reprinted as chapter 24 in Davidson (1990).

Davidson, P. (1990), *Money and Employment: The Collected Writings of Paul Davidson*, 1, edited by Louise Davidson, London: Macmillan.

Eichner, A.S. (1976), *The Megacorp and Oligopoly, Micro-Foundations of Macro Dynamics*, Cambridge: Cambridge University Press.

Harcourt, G.C. and P. Kenyon (1976), 'Pricing and the Investment Decision', *Kyklos*, **29**.

Howells, P.G.A. (1995a), 'Endogenous Money', *International Papers in Political Economy*, **2**(2).

Howells, P.G.A. (1995b), 'The Demand for Endogenous Money', *Journal of Post Keynesian Economics*, **18**.

Kaldor, N. and J. Trevithick (1981), 'A Keynesian Perspective on Money', *Lloyds Bank Review*, no. 139.

Kalecki, M. (1933), *Essay on the Business Cycle Theory*, reprinted in *Collected Works*, 1, 65–108.

Kalecki, M. (1934), 'Trzy uklady' ('Three Systems'), *Ekonomista*, 3 (English version appears in *Collected Works*, 1, 201–20).

Kalecki, M. (1943), *Studies in Economic Dynamics*, London: Allen & Unwin.

Kalecki, M. (1954), *Theory of Economic Dynamics*, London: George Allen and Unwin.

Kalecki, M. (1971), *Selected Essays on the Dynamics of the Capitalist Economy*, Cambridge: Cambridge University Press.

Kalecki, M. (1990), *Collected Works of Michal Kalecki*, 1, edited by J. Osiatynski, Oxford: Clarendon Press.

Keynes, J.M.. (1936), *The General Theory of Employment, Interest and Money*, London: Macmillan.

Keynes, J.M. (1937a), 'Alternative Theories of the Rate of Interest', *Economic Journal*, **47**, 241–52.

Keynes, J.M. (1937b), 'The Ex-Ante Theory of the Rate of Interest', *Economic Journal*, **47**, 663–9.

Kregel, J. (1995), 'Causality and Real Time in Asimakopulos's Approach to Saving and Investment in the Theory of Distribution' in G. Harcourt, A. Roncaglia and R.

Rowley (eds), *Income and Employment in Theory and Practice*, London: Macmillan and New York: St Martin's Press.

Lipsey, R. and K.A. Chrystal (1995), *An Introduction to Positive Economics*, eighth edition, Oxford: Oxford University Press.

Modigliani, F. and M.H. Miller (1958), 'The Cost of Capital, Corporation Finance and the Theory of Investment', *American Economic Review*, **48**.

Moore, B. (1988), *Horizontalists and Verticalists*, Cambridge: Cambridge University Press.

Moore, B. (1989), 'The Endogeneity of Credit Money', *Review of Political Economy*, **1**, 65–93.

Moore, B. (1994), 'The Demise of the Keynesian Multiplier: A Reply to Cottrell', *Journal of Post Keynesian Economics*, **17**.

Robinson, J. (1974), 'History versus Equilibrium', *Thames Papers in Political Economy*, Autumn.

Sawyer, M. (1995), *Unemployment, Imperfect Competition and Macroeconomics*, Aldershot, Hants: Edward Elgar.

Sawyer, M. (1996), 'Kalecki on the Trade Cycle and Economic Growth' in J. King (ed.), *An Alternative Macroeconomic Theory: The Kaleckian Model and Post Keynesian Economics*, New York: Kluwer, forthcoming

Stiglitz, J. and A. Weiss (1981), 'Credit Rationing in Markets with Imperfect Information', *American Economic Review*, **71**.

Tobin, J. (1969), 'A General Equilibrium Approach to Monetary Theory', *Journal of Money, Credit and Banking*, **1**.

Wray, L.R. (1990), *Money and Credit in Capitalist Economies*, Aldershot, Hants: Edward Elgar.

6. Paul Davidson's rediscovery of Keynes's finance motive and the liquidity preference versus loanable funds debate

Fernando J. Cardim de Carvalho*

Among his numerous important contributions to the development of macro-economic theory in a post Keynesian perspective, Paul Davidson's rediscovery and interpretation of the arguments involved in the Keynes–Ohlin debate on the determination of interest rates certainly stand out. Largely ignored both by mainstream *and* non-orthodox scholars, the Keynes–Ohlin exchange was the first stage of a protracted discussion opposing two fundamental (and contrasting) perspectives on the role of money in modern capitalist economies and its implications for the understanding both of their long- and short-term dynamics. Involving, as it did, essential arguments pertaining to complex and interrelated processes, the debate was difficult to follow and many authors seemed to have lost their ways in its midst. Many others simply seemed to be unaware of its having ever taken place. Paul Davidson, in contrast, realized its importance and endeavoured to decode the terms of the exchange and to explore its implications. Carefully separating the issues involved, he was able to significantly contribute to the clarification of the concepts proposed by Keynes and to their development, both in terms of money supply and demand analysis and of the study of the dynamics of capital accumulation.

In fact, a paradoxical destiny was suffered by the debates, in which Keynes took part, that followed the publication of *The General Theory* in the late 1930s. Even though no one would dispute that *The General Theory* was to become one of the most influential books in the history of economic thought, the discussions between Keynes and his critics that were meant to enlighten the public as to the meaning of the novel concepts and models Keynes was offering in that work were largely ignored and/or forgotten, even by most (at least nominally) Keynesians.[1] A case in point is Keynes's

*The author is grateful to the National Research Council of Brazil (CNPq) for financial support.

1937 paper on 'The General Theory of Employment', where his approach to uncertainty, as opposed to calculable risk, was explained and its consequences explored, the existence of which was never acknowledged by mainstream Keynesians.[2]

Keynes's debate with Bertil Ohlin in the pages of *The Economic Journal* on the determination of interest rates had a slightly better fate, but the attention it has attracted has been far less than one would expect given the importance economists have assigned to its central theme, the determination of the interest rate. In this exchange, Keynes developed the approach presented in *The General Theory* according to which *the* interest rate is determined by the interplay of the demand for and supply of *money*, while Ohlin presented his Wicksellian view that the interest rate is determined in the *credit* market. The opposition between the two theories had ultimately to do with their diverging views of the role savings and investment play in each model, and thus related directly to the validity of Keynes's principle of effective demand.

In part, this debate fell into oblivion because the dominant view among macroeconomists, inspired by Hicks, came to be that there is no essential difference between the theories. It became accepted that liquidity preference and loanable funds were not really contrasting theories but actually complementary approaches to the determination of the interest rate. It was alleged that the Marshallian framework within which these theories had been formulated by early macroeconomists prevented them from seeing that general equilibrium required the joint consideration of money *and* credit markets in the determination of all prices, including the interest rate.[3]

Not all economists, however, shared the view that nothing of substance was being disputed in the liquidity preference versus loanable funds debate. The bland phrasing of the consensus argument should be replaced by the harsh words of those who considered this choice to depend on fundamental aspects of theory. For Leijonhufvud, for instance: 'Unlike the Cambridge Keynesians, I do not accept the Liquidity Preference theory of interest of Keynes's General Theory or any of the "lemmas" that flow from it. *I believe it to be theoretically unsound, empirically false, and practically dangerous*' (Leijonhufvud, 1981, p. 195, emphasis added).[4] Paul Davidson also considered the points raised in the Keynes–Ohlin debate to be of central importance: 'The Keynesian Revolution was aborted by those who claimed to be Keynesians but who disregarded Keynes's Treatise on Money and his finance motive revision' (Davidson, 1994, p. 110).[5]

The arguments developed by Keynes, Ohlin, Robertson and others that took part in the debate are, at first sight, difficult to evaluate. Most of the time the participants seem to be talking at cross purposes. After reading the whole set of papers, one is left with the impression that the most heated disputes were mostly due to a mutual lack of understanding as to what each author meant when creating concepts and advancing theoretical propositions. Most of the time, we see an author indicting his opponent for not being able to reach conclusions that in fact were implied in the way the first discussant defined a given concept but were foreign to the way his opponent viewed it. When the discussants fail to agree, they attribute the remaining dispute to each other's faulty logic instead of acknowledging that they often use the same words to refer to very distinct phenomena.[6] The difficulty, however, is not just a question of using a common dictionary. In fact, the impossibility of sharing a common language results from fundamentally contrasting views as to how a capitalist economy works, espoused by liquidity preference and loanable funds theorists. There are at least three different problems that the authors allow to get entangled: the macroeconomic roles played by saving and investment; the determination of the interest rate; and the foundation of a financial theory of capital accumulation, that is, the definition of financial preconditions for economic growth (Carvalho, 1994). These are interrelated but essentially diverse issues, the degree of separability between them depending on which particular macroeconomic theory is accepted. To further complicate matters, the boundaries between a monetary theory of interest and a credit theory of interest may be obscure when money is mostly created by banks as a result of supplying credit. This feature of modern bank-money economies may have even led many economists to assume that differences between the two theories of interest became irrelevant in modern times, if they ever were meaningful for capitalist economies endowed with developed banking systems.[7]

The complexity of the debate is mostly due to the fact that it encompassed all the major themes of the Keynesian revolution. In this paper, we try to recover the terms of Keynes's original arguments related to the sole issue of the finance motive to demand money and the determination of interest rates, in order to identify the most important of Davidson's contributions to this subject alone. Davidson was able to contribute significantly to the solution of most of the other riddles formulated in the original exchange but a more complete coverage would be impossible in the confines of a single paper. We begin by briefly sketching the original debate between Keynes and Ohlin, emphasizing the development of concepts and models originally presented in *The General Theory* related to the demand for money. The following section is then dedicated to a presentation of Davidson's interpretation and further exploration of the novel concepts offered by Keynes and points to new lines of research inspired by these studies. A summary concludes the paper.

KEYNES'S DEFENCE OF THE LIQUIDITY PREFERENCE THEORY OF THE INTEREST RATE

A key element of Keynes's macroeconomics is the rejection of the assertion that *the* interest rate[8] is the element that brings saving and investment into equality. According to Keynes, there was no direct, unambiguous relation between the act of saving and the interest rate. A distinction was proposed between an agent's *time preference*, that explained choices between consumption and saving, and his/her *liquidity preference*, that had to do with choices as to the form in which wealth should be accumulated. The decision whether to direct income to immediate consumption or to put it aside in the present to finance an act of consumption at an indefinite date in the future depended, according to Keynes, mainly on the agent's income. The decision to save in an uncertain world generally obeys a precautionary motive to reserve some of one's present income to guarantee that consumption standards will be preserved in the event of adverse developments. Saving is not the placement of a definite order for future goods, but the demand for wealth as such, that can be used if and when the occasion requires it.[9] An individual making this kind of choice naturally turns to liquid forms of wealth, monetary assets, that mostly represent wealth as such, that is, wealth in a general form, as Marx put it.[10] To enable someone to part with the safety that keeping liquid wealth gives them it is necessary to pay him/her for the risk he/she is going to accept. According to Keynes, it is here that interest comes into the picture: '... the rate of interest at any time, being the reward for parting with liquidity, is a measure of the unwillingness of those who possess money to part with their liquid control over it' (Keynes, 1964, p. 167). The interest rate (or the price of securities) is thus the variable that reconciles the demand for liquid assets with their availability.[11]

Keynes went on to argue that choices between the various forms of wealth should be only marginally affected by new income flows, and, therefore, by the flows of new savings and investment. Demands for the available classes of assets were influenced by their liquidity premia, expected returns, carrying costs and expected capital appreciation (or depreciation). These characteristics attached to the existing *stocks* of each given class of asset, not just to their newly available flows. The interest rate, therefore, was determined not by the need to allocate the saving *flow* between money and bonds (the only non-monetary asset in *The General Theory* model), but to allocate the value of wealth among the existing *stocks* of money and bonds. *The interest rate should be determined in a stock equilibrium model, not a flow equilibrium model.* As argued above, it performs the role of changing the price of the non-monetary asset in such a way as to induce the wealth holders to keep in their portfolio the existing stocks of money and bonds.[12]

Taking the interest rate to be the reward for parting with liquidity, and having money as the only liquid asset in *The General Theory*, Keynes then analysed the motives to demand money. He identified three such motives: to pay for planned transactions; to keep as a precaution against an uncertain future; and to speculate over the future behaviour of the price of bonds. The transactions demand was proposed as proportional to income; the speculative demand depended on the expected behaviour of the interest rate; and the precautionary demand was suggested, without much reflection, also to be proportional to income.[13]

Ohlin, in his critical examination of *The General Theory*, agreed that the interest rate was not determined by investment and saving, arguing that Keynes had shown them to be always equal to one another, but did not accept the proposition that it was explained by the supply and demand for *money*. Rather, he argued, the interest rate is determined by the supply and demand for credit. The credit market could be conceived as *gross* and *net*, depending on whether one was considering only the *flow* demand and supply or the *stock* demand and supply for credit.[14] The result would, in any case, be the same (Ohlin, 1937, p. 225). Be that as it may, it was not the demand and supply of money as such that counted, but of credit, a larger concept.[15]

Keynes rejected Ohlin's approach, arguing that all it did was to reintroduce investment and saving through the back door to determine the interest rate. In his view, Ohlin defined the supply of credit in such a way as to make it equal to saving, and the demand for credit as equal to investment so the credit market would ultimately be in equilibrium when investment equalled savings. Ohlin accepted Keynes's equality between investment and saving as a tautology. In his view, what really mattered was that the *propensity to save* and the *propensity* to *invest* are different phenomena. These propensities were the ultimate determinants of the supply and demand for credit and, thus, of the interest rate (e.g. Ohlin, 1937b, pp. 426–7).

Although rejecting Ohlin's approach, Keynes conceded that there was an important qualification to be made to his liquidity preference model related to investment. The demand for money to pay for projected investments did not fit well in any of the three motives to demand money described in *The General Theory*. When an investment plan was decided upon money was demanded to cover the interregnum 'between the date when the entrepreneur arranges his finance and the date when he actually makes his investment' (Keynes, 1937b, p. 665). Although it consisted in a demand for money to buy capital goods, like the transactions demand, it was much less stable than the latter, related to investment plans adopted because of expectations of *future* profits, rather than to *current* income. The *finance motive to demand money* applied to discretionary spending in general, not only to investment expenditures. Given the less stable nature of these demands, the finance motive would not share the routine character of the standard transactions demand for money. As Davidson would put it later, this new reason to demand money should be more fruitfully viewed as a *shift factor* than as one of the endogenous variables in a money demand model (Davidson, 1994, p. 126).[16]

The addition of the finance motive to the liquidity preference model led Keynes to argue that an increase in investments above the customary level would cause, *ceteris paribus*, the interest rate to rise, not because of the necessary stimulus to consumers to save more in order to finance the investment, but because the demand for money would rise above the existing supply. The pressure on the interest rate was not to be alleviated by an increase in thrift, but by an increase in the money supply. As Keynes put it: '[t]he ex-ante saver has no cash, but it is cash which the ex-ante investor requires ... For finance ... employs no savings' (Keynes, 1937b, pp. 665–6).

It is not, thus, a problem of abstention but of liquidity. Keynes went further. He argued that the problem related to money, not to income. The pressure on the interest rates would take place in advance of the investment expenditure (and therefore of income, and savings creation) because money would be taken out of circulation to pay for the planned purchases when the time came. When the investment was finally spent, money would be released, making it possible for the next investor to get hold of money to spend on buying capital goods at a future date (cf. Keynes, 1937a, p. 247). If the rate of investment were constant, this pool of money would act as a revolving fund in which the liquidity released by a spender would now be available to be held by another prospective spender. It was only if the rate of investment were accelerating that a liquidity problem would arise because the money spent by one investor would be less than what was needed by the next investor in line.

Ohlin, as did Robertson and others, reacted very negatively to this line of argument. From this point on, the whole debate got entangled in a game of words that meant very different things for each of the discussants. Robertson took the finance motive to refer to the set of liabilities issued by the prospective investor and argued that no one would be liquid by spending the money they borrowed but by being able to pay one's debts. Robertson, thus, took liquidity to mean that the balance sheet of the investor (and of banks) is in equilibrium in terms of the liabilities issued and the assets bought. Keynes replied that liquidity was released when spending took place because money held in advance of spending was now back into circulation. Liquidity in this sense has to do with supply and demand for money. None of the disputing sides to this argument seemed to recognize that they were talking at cross purposes. In fact, under the pressure of the critics, mystified by the use of the term 'finance' to mean a kind of 'money demand', instead of the more familiar meaning of issuing liabilities, Keynes made a difference between 'finance', the creation of money, and 'funding' the posterior allocation of savings that permitted investors to improve their balance sheet situation. Now finance and funding had a meaning closer to Robertson's concerns, but its relation to the finance motive to demand money remained unclear, as did the ideas on the revolving fund and the restoration of liquidity through spending – ideas which, in any case, Keynes refused to recant.

The debate ended in a conceptual mess, more from exhaustion than from enlightenment. Keynes clearly lost it in the sense that the majority of the economists, then and afterwards, seemed unable to understand his ideas, and retreated to the much more familiar, classically rooted, loanable funds model proposed by Ohlin and Robertson. Mostly, the debate was buried and forgotten by the mainstream. For those who remained faithful to Keynes, and to liquidity preference theory, however, important lessons were to be learned from Keynes's attempts to respond to his critics. Among these, Paul Davidson was certainly a pioneer.

PAUL DAVIDSON'S CONTRIBUTIONS

The Finance Motive to Demand Money

Loanable funds theorists commemorated Keynes's identification of a finance motive to demand money, related to investment plans, as a retreat from the view presented in *The General Theory* that the interest rate was a monetary variable, having nothing to do with the interplay between investment and saving. For some, although Keynes had insisted that saving still had no influence on the determination of the interest rate, to acknowledge that investment was one of its determining elements was a sign that liquidity preference was theoretically fragile. The refusal to accept that saving was also one of the determinants of the interest rate should be explained more by Keynes's idiosyncrasies than by theoretical rigour.

These theorists may have been misled by the use of the term 'finance' to denominate this new motive. The term is suggestive of a demand for credit rather than for money and Keynes's own attempt to distinguish between 'finance' (but not the finance *motive*) and 'funding' later in the same debate may have strengthened this intuitive meaning of the word. These two points, however, should be kept analytically separate, as we argued above. One relates to the need, in a monetary economy, that any buyer has to get hold of a given amount of money to be able to acquire goods in advance of the purchase itself.[17] The other has to do with the relationship between assets and liabilities in the balance sheet of the buyer (and its bank). The central point of liquidity preference theory as an element of Keynes's principle of effective demand is that although they are two different (though related) processes, neither of them requires a previous availability of savings or even plans by consumers to save in the future. According to the principle of effective demand, savings *result* from investment spending. An investor does not need savings to buy capital goods, he needs money. Money is created by the monetary authorities or by banks, when creating deposits. To satisfy the finance demand for money, banks have to be ready and willing to create deposits and the monetary authority to create reserves. It is the policy of the authorities and the liquidity preference of banks themselves that matter. Banks create deposits as they offer credit, so the creation of finance to trigger the investment process depends on the liquidity preference of banks as well as the willingness to issue their own (fully) liquid deposit liabilities in exchange for the less liquid debts issued by the prospective investor. Once the investment is made, income will be generated in the capital goods sector and demand will spread to the consumption goods sector to serve the demands of those who produce capital goods. This is the multiplier proposed by Keynes and its end-result is that consumers will have an additional amount of savings in their hands precisely of the same value of the investment originally made. Ideally, although it is unlikely that things happen this way, these savings would be used to fund the investor's debt, allowing him to settle his short-term debt with the banks that offered him finance at the beginning. Keynes's meaning of liquidity in this debate referred to banks' willingness to satisfy the finance demand for money. Robertson's concept of liquidity referred to the possibility of funding the investor's debt, allowing repayment of that debt to the banks. These are different issues, but Keynes's point is that savings are the starting-point of neither the money market problem nor the financial one.

One could say, then, that the central point opposing liquidity preference to loanable funds theorists is the role played by the banking system in modern economies. For Keynes, the banking system (including the monetary authority) is the creator of money, and money is what it takes for an investment plan to be implemented. 'This means that, in general, the banks hold the key position in the transition from a lower to a higher scale of activity' (Keynes, 1937b, p. 668). For loanable funds theorists, in contrast, banks are essentially intermediaries between savers and investors. Institutional characteristics, such as the fractional reserve system, give banks some latitude of choice, but their functions are ultimately limited to transfer of real resources from savers to investors in the amounts the two groups agree about. As a consequence, Keynes believed that interest rates had to reconcile banking policy with the preference of the public for monetary assets. Loanable funds theorists believe the interest rate reconciles the intertemporal preferences of the public with the technical possibilities open to investors.

These problems were first considered by Paul Davidson in the mid-1960s and have consistently been a concern of his from then up to his most recent book. Davidson's starting-point is precisely the distinction between the money market discussion and the distinction between finance and funding.

According to Davidson, the finance motive allows us to connect the monetary analysis of the *Treatise on Money* to the principle of effective demand of *The General Theory*. Davidson criticizes Keynes for having yielded, in the latter, to mechanistic models of monetary analysis, when proposing a transactions demand for money by households functionally related to aggregate income. In the *Treatise*, in contrast, Keynes related the demand for money to *planned* expenditures by households *and* firms, rather than to equilibrium incomes, giving a behavioural content to the transactions demand for money that was lost in the mechanistic approach. For Davidson, the finance motive recuperates the behavioural basis of the transactions demand for money. Money is demanded in advance of *planned* spending both of consumption and of investment. What differentiates them is the alleged routine character of households' consumption expenditures as opposed to the volatility of investment spending. The finance demand for money, thus, is a kind of transactions demand, since it refers to the need to get hold of money in advance of a purchase operation. But while the latter category would be applied to routine expenditures, assumed to be stably related to current income, the finance demand should be defined in terms of discretionary spending, that has no necessary relation to it. In these terms, the finance demand would explain *shifts* in the total demand for money as described by the three motives mentioned in *The General Theory*.

Alternatively, one could consider an enlarged transactions demand for money function, encompassing both the finance and the transactions motives, as Davidson proposes in Equation (4) below.

The consideration of the finance motive would illustrate Keynes's argument that in monetary economies one cannot separate real from monetary variables. In fact, while in the traditional formulation the transactions demand for money would be represented by

$$L = kY \tag{1}$$

the transaction plus finance demand would consider planned consumption and investment. Let us assume consumption (C) to be related to income (Y) and investment (I) to interest rates (i) according to the following functions (a,b,c,d being parameters):

$$C = a + bY \tag{2}$$
$$I = c - di \tag{3}$$

Then, the demand for money comprising both the transactions and the finance motive would be given as:

$$L = xC + yI = xa + yc + xbY - ydi^{18} \tag{4}$$

with x and y being parameters of the money demand function. As a consequence, if planned investment were to increase, money demand would also increase and, if this increase was not accommodated by the banks and the monetary authority, interest rates would increase. On the other hand, if the monetary authority and banks decided to accommodate the additional demand, money would be endogenous and the interest rate would stay put.[19]

Davidson stresses three important features of this model. First, it shows a crucial element of Keynes's economics, that is the integration between monetary and real variables, in the sense that shifts in the demand for goods result in shifts in the demand for money. Second, it shows the conditions in which a *crowding-out* effect may emerge but it also shows that the latter is a consequence of a *lack of money*, not a *lack of savings*.[20] It is liquidity preference, not thrift, that is at the root of the problem. Finally, it also refines the analysis of the influences to which the money demand function is subject, overcoming the mechanistic approach inspired by its treatment in *The General Theory*. The function is sensitive to changes in expectations (that control investment and consumption expenditures), income distribution, taxation, etc. An important corollary is that investment *does* have some influence on the interest rate but this does not mean any overture to the loanable funds model, because pressure caused by increasing investments (or increasing autonomous consumption or public spending for that matter) concentrates on the demand for money and is alleviated by changes in the supply of money and not by increasing thrift that does not necessarily affect either the liquidity preference of banks or the policy of the monetary authorities.

Finance and Funding

A related, but nevertheless distinct, aspect of this discussion turns around the concepts of 'finance' and 'funding'. These concepts were offered by Keynes in the attempt to dispel the mistaken understanding of his finance motive to demand money as a roundabout admission that investment and saving were important elements in the determination of the interest rate, if not the ultimate determinants, after all. Keynes flatly denied that his finance motive was a concession to loanable funds theorists' views of the role of desired (or *ex ante*) investment and saving. As Davidson noticed, investment could influence the demand for money as, for that matter, any other market operation, in the sense that it involves transactions that require means of payment to be completed. Saving, on the other hand, can have a similar influence to the extent to which it represents *non*-purchases, decreasing the transactions demand for money. In any case, an increased finance demand for money can be satisfied by an increased supply of money, not of savings.[21] Loanable funds theorists, according to Keynes, mistakenly collapsed the two stages of the financial side of the investment process, finance and funding, into one. For that reason, the different roles of money creation (finance) and saving allocation (funding) escaped them.

To mark the differences between these two concerns and the distinct question of how investments are to be supported in financial terms, Keynes advanced the concepts of finance and funding. Keynes's point here was to show, once more, that savings were not a determinant of investment and that purchases of investment goods actually involved, from a monetary/financial point of view, two theoretically different sorts of operation that loanable funds theorists tended to collapse into one. One type of operation had to do with the creation, by banks, of money to allow the purchase to be made. This involved no savings at all. Another operation had to do with the way investors structured the debts they had to incur to obtain the funds required for the investment to be made. This is where savers could play a direct or indirect role. This essential difference was pointed out by Davidson:

> This bank-created (non-resource using) finance [the creation of money] must be distinguished from the role of long-term financial markets which require the public to give up an amount of liquidity equal to real savings (i.e., unexercised income claims on resources) in the process of funding the investment. (Davidson, 1986, p. 101)

The originality of Keynes's approach was in proposing that it was never the *amount* of savings that mattered but *its form*. Through the principle of effective demand Keynes had shown that *aggregate* savings would always be generated in the right and sufficient amount to finance investments. An entirely different question, however, was whether these savings would be available to investors to fund their debts in the required time and adequate terms. Investors seeking long-term funding for the investments they make should observe the behaviour of securities prices to assess the right moment to offer their long-term obligations in the financial markets.

Keynes detailed his conception of the process mostly in relation to the placement of government bonds but he insisted that the basic arguments were also valid for private investors.[22] The central argument, in any case, was that although there would always be enough aggregate savings to *potentially* fund any realized investment, prices of securities (and interest rates) had to be such as to allow these savings to be channelled to investors seeking long-term financial resources, which was not a trivial question. Again, Keynes showed that, although interest rates had to do with the forms through which available savings would be offered to investors, *aggregate* saving was still irrelevant to determine their behaviour.

The understanding of these processes was much advanced by Davidson's works. First, Davidson precisely isolated the roles of banks and of savers in each stage of the process. To satisfy the demand for money, banks create money *ex nihilo*, as a bookkeeping operation. Investors (or, in general, deficit spenders), on the other hand, will need to issue obligations that are generally matched by the income streams they expect to receive from the assets they are buying. The time to do it is when aggregate income has increased to such an extent as to make the aggregate saving created by investment desired by savers: 'When the real investment has been completed and the associated real spending flows have already been completed, the investment underwriter can float the new issue, whose nominal value equals the purchase price of the investment' (Davidson, 1986, p. 105). Keynes had put this point before as follows:

> It may also help to clear up misunderstanding to point out that whilst saving takes place concurrently with investment (in the sense of the first acquisition of a capital good by an entrepreneur), the flow of funds (i.e., of money) available for investment (in the sense of the first acquisition of this capital good by a permanent holder) takes place subsequently, the bridging of this time-lag by 'finance' (i.e., by the supply of money) being the function of the credit system (which is solely concerned with finance and never with saving). (Keynes, 1939, p. 574)

Davidson shows that three important implications follow from the above:

1. The distinction between the concepts of finance and funding does not violate in the least Keynes's principle of effective demand according to which aggregate investment determines aggregate savings with aggregate income being the adjusting variable;
2. Aggregate savings pose no limits on investment expenditures, but the (financial) channels through which savings can be transferred to investors matter for the investment decision;
3. Financial obstacles in the way of investments are to be treated as flow of funds problems rather than as insufficiency of savings.

The first implication has been sufficiently explored in the post Keynesian literature, in which the concepts of finance and funding are located as stages of the investment process.[23]

The second point may be worth some recapitulation. The idea is to show that providing financial support to investments is also a question of liquidity preference and not of those intertemporal preferences that neoclassical theory believes to determine interest rates. Finance is supplied when someone re-taining liquid assets (or with the possibility of creating money) accepts to become less liquid, exchanging them for relatively illiquid assets. This is a question of liquidity preference, not .of thrift. Less obviously, however, fund-ing is also basically a question of liquidity preference. According to Keynes's principle of effective demand, there will always be an aggregate amount of savings generated in an economy equal in value to the investments realized, no matter how thrifty consumers are. Through the multiplier analysis, Keynes showed that consumers will eventually hold an amount of voluntary savings in their hands that is equal to the investment value spent by firms. Problems can never arise because savings are insufficient, but because consumers may decide to keep those savings in forms that are incompatible with the funding needs of firms. In other words, savers' liquidity preference may be incompat-ible with the demands for long-term credit from firms. As a result, investors will either have to become speculators in the sense of Minsky, accepting liabilities that are shorter than their assets, or will have to pay high interest rates in order to induce savers to part with liquidity.

Davidson discussed this problem in the context of the Kaldor–Pasinetti growth model by creating a variable to represent the savers' propensity to buy bonds out of savings, which is, of course, dependent on the agents' liquidity preference.[24] If households exhibit a strong liquidity preference, the interest rate needed to induce them to part with liquidity (by buying securities issued by deficit spenders) may be too high, no matter what their propensities to save may be. As Davidson argues, if this is the case and, for some reason, the monetary authority has difficulties in creating money and in accommodating the households' liquidity preference, investment may be reduced even if entrepreneurs are endowed with the required 'animal spirits' (cf. Davidson, 1978, ch. 11).

There is a third way out of that dilemma, which takes us to the third implication of the preceding discussion. If private agents' liquidity preference is too strong, financial institutions can emerge to bridge the gap between the demands of the public and the demands of investors. Financial institutions can *transform* assets. They may pool risks and information, being able to supply liquid assets to savers at the same time they offer better credit terms to investors. Credit-based systems, like the ones we find in continental Europe or Japan, place an intermediary between ultimate savers and investors, to reconcile liquidity preferences with investors' needs. In Davidson's words:

> If, therefore, the rate of return on placements [that is, the interest rate] is to be either kept constant or reduced as the stock of capital expands in a growing economy, then the banking system must absorb those titles which the public does not wish to hold currently, and the quantity of money will, in general, have to

increase by an amount that exceeds the cost of net investment in both fixed and working capital. (Davidson, 1978, p. 276)

More generally, Davidson argues that this accommodation is the function of the banking system *and* the financial sector (ch. 13). Financial intermediaries enrich, with their own liquidity preferences and their privileged access to the banking system, the possibility of combinations that allow aggregate savings to be ultimately transferred to deficit spenders in general and investors in particular. To a large extent, one of the main implications of Davidson's post Keynesian approach is the need to study the process of capital accumulation through a flow of funds perspective instead of the neoclassical focus on the savings and investment relation.

CONCLUDING REMARKS

Paul Davidson has contributed to exploring the financial and monetary theory of investment required by Keynes's principle of effective demand. He was able to disentangle the threads of the Keynes versus Ohlin–Robertson debate of the late 1930s, showing that its central issue is the role of liquidity preference and the policy of the banking system as opposed to thrift in the determination of the interest rate, defended by Keynes against the classical theory. Some important difficulties remain, however, to be tackled.

As the creation of money in modern economies involves the issuance of debt to be bought by banks, the determination of the interest rate as shown in that debate has to consider three different models: first, there is determination of a *stock equilibrium* between the supply and demand for money, opposing those with various spending plans to the creators of money, banks and the monetary authority; then we have to consider the multiplier, through which a *flow equilibrium* is reached in the goods market; finally, we have the question of funding the debts, in order to achieve a *stock equilibrium* in the financial market and to close the whole circuit.

The interaction between these models cannot be properly explored, however, within the original terms of the debate. In particular, when finance and funding needs are considered, one can no longer talk in terms of *the* interest rate. We have now to disaggregate the credit market into its different segments, into which different agents with different motivations and specific action timing take part. An important element to analyse in their operation is precisely the changes in the *structure of interest rates* that take place when an investment process is initiated. Keynes began an analysis of this kind in the *Treatise on Money*, examining the behaviour of short- and long-term rates of interest and their interrelationships. The development of these insights, integrating them into the generalized liquidity preference model and a flow of funds perspective, outlined here, is still to be done.

NOTES

1. Mainstream Keynesians seem to have never felt completely at ease with the school label Modigliani, in his debate with monetarists, preferred to be called 'non-monetarist' rather than Keynesian (Modigliani, 1977). Tobin was 'proud' to be Keynesian (Tobin, 1987). New Keynesians are not so sure. As Mankiw put it: 'If new Keynesian economics is not a true representation of Keynes's views, then so much the worst for Keynes', quoted in Davidson (1994, p. 299).
2. Again, among mainstream Keynesians, Tobin seems to be an exception. See Tobin's interview in Blaug (1990).
3. The complementarity thesis goes back a long way. See, e.g. Lerner (1947), Modigliani (1944).
4. Elsewhere in the same work, Leijonhufvud stated that liquidity preference was 'historically important' because 'many of the weaknesses of "Keynesian economics" really stem from it' (Leijonhufvud, 1981, p. 134n).
5. Because of their disregard of the finance motive introduced by Keynes in his debate with Ohlin, 'mainstream Keynesians [were encouraged] to develop a bastard Keynesian model that was a perversion of Keynes's own system' (Davidson, 1994, p. 122).
6. A clear example is Keynes's and Robertson's different meanings attributed to the concept of liquidity. Both authors insist on trying to make each other to admit implications that are foreign to what each of them takes liquidity to be, although Keynes at least seemed to be conscious of Robertson's particular use of the term (Keynes, 1973, p. 230).
7. Some Keynesians now adopt loanable funds theory without even mentioning that there may be some contradiction between this approach and Keynes's liquidity preference theory. See, e.g., Blinder (1989).
8. *The* interest rate should be understood as an index of interest rates, a price index, not as any particular rate. In *The General Theory* model there is only one non-monetary financial asset (bonds). The interest rate refers to this aggregate. As will be argued below, if this choice as to aggregation was useful in *The General Theory* to present the principle of effective demand, its usefulness is much less visible in models that explicitly acknowledge more disaggregated choices as to financial assets.
9. 'An act of individual saving means – so to speak – a decision not to have dinner today. But it does not necessitate a decision to have dinner or to buy a pair of boots a week hence or to consume any specified thing at any specified date. ... It is not a substitution of future consumption-demand for present consumption-demand, – it is a net diminution of such demand' (Keynes, 1964, p. 210).
10. Money becomes a 'liquidity time-machine' in Davidson's expression. See Davidson (1994, pp. 114ff).
11. 'It is the "price" which equilibrates the desire to hold wealth in the form of cash with the available quantity of cash' (Keynes, 1964, p. 167). To put it another way: 'The function of the rate of interest is to modify the money-prices of other capital assets in such a way as to equalise the attraction of holding them and of holding cash' (Keynes, 1937, p. 250).
12. See also Kregel (1985).
13. A very unfortunate step, according to Kahn. See Kahn (1954).
14. 'What governs the demand and supply of credit? Two ways of reasoning are possible. One is *net* and deals only with *new* credit, and the other is *gross* and includes the outstanding *old* credits' (Ohlin, 1937, p. 224, his emphasis).
15. 'The "market" for cash has no key position in relation to other markets' (Ohlin, 1937, pp. 225–6).

16. 'Investment finance in this sense is, of course, only a special case of the finance required by any productive process; but since it is subject to fluctuations of its own, I should ... have done well to have emphasized it when I analysed the various sources of the demand for money' (Keynes, 1937a, p. 247).
17. In this sense, it is a demand for money. To obtain through credit operations does not change the fact that someone must be supplying the buyer with the money he needs to make the purchase effective.
18. Cf. Davidson (1978, pp. 160–70).
19. Cf. Davidson (1978, pp. 178–9 and 1994, pp. 128–9).
20. In one of Davidson's favourite quotations from Keynes's works: 'The investment market can become congested through shortage of cash. It can never become congested through shortage of saving. This is the most fundamental of my conclusions within this field' (Keynes, 1937b, p. 669).
21. 'The ex-ante saver has no cash, but it is cash which the ex-ante investor requires ... For finance ... employs no savings' (Keynes, 1937b, pp. 665–6).
22. Keynes's arguments are extensively documented in Carvalho (1994).
23. Davidson (1986) presents a very concise version of his views on this point. This author has proposed his own view in Carvalho (1992, ch. 9).
24. See Davidson (1978, pp. 299ff).

REFERENCES

Blaug, M. (1990), *John Maynard Keynes: Life, Ideas and Legacy*, London: Macmillan.

Blinder, A. (1989), *Macroeconomics Under Debate*, New York: Harvester Wheatsheaf.

Carvalho, F. de (1992), *Mr Keynes and the Post Keynesians*, Cheltenham: Edward Elgar.

Carvalho, F. de (1994), 'Sorting the Issues out: The Two Debates on Keynes's Finance Motive Revisited (1936/7; 1983/6)', Instituto de Economia Industrial, UFRJ, Discussion paper no. 319.

Davidson, P. (1978), *Money and the Real World*, second edition, London: Macmillan.

Davidson, P. (1986), 'Finance, Funding, Saving and Investment', *Journal of Post Keynesian Economics*, **9**(1), Fall.

Davidson, P. (1994), *Post Keynesian Macroeconomic Theory*, Aldershot, Hants: Edward Elgar.

Kahn, R. (1954), 'Some Notes on Liquidity Preference', *Manchester School*.

Keynes, J.M. (1937a), 'Alternative Theories of the Rate of Interest', *The Economic Journal*, June.

Keynes, J.M. (1937b), 'The "Ex-Ante" Theory of the Rate of Interest', *The Economic Journal*, September.

Keynes, J.M. (1939), 'The Process of Capital Formation', *The Economic Journal*, September.

Keynes, J.M. (1964), *The General Theory of Employment, Interest and Money*, New York: Harcourt Brace Jovanovich.

Keynes, J.M. (1973), *The General Theory and After – Defence and Development, The Collected Writings of John Maynard Keynes*, Vol. XIV, London: Macmillan.

Kregel, J. (1985), 'Le multiplicateur et la préférence pour la liquidité: deux aspects de la théorie de la demande effective', in A. Barrère (ed.), *Keynes Aujourd'hui*, Paris: Economica.

Leijonhufvud, A. (1981), *Information and Coordination*, New York: Oxford University Press.

Lerner, A. (1947), 'Alternative Formulations of the Theory of Interest', in S. Harris (ed,), *The New Economics*, London: Dennis Dobson.

Modigliani, F. (1944), 'Liquidity Preference and the Theory of Interest and Money', *Econometrica*, January.

Modigliani, F. (1977), 'The Monetarist Controversy', *American Economic Review*, March.

Ohlin, B. (1937), 'Some Notes on the Stockholm Theory of Savings and Investment', *The Economic Journal*, Pt II, June.

Ohlin, B. (1937b), 'A Rejoinder', *The Economic Journal*, September.

Tobin J. (1987), *Policies for Prosperity*, Cambridge, Mass.: MIT Press.

7. Money as a 'time machine' in the new financial world

Gary A. Dymski

Paul Davidson's *Money and the Real World* (1972, 1978) established the methodological basis of post Keynesian monetary theory. He argued that the entry point of this approach must be fundamental uncertainty about the future, as characterized by Keynes (1936, ch. 12). This uncertainty makes liquidity – that is, 'being able to meet contractual obligations as they come due' (Davidson, 1994a, p. 18) – valuable, and explains why households and firms demand money and credit: money and credit provide liquidity and access to liquidity, respectively. Money is a 'time machine' because it can transfer wealth and spending power across time. Financial intermediaries are important, in turn, because in creating and redistributing money and credit they manage the economy's liquidity.

This paper acknowledges the lasting importance of these insights. At the same time, it argues that the economic significance of money and credit has changed since Davidson first termed money a 'time machine' in the early 1970s.[1] In Paul Davidson's conception, money is a universally available shelter from uncertainty. But 20 years of unceasing financial globalization and innovation by financial intermediaries have transformed the markets for money and credit; in consequence, today 'time machine' money is no longer available for a growing number of households excluded from mainstream financial participation. How payments are made, how and whether savings are stored, and whether credit can be accessed all depend on whether the household or business in question is included among, or excluded from, the ranks of citizens in the brave new financial world.

Two consequences of this financial transformation are discussed here. First, monetary policy interventions have very different effects in this new financial world than in the one it replaced.[2] Second, with the coming of this new world, economic conflict increasingly involves not just the division of labour, but the division between those with access to credit and financial security, and those without it. This second consequence has important ramifications for post Keynesian theory. As Harcourt and Hamouda (1992) have suggested, three distinct branches of post Keynesian theory – what they term the neo-Ricardian, Kaleckian, and Davidsonian approaches – coexist uneasily today. The entry point for the former two approaches is class conflict between capitalists and workers; as noted, the entry point for the third is Keynesian uncertainty. It is possible – indeed, common – to construct models of capitalist/worker conflict which take no account of uncertainty, and vice versa. In consequence, the connections and commonalities among these strands of post Keynesian theory have remained underexplored. But if the argument made here about financial transformation is right, conflict may enter in naturally in models emphasizing Keynesian uncertainty and monetary themes; and this conflict is closely correlated with the class conflict emphasized in the neo-Ricardian and Kaleckian approaches, while remaining independent of it. Conversely, conflict models may take monetary factors into greater account, inasmuch as access to financial resources is a crucial axis of conflict.

This essay highlights my profound debt to Paul Davidson; here, as often before, his insights have provided my point of departure. I was first guided to his work by the remarkable post Keynesians of the University of Massachusetts: Jim Crotty, Douglas Vickers, Donald Katzner and Randall Bausor. Paul Davidson has been consistently encouraging and tolerant as my own professional relationship with him has developed. My own path and those of many others have been eased by his prodigious efforts, especially in establishing the *Journal of Post Keynesian Economics* as a respected platform for research output. It is perhaps the success of Davidson's efforts that explains why he often draws the ire of orthodox thinkers. As Plato (1956) put it long ago:

> The Athenians … may think a man to be clever without paying him much attention, so long as they do not think that he teaches his wisdom to others. But as soon as they think that he makes other people clever, they get angry, whether it be from resentment, … or for some other reason. (p. 2)

By 'making clever' many younger post Keynesian economists, Paul Davidson has helped to sustain a Keynesian tradition rooted in bold philosophies and policies, not just in academic parlour talk.

DAVIDSON ON MONEY AND FINANCIAL INTERMEDIATION

In *Money and the Real World*, Davidson (1978) states his theoretical premises: the future is uncertain, production takes time, and economic decisions are irretrievably historical and affected by expectations about the future. Both households and firms must contend with a dilemma: to accumulate wealth via production, or by financing production, takes time; but time is the vessel that carries uncertainty, which can dash agents' hopes.

Money offers respite from this dilemma: 'the existence of money and spot security markets, in an uncertain world, permits decision-makers to store wealth without making simultaneous commitments for resource-embodying goods' (1978, p. 20). Non-monetary assets lack continuous spot markets and have a variable nominal price: hence, if plans do not work out or an emergency occurs which requires instantaneous outlays, non-money assets can be converted into money (liquidated) only at a potentially large premium. So:

> It is only in a world of uncertainty and disappointment that money comes into its own as a necessary mechanism for deferring decisions; money has its niche only when we feel queasy about undertaking any actions which will commit our claims on resources onto a path which can only be altered, if future events require this, at very high costs (if at all). (1978, p. 144)

In Davidson's analysis any good qualifies as money if its properties satisfy the functional definition of money: a zero elasticity of production; a zero elasticity of substitution; and a zero (or negligible) cost of shifting wealth so held from medium of exchange to store of value or vice versa. An agent who holds money possesses that form of wealth best suited to deferring decisions or changing one's mind.[3]

In any economy the degree of tension between accumulating wealth and remaining liquid depends on the efficiency of what Davidson terms its monetary system: its institutional arrangements for making and enforcing contracts and for clearing payments. An efficient clearing system reduces transaction costs and allows firms and households to use non-monetary financial assets to settle payments. Forward contracts for labour and other inputs also reduce transaction costs. More importantly, they allow a reciprocal transfer of uncertainty: by locking in some costs in advance, firms producing output shift some uncertainty on to input suppliers; at the same time, input suppliers reduce uncertainty about their own future income streams.[4]

Within the monetary system, argues Davidson, financial intermediaries reduce transaction costs by expanding the reach of the clearing system and facilitating access to stored funds. Banks are special among intermediaries because they issue liabilities which are used to settle debts and make payments. Intermediaries also reduce savers' and borrowers' exposure to uncertainty by offering them forward financial contracts. For agents with more wealth than they plan to spend immediately, intermediaries reduce uncertainty by guaranteeing them access to liquidity and/or by insuring against the risk of loss on invested principal. Intermediaries can also reduce uncertainty for agents whose expenditure plans exceed their available resources by supplying them with credit. Credit can reduce uncertainty in two ways for borrowers. First, by spending loaned funds immediately, borrowers can secure the resources to carry out production processes over time. Second, by retaining unspent loaned funds, borrowers reduce their exposure to unforeseen revenue downturns or cost increases.

In sum, Paul Davidson argues that the monetary system is the portal through which uncertainty enters economic processes. For households, portfolio decisions depend on relative prices and expenditure plans, which in turn shift with every revision in expectations about the future. For firms, the inherited stock of capital is a 'bridge between the plans of the past, the current expectations, and the anticipation about the enigmatic future'; whereas 'the inherited stock of money and securities is the link between past financing decisions, the current need for a medium of exchange, and the desire to store value for the future' (1978, p. 23). And firms' access to credit determines their degree of exposure to expectational shifts and changed conditions: the fragility of their bridge to the future. The monetary system – the entire institutionalized system which mediates contracts for delivery and payment – is, warns Davidson, a double-edged sword. On the one hand, used wisely, this system 'permits installation of productive capacity and the expansion of output at a rate that would be virtually impossible in a commodity money world' (1978, p. 316); but used foolishly, it can 'magnify the rush to uncertainty and thereby accentuate slumps' (1978, p. 317).

HOW DOES FINANCIAL INNOVATION AFFECT THE MONETARY SYSTEM?

In Paul Davidson's monetary vision, the key function of the monetary system is to minimize the potential damage to economic activity from agents' behavioural reactions to perceived shifts in the uncertain environment. This is best accomplished in turn if the banking system offers agents a time-machine money; for then a run to liquidity (to money) will not destroy the reserves on which the monetary system has constructed its networks of credit. Financial intermediaries thus retain the ability to use the economy's pool of liquidity productively under varying conditions. Intermediaries are not themselves immune to the impact of shifting degrees of uncertainty; they are just as prone to overexposed balance sheets in periods of liquidity shortage, and as likely to crave liquidity, as any other firms (Davidson, 1994a, p. 136; Dymski, 1988).[5] The point is that a monetary system which conserves available liquid funds within its banking system can recover quickly from adverse circumstances and expectational shifts, since its intermediaries' lending capacity will not be damaged whenever firms and households adjust their plans.

By implication, much financial innovation is economically beneficial. Innovations that increase the number of money substitutes; that reduce transaction costs; that increase the type and variety of contracts for the delivery of goods, services, or assets across time, all enhance monetary efficiency. Similarly, as the variety of intermediaries specializing in different credit and payments sub-markets grows – that is, as financial development in the sense of Goldsmith (1969) occurs – the monetary system grows more efficient, *ceteris paribus*.

But *ceteris* is not invariably *paribus*. Davidson himself has repeatedly emphasized that the social world is 'nonergodic' or non-repetitive and hence a 'transmutable or creative reality' (Davidson, 1994b). Nothing remains what it was. Social relations are historically relative and, at the same time, unpredictable: current outcomes and states cannot reliably predict future outcomes. This non-ergodicity generates uncertainty. It also implies that money itself is 'a social phenomenon' (in a passage from Harrod quoted by Davidson, 1994b, p. 6). Money and credit are not pre-given categories with fixed properties, but historically contingent arrangements. As a result there is no reason to think financial changes will lead only towards economic progress: changes that accelerate economic growth in some ways may slow it in others.

Consider two adverse effects of recent financial changes. First, some financial innovations may increase uncertainty in some ways. Arguably the large volume of index trading in secondary asset markets increases their volatility; and the proliferation of over-the-counter financial derivative contracts creates illiquid risks of unknown magnitude for many firms operating in sophisticated financial markets.

This point is not pursued here. Rather, the remainder of this paper explores a second adverse effect: the reduction of financial access for poorer households and smaller firms, even as financial options for wealthier households and established firms have multiplied. In effect, the monetary system now functions differently for different classes of economic agents, in ways not anticipated in Davidson's analysis. Making this argument requires a selective review of US experience. Space limitations preclude a discussion of financial change in other nations.

THE NEW DEAL SYSTEM AND 'TIME MACHINE' MONEY

The *laissez-faire* US banking system collapsed amidst the Great Depression due to numerous weaknesses. This system's guarantees of liquidity rested with a Federal Reserve that was ambivalent about its 'lender of last resort' role. Many households were outside the banking system; and most did not own, but rented housing. The stock market and real estate booms of the 1920s induced banks to overcompete for deposits, which were often used to acquire financial assets for speculative gain.

Wide-ranging reforms in the 1930s addressed these weaknesses. New acts and regulations rebuilt the US monetary system on the basis of two principles: market segmentation and universal coverage. Banking markets were separated geographically and competition for savings and for loans was strictly limited. Banks and thrifts (savings and loan associations) were provided with deposit insurance; the Federal Reserve made clear its resolve as a lender of last resort.

These changes revolutionized the US monetary system and restored public trust therein. This encouraged the rapid expansion of money substitutes (especially bank deposits) and hence a more efficient payments system. Many firms shifted their payrolls from cash to chequing systems (Caskey, 1994). The postal savings system was widely used by working-class households, and cheque-cashing stores sprang up. Meanwhile, banks' branch networks grew, eventually covering most market areas densely; commercial banks eventually collected most liquid household savings and short-term financing for local businesses. Savings and loan associations provided the principal savings vehicle for household financial savings and supplied long-term mortgage loans to facilitate the spread of home ownership. Restrictions on competition and government backing allowed banks and savings and loan associations to subsidize loans to smaller borrowers with the proceeds from blue-chip loans, while subsidizing deposit services for smaller savers with earnings from larger savers. Localized networks of banks and savings and loan associations provided integrated mechanisms for gathering and channelling small savings.

At the same time, President Roosevelt's reluctant embrace of Keynesian policies stimulated employment and eliminated the debt–deflation cycles of the pre-Keynesian economy. Pushed by union militancy and encouraged by macroeconomic stability, many non-financial firms began signing forward labour contracts and offering stable jobs. This, together with the ready availability of savings and loan associations financing led to the proliferation of home ownership; and this fed the virtuous growth cycle more, since new home owners needed new suburbs. Stable profit rates provided much of the funds needed for corporate investment spending; much of the rest was raised by auctions of equity shares to the very wealthy and their trust funds.

In sum, the New Deal banking system provided a stakeholding vehicle for the broad mass of Americans.[6] Davidson's depiction of money and financial relations characterizes it well. Dense networks of interlocking forward contracts conferred price and employment stability; financial intermediaries uniformly facilitated higher levels of economic welfare by offering common savings and financing vehicles to small and large, rich and working-class agents alike. Because of this uniformity of financial options, most households held their wealth in deposits within the US banking system, in its banks and thrifts. In the stable macroeconomic climate, banks routinely absorbed the risks associated with making credit broadly available to firms and households.

FROM THE NEW DEAL SYSTEM TO THE BRAVE NEW FINANCIAL WORLD

In the 1960s macroeconomic pressures and growing sophistication by banks and their larger customers began to break down the New Deal banking system. Banks' near-monopolies over household savings and credit supply were gradually undermined. Periodic bouts of 'tight money' designed to rein in inflationary pressures led to disintermediation (the flight of deposit funds out of banks) by wealthy depositors, sometimes into the Euromarket. In consequence large US banks began conducting increasing portions of their lending offshore.

In the 1970s still more financial innovations further compromised the integrated character of investment and savings under the New Deal system. Money market mutual funds were created; these funds provided upper-income and even middle-income households with a liquid, interest-earning alternative to bank deposits. Disintermediation from the banking system increased from a trickle in the 1960s to a flood in the late 1970s. This savings outflow compromised banks' lending capacity, leading in short order to the establishment of robust, liquid corporate bond and paper markets. The 'blue-chip' corporations that had been the backbone of banks' commercial and industrial lending turned to these direct credit markets for most of their financing needs (see table 7.1 in Kashyap and Stein, 1994, p. 231).

The US and global macroeconomic environments were also undergoing fundamental changes. The Bretton Woods system of fixed exchange rates broke down in the early 1970s. Two oil price shocks, trade imbalances, and uncoordinated recovery/recession cycles led to roller-coaster exchange rate movements. The Euromarket experienced explosive growth: OPEC wealth from the oil price shocks was recycled through this market to oil-importing and developing nations. Further, as macroeconomic instability increased, the secure long-term, high-wage industrial jobs that had anchored the US economy came under attack. Inflation-indexed union contracts bore much of the blame for stagflation at this decade's end; the 1980s and 1990s have subsequently seen the dismantling of this 'Fordist' job structure (Amin, 1994). The 'flexible specialization' production system that has gradually emerged since the mid-1970s features many more short-term, temporary contracts, less job security, and lower wages (Mishel and Bernstein, 1994). Unions have either disappeared or accommodated these changes, usually by trading security for older workers against concessions for new workers.

High rates of price inflation led to unprecedented nominal interest rates. Banks had to borrow at these high rates to replace the funds they lost through intermediation. This in turn violated the integrity of the New Deal banking system: banks and savings and loan associations could no longer remain at the centre of the savings/investment process by absorbing (as much) liquidity and default risk. Mortgages and other long-term loans often yielded less than it cost to carry them; loan defaults rose dramatically. The pressure on the banking system was further fuelled by intensifying intra- and international competition. Bank and savings and loan associations failure rates climbed to levels not seen since the Depression.

Congress and regulators stepped in to salvage the banking system. Four banking acts through the 1980s brought deregulation and the end of the New Deal system. Banks and savings and loan associations were given more freedom to set deposit rates, make loans, buy and sell in financial markets, and even (in some states) participate in underwriting and capital-provision. The government extended additional guarantees and took on more risk: deposit insurance was increased; the securitization of home mortgage debt, under cover of implicit governmental guarantees, was expanded; and the Federal Reserve expanded its lender of last resort role to include the salvaging of banks deemed 'too big to fail'. A lax regulatory approach to bank mergers and to the disposition of failed intermediaries further sped this transition.

How have banks and other lenders reacted to the new competitive challenges and freedoms of the 1980s and 1990s? Some, especially smaller institutions, have tried to maintain business as usual in their traditional loan and customer markets. Others have outpaced these institutions by pursuing new earnings strategies: targeting new loan and deposit customers, opening new lines of business and reducing their risk exposure. These banks and savings and loan associations are leading the US monetary system into a brave new financial world. Indeed the small town or neighbourhood bank is nearly extinct; larger banks with a presence in multiple states and in multiple product lines are becoming the norm.

A key feature of the new aggressive banking strategy is a rethinking of how earnings are generated. Since 'blue-chip' borrowers are no longer to be had, banks have sought out new loan customers in emerging markets, especially overseas. Many lenders derive profit from fee-based income as much as, or more than, from interest margins earned over time. They have also exploited computer technology to cut loan-making costs: loan decisions are increasingly made on a quantified basis that emphasizes standardized balance sheet and cash flow data (not 'character' as in an earlier day). In every area of banking activity, lenders are seeking out lower-cost methods of delivering services; since financial intermediation is labour-intensive, this search invariably leads to workforce downsizing. Bank branch offices have been rigorously pared in the past 15 years; many more branch closures could still occur.

Apart from reducing costs, intermediaries are calculating net returns on the basis of the bundles of services they sell to different customer groups (Burton, 1994). Customer groups whose businesses yield positive net returns are encouraged with special rates, promotions and fee forgiveness, even while fees are raised for groups with negative net returns. So whereas the New Deal system effectively brought about cross-subsidies between wealthy and poor households, and between large and small businesses, in today's monetary system cross-subsidies are used as marketing tools: reduced fees on one product attract income-generating customers for other products.

The retail banking business has been transformed. On the liability side the major banks have shifted 'upmarket' toward upper-income, wealthier customers. Indeed, New Deal US banking markets, which featured (near) universal access and standardized savings/transactions instruments for all, have broken into three distinct segments. At the top end are the 'super-included': the wealthy, whose financial needs are catered to personally by diverse sets of brokers, bankers and advisers.[7] Most households fall into the middle segment, which has ready access to a standardized set of savings/borrowing options such as credit cards, mutual funds and money market accounts. A broader range of product choices is available to this segment than in the New Deal system, and more firms compete to offer these standardized services. This intense competition explains why these households enjoy some cross-product subsidies: for example, transaction fees are routinely waived in exchange for hefty minimum account balances.

On the bottom are the unbanked, who face financial exclusion. The unbanked are unable to maintain bank accounts due to low savings rates and rising bank service fees.[8] In consequence, the unbanked conduct their financial business through a network of informal firms – cheque-cashing outlets, money-order firms, grocery stores – at substantially higher fees than the same services would cost in banks or savings and loan associations.

The same kind of customer differentiation has occurred on banks' asset side. As lenders replace local lending officers with centralized computer programs, borrowers' access to credit depends on their ability to pass a set of standardized creditworthiness criteria. Here too the customer base splits apart. On one hand are the larger, experienced firms and wealthier households; these units' healthy balance sheets and track records easily qualify them as desirable borrowers. On the other hand are smaller firms and poorer households, with worse financial 'fundamentals' and slimmer experience. Under standardized creditworthiness criteria, these units appear uniformly undesirable; and the local loan officers capable of sorting good from bad risks in these populations have largely been reassigned, retired or laid off.

Lenders compete to service upper-income households and established firms; often these units receive unsolicited offers of credit, and have access to deep lines of credit should they be needed. By contrast, marginal borrowers must seek out credit informally. Small businesses must rely on trade credit, relatives, and their owners' credit cards and housing equity; poorer households must turn to finance companies or, in extremity, to pawnbrokers.[9] Generally these alternatives are less desirable than bank credit: they are usually more costly; and fewer funds are usually available from any one source, so either multiple sources must be tapped or the borrower must function with inadequate credit. In sum, intermediaries' customer bases have bifurcated: one group is left with costless access to money and plentiful credit, and the other with costly money and limited access to borrowing.

In addition to customer shedding, banks have shed credit risks and, in some credit markets, shifted from an intermediary to a broker role. Banks have shed risk in part by replacing fixed-rate with variable-rate loans in most credit transactions. When they do not make variable-rate loans, banks have increasingly protected themselves against risk by securitizing credit – that is, by bundling and selling off their loans to insurance companies, pension funds, mutual funds and overseas investors. Indeed, over half of all mortgage debt is now securitized, and securitization for credit card debt is expanding rapidly.

THE ROLES OF MONEY, CREDIT, AND INTERMEDIATION RECONSIDERED

In Paul Davidson's view, the economic functions of the monetary system are increasing transactional efficiency and reducing the consequences of uncertainty for non-financial units. Financial intermediaries accomplish the first function by making available low-cost access to liquidity, and the second by making available patient, long-term credit, thus allowing borrowers to stabilize cash flows by making long-term forward contracts for goods and services.

The changes in financial intermediation reviewed above have eroded these functions for growing portions of the household and firm population.[10] Lenders' splitting of customer bases results in the oversupply of financial services for some, and the denial of financial services – or their provision only at high cost – to others. Households and firms excluded from lenders' competition for customers are more exposed to the costs and losses of operating in a fundamentally uncertain environment. They are less able to make long-term contracts, pay more to execute transactions, and (in the case of firms) operate at smaller, less efficient scales than they otherwise would.

Lenders' shedding of credit risk also makes the monetary system less functional in reducing uncertainty within the economy. In operating as brokers – that is, in selling off the credits they originate, instead of holding loans to maturity – lenders are no longer absorbing risks they routinely took on under the New Deal system.[11] Financial intermediaries have almost universally shed interest-rate risk by issuing variable-rate loans, which shift this risk to borrowers.

So some customers have more access to money and credit, at better terms, than ever, while others face higher financial costs and reduced capacity. The bifurcation of customer bases has redefined the relationship between banks and the communities within their market areas. Banks and savings and loan associations are no longer the focal point for integrated, localized savings/ investment processes. Increasingly they are the localized purveyors of standardized financial contracts and services. Those smaller banks that retain the older model find it difficult to attract wealthier, higher-margin savers, and to retain larger, lower-cost borrowers. Needless to say, bank branch closures have largely occurred in 'marginal' communities whose residents represent a smaller marketing potential than the residents in communities elsewhere.

Financial intermediaries' reduced willingness to transform maturity and to reduce uncertainty through longer-term credit contracts reflects the real-sector shift from stable, Fordist employment and production contracts to short-term, contingent production arrangements. Firms that have lost stable forward contracts for goods and services are less desirable as borrowers, especially long-term borrowers. The workers that these firms employ have less stability in projected income flows, and hence are also worse prospects for mortgage and long-term consumer debt.

A positive feedback loop exists among increasing macroeconomic instability, the rise of flexible production systems, and banks' shift away from a risk-bearing (and hence uncertainty-reducing) role *vis-à-vis* its customers.[12] Long-term credit and secure lines of credit allow borrowers to reduce uncertainty by making fixed-price forward contracts; lenders' stricter criteria for these arrangements force borrowers to shift to shorter-term contractual arrangements for goods and services.

In sum, whereas the New Deal monetary system's risk-bearing intermediaries and broad cross-subsidies encouraged wealth building by units without equity, the monetary system of today erects barriers to units without equity, while enhancing access for households that are already wealthy and for firms that are well capitalized. These characteristics make the new monetary system more prone to instability: well situated units can more easily mobilize funds to pursue opportunities in boom periods, leading more quickly to oversaturation and to bust periods.

We turn now to the impact of financial transformation on money itself. Recall Davidson's three-part definition of money as a good with zero elasticity of production, zero elasticity of substitution, and a zero cost of shifting from store of value to means of payment (and back). In the New Deal monetary system, high-powered money (reserves) and bank demand deposits satisfied Davidson's definition. Both reserve money and demand deposits were broadly available at low cost to most households and firms. However, financial transformation has created a social world with two types of money, one for the rich and one for the poor. These monies have different properties: the money available to the poor only partially satisfies Davidson's definition.

Consider the monetary arrangements available to a lower-income 'unbanked' household in today's monetary system. Any working members of this household receive payment either in cash or in the form of a cheque deposit. Neither can be used to make payments costlessly. A pay cheque may be converted, for a fee, into cash and money orders (used to pay utility and rent bills) at a cheque-cashing store. Cash may be converted into money orders only for a fee. This household has no ability to store value in the form of money, unless it literally stashes cash into a crack in the wall or under grandma's mattress. In effect, money is available to this lower-income household only on terms that violate the first and third elements of Davidson's definition of money.

Households with high incomes, by contrast, can readily obtain monies that entirely satisfy Davidson's definition. Indeed, the proliferation of liquid mutual funds and 'interest-plus' cheque accounts has expanded the range of assets that qualify as money for these households. Further, wealthy households with lines of credit can access money on demand: they have the power to force financial intermediaries (those issuing these credit lines) to provide them with cash by selling off securities. So the wealthy – the 'super-included' – do not have to choose, as under the previous system, between a completely liquid money and interest-earning securities.

This shift increases the tendency of the monetary system towards instability. When wealthier households hold completely liquid assets in the form of mutual funds or interest-plus cheque accounts, they actually have in hand securities that can be instantaneously and costlessly converted to money on demand. For while these units' liquid assets are effectively money from their perspective, they are money substitutes in the context of the financial system; if a unit holding such money substitutes exercises its claim on liquidity, the intermediary in question has to sell assets to obtain high-powered money. So the intermediaries that successfully solicit the business of these households by selling them money substitutes are effectively promising to absorb any capital gains or losses that result when these units' claims on liquidity are exercised. In a crisis period, more such intermediaries will be chasing the available pools of money so as to meet their contractual obligations.

IMPLICATIONS OF FINANCIAL TRANSFORMATION

The changes in money and financial intermediation described here have ramifications for monetary theory, for monetary policy, and for the nature of distributional conflict in the economy. This section examines these in turn.

Monetary Theory

The New Deal monetary system was based on universal access to uniform financial services, and on segmented participation by financial intermediaries in financial markets. The new monetary system now emerging is unifying the markets in which financial intermediaries participate; but it is segmenting customers' access to intermediaries, replacing a universal monetary system with a stratified one.

Lower-income households cannot shift among financial assets in the wake of heightened uncertainty. These households no longer store wealth within the monetary system. For privileged households, heightened uncertainty no longer triggers a flight into liquidity. For this new financial citizenry, liquidity is available on demand from the diversified financial firms that provide these citizens' packages of financial services; so adverse shocks do not generate the portfolio shifts they did in the past. However, the intermediaries that provide 'money' for their prosperous customers must absorb more risks on their behalf even while competing in a more volatile and hence uncertain financial world.

In the new financial system the wealthy are oversaturated with savings, payments, and underwriting alternatives. Liquidity is available to these households in several forms. Money is now, increasingly, not just a stock but a power: the command over liquidity, guaranteed by institutions protected by Federal Reserve underwriting. This power is evident in cash management accounts at mutual funds, in lines of credit, in the plethora of credit cards. These instruments provide instantaneous buffers against shifts in the degree of uncertainty. Whereas access to the time-machine property was once conveyed by maintaining a stock of money, it can now be conveyed by financial power and wealth itself. In the old monetary system, what decision makers stored against the uncertain future was a stock, a thing; what is stored now is a power, detached from any stock.

These shifts clearly require some new thinking by those developing monetary theories concerned with institutional realism. For example, Davidson's analysis, the centre of attention here, proceeds in terms of representative firms and households. The bifurcations now emerging in the new financial system will make it important to consider representative households and firms of two types – the rich and poor, on the one hand, and the well capitalized and the marginal, on the other. It also becomes increasingly important to take into account the differential power of units operating in the monetary system. This topic is developed further below.

Monetary Policy

These shifts in money and in what banks do affect monetary policy. Recall Davidson's characterization of how shifts in uncertainty affect credit (and endogenous money) flows. Shifts in perceived uncertainty might cause either non-bank units or banks to run to liquidity. Under the New Deal system, non-banks' run to safety involved principally a shift in which types of deposit instruments were held, and in what proportions; the reserves anchoring these deposits remained within the banking system. Given this conservation of reserves, the key determinant of the level of credit flows is the attitude of banks towards lending. If they are willing to become illiquid and put their reserves at risk, credit and economic activity will expand; but if they are sufficiently cautious, they will not lend even if free reserves are created.

In this context, activist monetary policy *per se* – the creation or removal of free reserves in the banking system – only indirectly determines the level of banks' credit flows to firms and households. For Davidson, the key determinant of bank lending, and hence of the real target of monetary policy, is banks' confidence level, and this in turn depends on banks' assessment of the threat posed by uncertainty.[13] So expansionary monetary policy might *appear* to stimulate lending and hence investment spending, but the stimulus occurs more fundamentally because the Fed's actions convince lenders and borrowers that uncertainty and hence illiquidity poses a decreased threat.

Three key differences in the effects of monetary policy in the new financial world can be identified. First, the relationship between bank reserves and bank liabilities is looser. Reserves move more fluidly into and out of the banking system, and can be purchased in ever more markets. However, these markets are interlinked globally, with prices that shift with every rumour and every hint of a rumour. The intermediaries that need more reserves to respond to their customers' uncertainty-driven shifts can acquire these only in markets that themselves are ultrasensitive to the degree of uncertainty.

A second difference in monetary policy derives from the emergence of money as a power and not just as a stock. Previously intermediaries supplied loans of determinate size; now they provide ever more lines of credit (money power) to households and firms. These contracts make intermediaries liable to create credit on demand up to whatever limits their customers demand. Thus a large portion of the credit expansion *by* banks at any point in time (say, in the wake of expansionary monetary policy) may actually be forced *on to* banks by their current client relationships. Lines of credit will be drawn on more heavily, *ceteris paribus*, in adverse economic environments, when uncertainty is high; thus, banks will be forced to borrow under adversity to meet credit commitments they originally made to acquire customers in robust economic environments.

Banks' stratification of customer bases and their greater reliance on standardized criteria for loan decisions account for yet a third difference in monetary policy today. The firms and households that lack access to money power, and hence to lines of credit, are those who might benefit if banks' willingness to lend increased. However, these firms' and households' balance sheet positions and net income flows are chronically weak, especially in the wake of the adverse circumstances that usually accompany tight monetary policy. Thus, these firms and households will be less likely to pass the lending screens imposed by lenders if and when these lenders do expand credit. As a result, lenders today will most likely try to sell more credit to prequalified borrowers, or to take customers away from competitor firms, as a way of expanding their lending activity and customer base. This credit competition will exacerbate uneven spatial development and unequal economic opportunity, rather than lifting all boats to prosperity (Dymski, 1996).

The first two shifts – banks' greater need to purchase reserves at rates reflecting an uncertainty premium, and banks' large volume of lending precommitments due to their proliferating lines of credit – imply that lenders are less likely to adopt credit policies that lean against the wind. The third shift – the stratification of the loan–customer base – implies a shrinkage in the money multiplier. Taken together these shifts render monetary policy even less effective than in the past as a stabilization tool. Ironically, these same shifts will also tend to increase financial instability: the increased availability of lines of credit will make upper-income households less prone to rein in spending excesses before their balance sheets become fragile; and overcompetition for desirable financial customers and borrowers may weaken financial intermediaries' balance sheets and lead to overlending, as in the commercial real estate boom of the 1980s. In consequence, more 'lender of last resort' interventions may become necessary.

Distributional Conflict in the Economy

As noted above, Harcourt and Hamouda (1992) have suggested that post Keynesian economics contains three branches: one is work in the monetary tradition associated with Paul Davidson; a second (Kaleckian) branch explores paths opened by the late Polish economist into understanding capitalist dynamics and crisis, as well as political and distributional class conflict; and a third 'neo-Ricardian' branch extends Piero Sraffa's work on long-run economic reproduction.[13] The first and second branches both appreciate the importance of monetary factors, including banks' willingness to lend and their ability to endogenously create money. The second and third branches both emphasize class conflict.

Standing in the way of deeper exchanges among these different post Keynesian approaches are several methodological and substantive disagreements. For the Davidsonian approach, fundamental uncertainty is the *sine qua non* of a post Keynesian model; but for the other branches it is the presence of class conflict. Kaleckian models often use deterministic dynamical equations, which do not incorporate Keynesian uncertainty. The problem is that Davidsonian models are necessarily monetary, in the sense of allowing for purely financial (nominal) forces to affect real outcomes; but often models of class conflict are solely real (regard financial forces as purely passive). Consequently, a challenge for post Keynesian economists is to build bridges among these different branches.

The central challenges are to bring distributional conflict into monetary models, and in turn to incorporate monetary elements into class conflict models. Some theorists, such as Jarsulic (1988) and Skott (1989), have addressed the former challenge. These authors have suggested models in which the resolution of distributional conflict between workers earning wages and capitalists earning profits (or rent) depends on credit market outcomes – different interest rates and/or investment/savings balances lead to different levels of real wages and profit.

This chapter suggests another way of incorporating financial relations into models of conflict and growth. Apart from conflict over income shares and unemployment levels, conflict exists between those with access to liquidity and financial services, and those without it; in effect, this conflict arises because different agents have different levels of exposure to uncertainty. This financial access conflict exists within both the capitalist and working classes; for while income source (wages or profits) correlates closely with the degree of financial access, it does not correlate perfectly – and this difference increasingly matters.

Among capitalists – those who (directly or indirectly) employ the labour of others in production processes aimed at making profit – some have assured access to liquidity and to expansion financing, but others do not. Those without it – including many minorities and women, and the owners of newer and smaller firms – operate at a considerable disadvantage. They are less able to tap lines of credit to meet production demands, to meet new market trends through investment, and to survive periods of stagnant demand or costly supply. Similarly, within the working class, workers with assured access to borrowed funds (credit cards) and with means of financial savings have a considerable advantage in periods of recession or of secular downturns in labour demand, compared to households that lack these financial resources.

The shifts described above in financial intermediaries' behaviour have significantly increased the importance of these intra-class conflicts over financial access. In the old financial regime, banks serviced large and small firms more uniformly; now, more small firms are unable to obtain access to working capital or to expansion financing, while larger and more experienced firms have more access than before. So the competitive playing field has tilted towards large firms and large capitalists. Similarly, the bank deposit account has become more costly and less available for workers whose earnings are more sporadic or lower. Increasingly wage earners fall into both the unbanked and financial citizen categories. Workers with large amounts of financial assets and with assured access to liquidity have not just a job, but a financial position to protect. Meanwhile, workers with worse jobs are losing access to the financial resources that allow them to survive periods of downturn in labour demand. Clearly, the playing field between the financially empowered sector of capitalists and the financially disenfranchised sector of workers has tilted notably against workers because of these two sides' different degrees of financial access and security.

In the terminology suggested above, the three financial customer categories of firms and households – the unbanked; the 'process-included'; and the 'super-included' – can be regarded as contending for the limited services (credit and liquidity guarantees) that the structure of financial intermediation can offer at any point in time. A central point made above is precisely that the explosion of credit and liquidity alternatives for the new financial citizens has come at the expense of the financial access of the unbanked and financially marginal.

In any event, the struggle between haves and have-nots has two dimensions, not one: how high are real wages and unemployment rates; and who has access to credit and liquidity. The exposure of financial citizens and of the financially marginal to shifts in uncertainty is very different. So workers are at risk in any struggle with capital not just of losing their jobs (or facing lower wages), but of losing their financial privileges – and especially their ability to accumulate wealth and to maintain a buffer against uncertainty.

CONCLUSION

Paul Davidson's notion of money as a time machine emphasizes the tension within any monetary system between protecting the value of accumulated wealth and accumulating still more wealth. This tension centres on households' choice of whether to hold money or risky assets, and on banks' choice of whether to buy securities or to lend. Innovations in the past two decades have set in motion changes that have allowed high-margin financial customers to avoid this trade-off. But the intensifying competition for these desirable customers has led banks to cut operations and eliminate cross-subsidies that once permitted full financial participation by lower-income households and by smaller firms. Consequently these less desired financial customers face new barriers to financial access.

In the wake of these changes money is no longer the time machine it was for many households and firms. This has consequences for both theory and policy. For post Keynesian theory, maintaining descriptive accuracy will mean taking into greater account a form of economic conflict often overlooked until now – that between those with, and those without, access to diversified, low-cost means of saving and of borrowing. Indeed, conflict models should generally take monetary factors into greater account, given that one axis of conflict increasingly revolves around access to liquidity and to financial resources.

In terms of policy, the emerging monetary system is reversing the momentum of change initiated with the New Deal monetary system. That older system enhanced access to uniform financial services, while segmenting the activities of financial intermediaries in financial markets. The new monetary system now emerging is unifying financial intermediaries' participation in financial markets; but at the same time it is also segmenting customers' access to intermediaries, thus replacing a universal monetary system with a stratified one. So the nearly universal banking 'public' of the past is dividing into several non-intersecting customer bases. And given the ongoing processes of deindustrialization in this post-Fordist era, this financial restructuring is making access to financial resources and buffers against uncertainty all the harder to obtain for precisely the households and firms that most need it.

Perhaps financial intermediaries can survive the volatile 1990s by shedding the behaviours that made them functional within the economic order; but can US society survive if many of its citizens are permanently denied not just secure jobs, but any buffer against uncertainty and any access to financial capital? Must Paul Davidson's lessons about the terrors of uncertainty be learned anew at the dawn of the new century?

NOTES

1. For example, this phrase appears in Davidson (1994a, p. 94).
2. The historical and institutional assertions made below are introduced with minimal references. These assertions synthesize aspects of my continuing research into this topic; this research has appeared, with extensive documentation, in Dymski (1996), Dymski and Pollin (1994) and Dymski and Veitch (1996).
3. This list is drawn from Davidson (1978). Davidson (1994a, ch. 6) revisits this ground, and eliminates the third property of money, which can be derived from the first two. It is listed explicitly here for analytical convenience.
4. Transfers that shift some possible costs of uncertainty on to others appear to reduce uncertainty. This reduction is apparent, not real. A firm can promise to purchase labour services in advance; but it cannot guarantee that it will avoid failure or takeover before this promise is realized.
5. Davidson himself has long been sensitive to this; his 1978 book (pp. 184–5) recalls and amplifies on Keynes's observation that banks hold the key role in the transition from lower to higher levels of economic activity.
6. It did not extend evenly to all. Banks and savings and loan associations often did not locate or lend in minority neighbourhoods. Given rampant segregation, minority households and businesses faced higher transaction costs and less access to credit. See Dymski and Veitch (1996).
7. Leyshon and Thrift (1996) suggest this terminology.
8. Caskey (1994, p. 89) reports that whereas 35 per cent of all banks offered no-fee cheque accounts in 1977, only 5 per cent did in 1991; and he presents evidence that fees and minimum balances have skyrocketed.
9. Caskey (1994) has described pawnbrokers as the short-term credit market for the poor. However, this description overstates the case. Pawnbrokers lend on the basis of terms and conditions that are substantially more onerous than those of banks. In effect, pawnshop credit is solely an avenue of emergency spending, for most who use it; it facilitates asset decumulation, but seldom if ever asset accumulation.
10. Caskey and Peterson (1994) show that the proportion of all households with a bank account dropped from 90.5 per cent in 1977 to 86.5 per cent in 1989. This entire decline was accounted for by the bottom sixth in income terms, 70.3 per cent of whom had bank accounts in 1977, versus 59.2 per cent in 1989. No figures are available for the share of small businesses that lack access to formal bank financing.
11. Securitized loans *are* held to maturity by other financial firms – typically, by insurance companies, pension funds, mutual funds, and overseas investors. However, the monetary system becomes less efficient in absorbing risk in that the intermediaries that previously held these credits were transforming maturity – that is, financing longer-term assets with short-term liabilities.
12. Since the prospects of repayment and/or of payment to term by borrowers are much more uncertain, loan securitization and risk shedding serve to disconnect the institutions originating debts from the longer-term risks to which these debts give rise.
13. Sawyer (1985) has argued that post Keynesian theory should be rechristened post Kaleckian macroeconomics. Dymski (1995) discusses these different strands of theory from a monetary perspective.

REFERENCES

Amin, A. (1994), 'Post-Fordism: Models, Fantasies and Phantoms of Transition' in A. Amin (ed.), *Post-Fordism: A Reader*, London: Basil Blackwell, pp. 1–40.
Burton, D. (1994), *Financial Services and the Consumer*, London: Routledge.

Caskey, J. (1994), *Fringe Banking: Check-Cashing Outlets, Pawnshops, and the Poor*, New York: Russell Sage Foundation.

Caskey, J. and A. Peterson (1994), 'Who Has a Bank Account and Who Doesn't: 1977 and 1989', *Eastern Economic Journal*, **20**(1), 61–74.

Davidson, P. (1972), *Money and the Real World*, London: Macmillan. References in the text are to the second edition, 1978.

Davidson, P. (1994a), *Post Keynesian Macroeconomic Theory*, Aldershot, Hants: Edward Elgar.

Davidson, P. (1994b), 'The Concepts of Uncertainty and an External Economic Reality in Economic Theory', mimeo, The New School for Social Research, New York.

Dymski, G. (1988), 'A Keynesian Theory of Bank Behaviour', *Journal of Post Keynesian Economics*, **10**(4), Summer, 499–526.

Dymski, G. (1995), 'Kalecki's Monetary Economics' in J. King (ed.), *An Alternative Macroeconomic Theory: the Kaleckian Model and Post Keynesian Economics*, Amsterdam: Kluwer.

Dymski, G. (1996), 'Economic Polarization and US Policy Activism', *International Review of Applied Economics*, **10**(1), 66–83.

Dymski, G. and R. Pollin (1994), 'The Costs and Benefits of Financial Instability: Big-Government Capitalism and the Minsky Paradox' in G. Dymski and R. Pollin (eds), *New Directions in Monetary Macroeconomics: Essays in the Tradition of Hyman P. Minsky*, Ann Arbor, Mich.: University of Michigan Press, pp. 369–401.

Dymski, G. and J. Veitch (1996), 'Financial Transformation and the Metropolis: Booms, Busts, and Banking in Los Angeles', *Environment and Planning A*, forthcoming.

Goldsmith, R. (1969), *Financial Structure and Development*, New Haven, Conn.: Yale University Press.

Harcourt, G. and O. Hamouda (1992), 'Post-Keynesianism: From criticism to coherence?' in C. Sardoni (ed.), *On Political Economists and Modern Political Economy: Selected Essays of G.C. Harcourt*, London: Routledge, pp. 209–32.

Jarsulic, M. (1988), *Effective Demand and Income Distribution*, Boulder, Col.: Westview Press.

Kashyap, A. and J. Stein (1994), 'Monetary policy and bank lending' in G. Mankiw (ed.), *Monetary Policy*, Chicago, Ill.: University of Chicago Press for the National Bureau of Economic Research, pp. 221–56.

Keynes, J.M. (1936), *The General Theory of Employment, Interest and Money*, London: Macmillan.

Leyshon, A. and N. Thrift (1996), 'Geographies of Financial Knowledge', *Environment and Planning A*, forthcoming.

Mishel, L. and J. Bernstein (1994), *The State of Working America*, Armonk, NY: M.E. Sharpe.

Plato (1956), *Euthyphro, apology, crito*, translated by F.J. Church, Indianapolis, Ind.: Bobbs-Merrill, The Library of Liberal Arts.

Sawyer, M. (1985), 'Toward a Post-Kaleckian Macroeconomics', in *Post Keynesian Economic Theory*, Armonk, NY: M.E. Sharpe, pp .146–79.

Skott, P. (1989), *Conflict and Effective Demand in Economic Growth*, Cambridge: Cambridge University Press.

8. Endogenous money and the 'state of trade'

Peter Howells

In 1972, in my first teaching post, I was trying, with only limited success, to persuade my colleagues and students of the importance of a sound knowledge of economic history, at least of more recent times. Though I still believe that no amount of theory is an adequate substitute for knowing what actually happened, it was clear that I was not going to make much of a living from pressing this advice on others and that some diversification was called for. Since my prime interest as a historian lay with the interwar period and the life and ideas of Keynes there was never much doubt that diversification meant macroeconomics. (There was no shame or danger in those days in admitting one's Keynesian credentials – in the UK that came later.) I set myself the task of rereading Keynes and was much perplexed by the emphasis on money and the way in which this had become lost in the standard, so-called, Keynesian expositions of macroeconomics of that period. On the other hand, such monetary textbooks as there were had little connection that I could see with Keynes or with the institutional realities of which (as a historian) I was still keenly aware. In the circumstances, I could hardly have resisted a book with the title of *Money and the Real World*. It was a revelation. Above all, it taught me that I did know something useful about money and that what I knew had come from Keynes (*Treatise* as much as *General Theory,* in fact). Paul's book was quickly followed by Victoria Chick's *Theory of Monetary Policy* and I knew then that monetary economics would yield enough fascinating questions to last me a working lifetime. It has.

This paper combines a number of themes in which I have long been interested. One is the demand for bank lending and the question of whether this may be affected increasingly by what one might call 'speculative' expenditures – using the term to include spending on secondhand assets as well as financial assets – which are not recorded in national income statistics. This relates to another issue, which is the common tendency to treat PT as equivalent to PY in discussions of the quantity theory. Not only may this obscure some of the insights of original work in the quantity theory framework, it is clearly wrong if non-GDP spending is diverging from GDP expenditures. The third theme is the endogeneity of money supply. The core of the endogeneity thesis, which we might summarize as 'loans cause deposits' has seemed to me self-evidently true for many years.[1] But I have become increasingly interested in the process whereby the supply of (loan-created) deposits is made consistent with increases in the demand for money. How is it that the desires of one group of agents with one set of motives ('borrowers') come to match the desires of another group with a different set of motives ('wealth holders')?

This chapter explores the relationship between the endogeneity of money supply and the quantity theory. In particular, the paper questions whether endogeneity of money necessarily destroys the QT assertion that causality runs from money to output and prices. It looks at two situations in which the direction of causality might still run in some degree from M to PY. The first involves the possibility that new money has its origins partly in loans to finance speculative activity, i.e. in total spending (PT), rather than in spending on final output (PY). The second involves the possibility that loan-created deposits (whatever their origin) might not be matched by the demand for new money. Furthermore, this chapter emphasizes areas for future research, first, in the relationship between total spending (PT) and spending on final output (PY); second, on the interaction between the demand for loans and the demand for the resulting deposits.

We begin, in the next section, with some remarks about the origin of the equation of exchange and the tendency to treat PT as equivalent to PY in many circumstances. We shall note some evidence that PT and PY have diverged in the UK in recent times and thus that they were *not* equivalent, at least for this time and place. We then turn to the argument that endogeneity of money means that causality runs from spending to money, and not the other way as required by the quantity theory. We shall see that the argument relies upon 'new money' being created by loans which are dependent upon the 'state of trade' which, in its usual interpretation, corresponds to PY, and thus 'PY causes M'. But we shall question whether the emphasis on firms and production as the source of loan demand and new money is excessive. Personal sector borrowing rose much more rapidly than borrowing by firms in the 1980s in the UK and much of that borrowing was for (secondhand) house purchase, included in PT, but excluded from PY. In the next section we ask whether it matters if new money has its origin in PT rather than PY. We note that in certain circumstances a 'PT causes M causes PY' sequence might be possible. In the penultimate section we consider a further possibility which might lead to an 'M causes PY' sequence. This arises when the flow of new loan-created deposits is not matched by a demand for new money.

In the final section we summarize and conclude.

THE EQUATION OF EXCHANGE: *PT* OR *PY*?

As any first-year student knows, the equation of exchange is merely an identity. If, for example, we write:

$$MV = PY \tag{1}$$

we are merely saying that current output at market prices (*PY*) is equal in value to total spending on current output (*MV*). Notice that the spending denoted by *MV* is restricted to spending on current output precisely because we define *V* as the ratio *PY/M*. We could, if we choose, make *MV* denote *total* spending (on current output, intermediate goods, secondhand goods, financial assets etc.) by defining *V* as the ratio *PT/M*, where *PT* stands for the nominal value of *total* transactions. Since the latter is bound to be larger by some multiple than spending on national income, the value of corresponding *V* ('transactions' velocity) is bound also to be larger than the value of the *V* ('income' velocity) linking *M* to *PY*. Briefly, then:

$$V_Y = PY/M < V_T = PT/M \tag{2}$$

Of the two versions, the transactions version of the equation of exchange is the older, going back at least to the eighteenth century when Hume and others developed it into the quantity *theory* of money as part of an attack on the mercantilist tendency to identify money with wealth (Visser, 1974; Chrystal, 1990).

What this attack, and the transition from identity to theory, entailed is also well known. It required a plausible argument that changes in the quantity of money would lead (eventually and short-run impacts notwithstanding) to a rise in prices. There would be no lasting effect on total transactions, output or *real* income. This was achieved by placing severe restrictions on the behaviour of velocity and on the volume of total transactions. The value of *V*, it was argued, could change only slowly over time, being determined by: (a) the frequency with which income is received; (b) expenditure patterns and the timing of payments; (c) the degree of vertical integration of industry; and (d) the extent to which credit is used. These restrictions had the effect of making the effect of changes in *M* on total spending (*MV*) predictable. As to the effect in turn of changes in total spending, this could be made predictable and could also be made to fall upon the general level of prices if *T* is determined by real variables (such as resources and techniques of production) so that this too can change only slowly over time.

In this form (and with no reference to the demand for money) the quantity theory was popularized by Fisher (1911). In the light of what was to follow, however, it is very interesting to observe that in 1926 Fisher was distinguishing between two classes of transactions, namely those involving finished output (real income), which he called 'income transactions' and identified as PT_1, and 'financial transactions' or PT_2. In this version:

$$MV = PT_1 + PT_2 \qquad (3)$$

By contrast, the income version of the equation of exchange is more recent, having its origin in the work of Marshall, Pigou and the early Keynes on the Cambridge equation, and in Friedman's revised quantity theory. Nonetheless, moving from identity to *theory* requires similar restrictions on V and Y. In the income version, the arguments for stability of V and Y are provided by a stable demand for money function and the vertical Phillips curve, respectively, and have naturally been the source of much controversy, much of it spilling over into the textbooks as arguments about the elasticities and stability of components of the *IS* or *LM* schedules.

By contrast, another similarity between the two versions has gone *comparatively* unremarked. This is that both versions assume that the money supply is exogenously determined. It makes no sense to discuss whether the impact of ΔM falls upon P or T (or Y) unless M is the independent variable.[2] In Fisher's day, this may have been an easy assumption to make given the state of the banking system (Chick, 1986; Niggle, 1990). Keynes, after all, was willing to make the same assumption in *The General Theory* (Keynes, 1971, VII, especially 206–7).[3]

In the 1970s and 1980s, the income version of the quantity theory became a useful and popular framework for emphasizing the importance of monetary rules (in the days before independence of the central bank came to be seen as the only source of policy credibility). Hence interest in the equation of exchange was often in the form of interest in *rates of change*. Typically, the question involved finding the rate of inflation implied by a given monetary rule, or finding the monetary target consistent with zero inflation. Provided that Y is some fixed proportion of T and provided that the average price of T maintains a fixed relation to the average price of Y then it does not matter whether we write the identity in income or transaction form.

But why should we assume that T bears some stable relation to Y? We noted earlier that total transactions comprised transactions in finished goods and services (Y). It also includes intermediate transactions – arising in the course of production of finished goods and services; transactions in secondhand goods – of which houses would form a large proportion by value: and financial transactions – some arising from the current financing needs of the production process but the vast majority resulting from the continuous rearrangement of portfolios by wealth holders, unconnected with any real economic activity. These latter categories, the difference in other words between Y and T, constitute roughly what Keynes in the *Treatise* called 'business transactions'. Expressed in relation to 'business *deposits*', these transactions gave rise to 'V_2' a measure of velocity which focused upon funds used for non-income purposes. We can agree with Keynes that some of these expenditure categories are likely to change only slowly over time and in so doing are likely to move with Y. Intermediate transactions, for example, reflect the degree of vertical (dis)integration in the production process and are not likely to be subject to sudden shocks. By contrast, transactions in secondhand (real) assets or in financial assets:

> ... need not be, and are not, governed by the volume of current output. The pace at which a circle of financiers, speculators and investors hand round to one another particular pieces of wealth, or title to such, which they are neither producing nor consuming but merely exchanging, bears no definite relation to the rate of current production. The volume of such transactions is subject to very wide and incalculable fluctuations. ... (Keynes, 1971, V, 42)

Would anyone watching the gyrations of asset markets over the last 25 years doubt it?

Unfortunately, the measurement of total transactions is no easy matter. In the UK the Central Statistical Office regrets being unable to provide a measure of transactions velocity and offers the standard income velocity (GDP/money stock) instead, admittedly as second-best. And it is indeed a cause for regret. GDP, or some variation thereon, is used as the scale variable in countless demand for money investigations and in estimates of the demand for bank lending. The rationale in both cases is that the demand for money (and credit) are related to people's spending plans. But why should either follow only the plans to buy newly produced goods and services?[4]

In recent years, there have been attempts to incorporate movements in total transactions in both areas of empirical work. A few years ago, Howells and Biefang-Frisancho Mariscal (1992) estimated short-run demand functions for (UK) bank lending using PT rather than PY (i.e. GDP). More recently, Palley (1995) estimated demand functions for (US) M1 and M2 using consumption spending (rather than GDP) but adding variables which proxied for, rather than measured directly, the volume of transactions in real estate and in financial assets (Palley, 1995). In both cases, the results were improved by these attempts to recognize the relevance of non-income transactions, compared with reliance on a GDP variable.

Such work suggests that total transactions do matter, that is, they must have behaved in a way which differs from GDP. As we noted above, it is no easy task to measure total transactions but the potential rewards would seem to make serious efforts worth undertaking. For the UK, future researchers might look at a paper by Bain and Howells (1991).[5] This explains that in the UK all transactions involving bank deposit transfer are centralized in the UK in the records of the Association for Payments Clearing Systems (APACS). Such transfers occur in different ways. Some involve the physical clearing of cheques while some are electronic transfers, for example. APACS publishes a series for each and the simple approach, naturally, is to aggregate the series. The result excludes all payments in cash and thus is an underestimate of the absolute value of transactions. On the other hand, unless we suppose that there are sharp fluctuations in cash payments as a proportion of the total, its trend should indicate something reliable about the total value of payments. A more serious shortcoming in the aggregation approach, however, is the possibility of some double counting, a single transfer being recorded in more than one series. This is a product of institutional peculiarities of the UK banking system and it is something which future researchers on transactions would have to address. Nonetheless, again, unless one supposes that there are significant changes in the degree of double counting, the trend may be indicative. Figure 8.1 shows UK total transactions, measured as we have indicated,

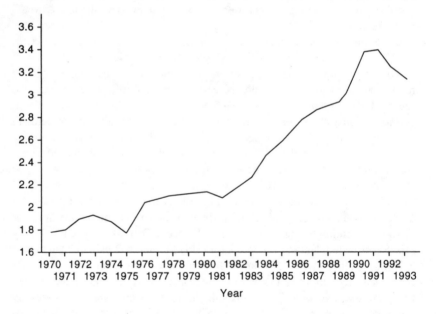

Sources: GDP figures are from the UK Central Statistical Office's macroeconomic database held at the University of Manchester Computing Centre (MIDAS). Series code is CAOB. Figures for transactions are taken from the *Yearbook* (various issues) of the Association of Payments Clearing Systems (APACS).

Figure 8.1   Total transactions/GDP (PT/PY)

as a ratio to UK GDP. The results are startling. It is not quite true to say that the ratio is stable in the 1970s; there is some upward drift. But there is a dramatic change in 1981, after which total transactions rise very rapidly relative to GDP. While the figures may be imperfect, the *variation* in the ratio cannot be dismissed by reference to fluctuations in cash payments or in double counting.

Clearly, henceforth, we should not just assume that *PY* is equivalent to *PT*.

THE STATE OF TRADE

Money is made endogenous, first because banks supply loans (and thus create deposits) on demand. This in turn depends either upon central banks accommodating the resulting demand for reserves at the going rate of interest (e.g. Moore, 1988) or upon banks' innovative behaviour being always sufficient to enable them to stretch the available reserves more thinly (e.g. Pollin, 1991). But money is endogenous fundamentally because the origin of the demand for loans lies within the economic system and not with some independent discretionary action by the authorities. The question for this section is, does the demand for loans derive from plans to spend on finished output or on all spending plans?

Hitherto, in the endogeneity literature, it has been the behaviour of *P* and *Y* which has been held responsible for the demand for bank loans and the channel through which these operate is firms' demand for working capital. If, for example, output is expanding (at constant prices), firms need more inputs and, since production takes time, they have to meet higher input bills before the proceeds of sales can be realized (Davidson, 1994). Likewise, if costs are rising (volumes given) higher input bills have to be met. In practice, of course, some combination of both is likely to be the case and thus the norm is for the stock of bank loans to be expanding. That is, flows of net new loans (and new deposits) are normally positive. When it comes to being more specific, for empirical purposes for example, cost variables include wages and productivity (often based upon some version of Weintraub's, 1978, wage theorem), raw materials, especially imports, and taxes (Moore and Threadgold, 1985; Moore, 1988).

This element of the endogeneity hypothesis should not be underestimated, since it is this (and this alone) that reverses the causal arrow in the quantity theory. If the only reasons for monetary expansion are increases either in the cost or volume of production which are already occurring, then expansions of the money supply must be responses and not causes. And this follows through into a direct confrontation with policy measures derived from the quantity theory. If the money supply increases only in order to allow firms to function under conditions of exogenously rising costs, then quantitative restrictions on monetary growth will have no effect on rising prices except in so far as they cause sufficient disruption to the economic system, through bankruptcies etc., eventually to cause a reduction in cost pressures.

None of this follows from the other elements of the endogeneity paradigm. For example, loans could still be demand-determined, and central banks could still choose always to accommodate; banks' own liquidity preference may affect the shape of the so-called money supply curve. All of this could be true and yet resulting deposits would have major effects on prices (and output) provided only that the demand for loans were independent of the volume or cost of production.

Certainly, the conditions under which firms produce seem obviously relevant to the demand for bank loans for all the reasons we have given above. But is the emphasis in the endogeneity literature on firms and the time dimension of production excessive? Do changes in these conditions provide the whole explanation for the level of borrowing from banks? Might it be possible, for example, that the demand for loans (and the supply of deposits) might be driven by other factors? For the UK at least it is worth noting the dramatic change in the composition of bank lending in recent years. Lending to the personal sector accounted for about 12 per cent of the total stock of outstanding bank loans in the second half of the 1970s, barely different from what it had been 20 years before. Beginning in 1980 it rose rapidly and steadily to reach 29 per cent of the total by 1990, and has edged very slightly upwards since then. The change in flows was necessarily more dramatic. When the stock proportion was stable, the proportion of total new lending going to the personal sector naturally ran at a similar level – 12–13 per cent in the 1970s. During the 1980s, however, lending to the personal sector varied from 30 to 40 per cent of total new lending. In the 1970s, the proportions of new lending going to the personal sector and to manufacturing industry were roughly equal. By the 1990s, the proportion of lending going to the personal sector was three times the proportion going to manufacturing industry.[6]

Clearly while the proportion of loans going to the corporate and personal sectors is changing, the two flows cannot both be following a common source. Corporate borrowing may have been determined largely by changes in the total production bill but the sources of the surge in bank lending to the personal sector are easily traced to banks entering the home loans market[7] (for reasons now well documented), at a time when house prices rose dramatically relative to the price of output and indeed to the price of most other assets.[8] Hence, as we commented in the last section, our attempt to estimate a demand function for UK bank lending after the mid-1970s succeeded with *PT* but not with *PY* as the scale variable.

In these circumstances, and they are not likely to be unique, it is difficult to explain the endogeneity of money by reference to 'the state of trade' if the latter is interpreted, as it usually is, as a reference to price and/or quantity conditions facing firms in the production process. In the circumstances that we have described here, bank loans (and deposits) have been driven in part by circumstances quite independent of the state of *production*. Money has been made endogenous, in other words by *PT* rather than by *PY*. Just how general these circumstances are deserves further investigation. It is curious that in an era when money *supply* (and its control) was felt to be so important in some circles, money *demand* studies flourished while the demand for bank lending was scarcely investigated. And when it was, the emphasis was largely upon the corporate sector (Cuthbertson, 1985; Moore and Threadgold, 1985) based, presumably, on the evidence of the 1970s that it was corporate demand which dominated. Certainly the idea that new bank lending originates solely with firms and reflects their production plans now seems very naive. Much has changed in the last 15 years and a great deal of interesting work waits to be done here.

The next question is 'does it matter?' Can deposits created by essentially speculative activity have any impact on the economy, different from the impact of deposits created in the wake of production? We turn to this next.

SPECULATION AND THE DEMAND FOR LOANS

We have just seen that there is every reason to suppose that the loans which create deposits have had their origin to some degree in a demand for funds for speculative purposes in recent years. That is, the demand for such loans has been driven by *PT*, which in turn, we know, has diverged from *PY*. Does widening the origin of loans (and deposits) make it more or less likely that the resulting new money can cause price or output changes? In terms of causal arrows, is '*PT* causes *M* causes *PY*' a possibility?

As we saw in the last section, the causal sequence of the quantity theory requires money to be created independently of *PY*. Thus anything that separates the origin of new deposits from *PY* seems to threaten trouble. If, for example, *PT* were ultimately the source of newly created deposits which were then used to spend solely on finished output, then *PY* must be affected. Even where *PT* does not diverge from *PY*, *PT* is a substantial multiple of *PY*. An increase in *PT*, financed solely by lending, would create an increase in deposits which would finance substantially more than any corresponding increase in *PY*. But this overlooks the rather obvious fact that while people borrow for secondary or speculative transactions, they also hold money balances which reflect those spending plans. Just as the demand for loans may sensibly be related to the *total* amount of spending which people plan to undertake, so too may the demand for deposits. This is the issue which Palley (1995) addresses. Adding variables for housing and financial transactions improved the performance of the demand for money function.

Clearly, introducing the possibility that speculative expenditures are an additional source of demand for loans, and thus an additional source of deposits, increases the possibility of an increased divergence in the flow of new deposits and the demand for them, provided that we think of demand as being rooted only in *PY*. But just as a demand for loans and deposits emanates from income transactions, we may suppose that if some demand for loans has its origin in speculative spending then so too does a demand for deposits. We cannot then say, *a priori*, that there is any particular implication for expenditure which follows from a *PY/PT* divergence.

There is, however, an implication for velocities, which we can see if we rewrite the last two paragraphs, distinguishing between income and transactions velocities. New loans and new money generated by *PT*, we said, will lead to excessive spending on *PY*, if the decision to hold money is

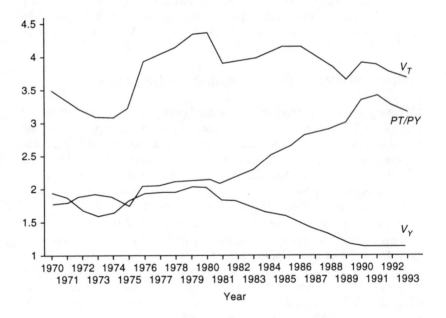

Sources: M4 figures are from the UK Central Statistical Office's macroeconomic database held at the University of Manchester Computing Centre (MIDAS). Series code is AUYN. V_T and V_Y are calculated by dividing M4 by transactions and GDP respectively.

Figure 8.2   Behaviour of three ratios, PT/PY, V_Y *and* V_T

based solely upon *PY*. This amounts to saying that income velocity, V_Y, is given. That it does not in practice do so reflects the fact that money is also held in respect of plans to spend on non-income transactions. This is just another way of saying that transactions velocity, V_T, may be stable or at least more stable than V_Y. If this is the case, then we should expect to find that at times when *PT* shows a higher rate of growth than *PY*, and thus new deposits grow more rapidly than the *PY* requirements, income velocity will fall.

Figure 8.2 shows the behaviour of three ratios. First, it takes the *PT/PY* ratio from Figure 8.1. On top of this, it superimposes income velocity (GDP/M4 = V_Y) and transactions velocity (total transactions/M4 = V_T). We can see very clearly a confirmation of the relationships we have just discussed. In particular, the moment that *PT* grows more rapidly than *PY* (in 1980/81), income velocity (V_Y) falls. *Income* velocity, we can see, fell quite sharply, from roughly 2 to roughly 1. Indeed, as we know, it fell so sharply in the early 1980s that monetary targets were abandoned. By contrast, *transactions* velocity fluctuates around 4, showing as clearly as anything could that the money supply (and bank credit) grew in line with total rather than income transactions during the 1980s.

THE DEMAND FOR ENDOGENOUS MONEY

Provided that V_T is stable, a growth in money supply which follows *PT* rather than *PY* may have little consequence for aggregate demand, since any divergence in *PT/PY* will be reflected in a change in V_T. Does this mean though that endogenous money can never cause changes in *PY*? Let us ignore for a moment the question of whether new deposits are generated by loans for the state of trade or loans for speculation. Whatever the origin of loans, it lies with a group of agents who are distinct from those who must ultimately hold the deposits which result. Borrowers are making an income/expenditure decision; money holders are making a portfolio decision. Not everyone is in debt to banks – borrowers from banks are a subset of the community; everyone holds money – money holders are the whole community.[9] No amount of wishful thinking can change this. Does it seem likely that two distinct groups of agents with distinct motivations are going to make coincident decisions without some powerful mechanism forcing a coordination?

And coordination there must be. Since we define money as certain types of asset held by the non-bank private sector and since we assume that agents have a choice about how they hold their wealth, then it follows that whatever the desire for credit may be amongst deficit units, this can only create deposits which the community is willing to hold.

The problem can best be put in *ex ante* and *ex post* terms. *Ex ante*, deficit units plan to borrow L of new loans per period. Meanwhile, holders of money plan to expand their holdings of deposits by D per period where, let us assume, $L > D$. But *ex post*, actual new loans must match actual new deposits, $L^* = D^*$, through the banks' balance sheet identity. What mechanisms or processes are responsible (in this case) for *reducing* the flow of actual loans relative to initial plans and *increasing* the demand for money relative to planned levels?

We answer this in a moment, but first we offer one more statement of the problem in a way that helps us keep it in proportion. The demand for *new* loans originates with one group of agents whose decisions are based to some degree upon the state of trade, or speculation, or both. This demand, if carried through spontaneously and with no constraints, will create an equal quantity of deposits. At the same time, the state of trade, or speculation, or both, will give rise amongst wealth holders to an increase in the demand for deposits, for transactions or asset purposes, as the case may be. Thus, whatever is driving the demand for loans (and supply of new deposits) is also pushing the demand for new deposits at least in the same direction. In exceptional circumstances, the demand for loans *and* deposits may expand by exactly equal amounts (and there is no problem). Furthermore, there will be many agents, firms in particular, who *are* simultaneously holders of deposits and debtors of banks. If they, or households in a similar position, find their receipts of money payments growing more rapidly than they intend, the 'excess' of these receipts will be devoted to repayment of some or all of their existing bank loans. Thus new loans in the aggregate turn out to be less than the aggregate planned by new borrowers.

This idea, that realized lending could never create excess deposits because any potential excess would always be used to repay existing loans, is stated most clearly in Kaldor and Trevithick (1981). But it is essentially the same as the 'reflux' principle which features in Graziani (1990), Lavoie (1992) and, though illustrated with reference to notes rather than deposits, Robinson (1956). According to the reflux principle, firms (notice the stress again upon firms as the source of borrowing) wishing to create output by an amount which increases their costs by, say, 100, have no option but to borrow the 100 from banks to cover the period between paying for the inputs and realizing the proceeds from sale of the output. However, when the output is finally sold, for 120, say, firms use the proceeds to retire some of the debt. How much to retire is a decision which rests with firms. Running at a higher level of output, henceforth, they may feel inclined to hold larger money balances and to be able to support more debt. There is some increase in indebtedness and a corresponding increase in the money supply. The point is that, seen from the firm's perspective, the decisions on money and debt are really two parts of the same decision. There can be no coordination problem. Furthermore, the decision is made voluntarily.

Both the appearance of common terms in the loan and deposit demand functions and the reflux principle mean that the demand for loans and the demand for deposits are not entirely independent, and doubtless work to prevent complete divergence about decisions on both. However, this is a long way from providing a mechanism which coordinates the two. The problem facing the reflux principle is that not everyone has a bank overdraft, a point that has been stressed by others (Cottrell, 1986; Chick, 1983, p. 273, 1986). Of course it is possible to argue that any 'surplus' (for example) deposits will get passed around until someone with a loan feels able to use them to reduce his or her debt. But this is only stating the obvious that loans must ultimately (i.e. *ex post*) equal deposits. The interesting question is whether the 'passing around' has any consequences.

A number of possibilities can be found in the monetary literature, not all of them put forward deliberately as a response to the question of how the demand for loans and the demand for deposits are to be reconciled. We have examined them at some length elsewhere (Howells, 1995a,b; Arestis and Howells, 1994) and so refer to them only briefly here.[10]

One logically satisfactory possibility is unfortunately one which we must dismiss immediately. This is that the economy is in the liquidity trap, where any increase in the quantity of money is willingly held with no need for adjustments in other variables, because the fear of impending capital losses is so strong. This is not to deny that the desire for liquidity may at some times and places be very strong, but we need an altogether more general mechanism.

In the short run, one might appeal to Laidler's (1984) buffer stock notion. The 'equilibrium' demand for money associated with other variables is not a unique value but a range. Within upper and lower limits agents are prepared to accept fluctuations in money holdings as the cheapest way of coping with uncertainty. But once those limits are reached, of course, our question reappears.

Ironically, though certainly relevant to the case of endogenous money, the buffer stock model was originally developed to analyse the response of wealth holders to changes in a money stock which was unambiguously exogenous. A third possibility which we might consider comes directly from the endogeneity tradition. This is Moore's (1988, 1989) concept of 'convenience lending'. The origin of the idea is uncontroversial. Deposits are means of payment and thus are always acceptable as a means of payment. Since sellers have no idea whether the payment they are receiving is a transfer from a positive balance or the fruit of some overdraft agreement, all loan-created new money is willingly accepted. The increase in the deposits of those who receive them

Moore calls 'convenience lending' (to the banking system) because no inducement is required to make agents accept the deposits; they sacrifice nothing in getting the deposits which appear in effect as a windfall. But all of this is reasonable only as an explanation of why agents accept deposit transfers as payment. It is a rather elaborate way of restating the old adage that what makes an asset 'money' is acceptability. But this is not addressing the question of the demand for money which is a question of why people are willing to *hold* the deposits after they have received them (Meulendyke, 1988; Goodhart, 1989, 1991). As a theory of the demand for money 'convenience lending' is saying that the demand for money is perfectly elastic at prevailing levels of interest, income etc. The fact that agents may require no inducement to accept transfers of bank deposits does not mean that *at some point*, or beyond some quantity, they will not require inducements to keep them there when faced with an infinite array of alternative financial assets with alternative risk, liquidity and return characteristics. Its failure as a theory of 'perfectly elastic' money demand is apparent in a passage in Moore's (1991) debate with Goodhart.

> Suppose all wealthholders were to ... have their transactions balances swept into higher-interest-earning, nonbank liabilities. The issuers of these liabilities would then find themselves with higher money balances, and the distribution of deposit ownership would change. But so long as these economic units did not use their sweeping proceeds in turn to repay bank loans, or turn them in for cash, there would be no change in the total quantity of deposits. (Moore, 1991, p. 130)

This is just stating the basic textbook version of the downward-sloping money demand function. Agents with excess money balances buy alternative financial assets, pushing up prices and lowering yields. The money supply, however, remains unchanged at its (previously 'excess') level. In the aggregate, demand is brought up to match supply by the fall in interest rates.

And this is the mechanism that we would endorse, albeit with some modification. The standard version of adjustment to monetary equilibrium which Moore provides is (some irony here, surely) intended to explain the adjustment of demand to an exogenous supply. In a world of endogenous money it is only part of the demand–supply reconciliation process, however. Certainly the purchase of financial assets and the resulting fall in yields makes people more willing to hold 'excess' deposits. But the financial assets concerned are someone's liabilities, issued originally as an alternative to, *inter alia*, borrowing from banks. The fall in yields on such assets represents therefore a reduction in the cost of non-bank finance relative to the cost of borrowing from banks: the demand curve for bank lending shifts inward. Thus the mechanism, which now involves two interest rate differentials, provides not just for an increase in quantity demanded, it also works to reduce supply.

In principle, the question of whether interest differentials are implicated in the reconciliation of the demand for loans and the demand for deposits is one which is open to empirical investigation. In the UK, at least, money's own rate can be calculated with reasonable precision and rates are published on a variety of non-money assets. The other differential (between rates on non-money assets and on bank lending), however, poses insuperable problems since it requires detailed information on bank loan rates which is unpublished and which banks, perhaps understandably, are reluctant to supply. This rules out any direct investigation of its role in both demand for loan and demand for money functions. An interesting first step, however, would be to establish at least some interaction between the demand for money and the demand for loans. Some years ago Moore (1989) conducted a series of Granger–Sims causality tests on various measures of (US) money, the monetary base and bank lending, and found generally speaking that loans caused deposits and base and (again generally) that there was no feedback. This is what one might expect, if the demand for deposits plays no part in loan creation. If, however, we are correct in supposing that the two demands do not always coincide, *ex ante*, then we might well expect such tests to show two-way causality. Bearing in mind the improvements that have recently taken place in econometric techniques in this area there is a strong case for investigating the UK data.

The point of this discussion is that it is possible to see both (i) how new, loan-created, deposits could *ex ante* exceed people's willingness to increase money holdings, given current prices, interest rates, income etc. and (ii) how, *ex post*, such a discrepancy could be resolved. And this raises a crucial difficulty for the argument that endogenous money reverses the direction of causality in the quantity theory. Granted that new money has its origins in loan demand resulting from changes in PY or PT (and the causality is reversed), is it possible for the newly created deposits to exceed demand and then to lead to adjustments which feedback to PY (or PT)? We have stressed changes in interest differentials as a fairly innocuous adjustment device. (After all, we can invoke the appropriate elasticities in order to prevent the adjustment process having much effect on prices or quantities.) But others would doubtless ask why 'excess' deposits should only be used to buy financial assets, rather than goods and services in general.

CONCLUSION

It is commonly held that if the money supply is endogenously determined, then changes in the quantity of money must be caused by other variables in the system and thus cannot themselves be responsible for changes in output or prices. Logically, this does not strictly follow, for two reasons.

First, money's innocence in the endogeneity schema follows from the assumption that the variables in the economic system which cause money are the same variables that would have to be affected by changes in money if money were to cause changes in aggregate demand. Hence the emphasis upon the 'state of trade' as the source of endogeneity. If it is the price or quantity of output (PY) which causes money, then the new money is used to satisfy the needs of PY and nothing more. But money would still be endogenous if it were determined by variables, provided that they were variables whose values were determined within the economic system. If these variables are independent of PY, then it becomes *possible* for money to be generated in quantities which do not match the needs of trade and thus an excess (or deficiency) which will cause a rearrangement of assets from which all sorts of consequences (including consequences for PY) could follow. Thus, if bank loans (and new deposits) follow PT when PT diverges from PY, money *could* be created in quantities which have repercussions for spending on PY. Whether this happens is an empirical question and depends upon the demand for money. If that too follows PT, i.e. V_T is reasonably stable, all will be well, though V_Y must of course fall. This seems to have happened in the UK in recent years.

Second, money's innocence also relies upon the assumption that if money is determined within the system (by PT or PY), then it follows that it is created in quantities which just match the demand for it. Broadly, the demand for new loans (and the supply of new money) will move together since both depend upon PY (or PT). But 'broadly' does not mean that *ex ante* decisions to take out new loans must match exactly the *ex ante* demand for new deposits. The process of continuous adjustment involves expenditure on other assets, goods and services and thus, directly or indirectly, affects aggregate demand. Once again, the precise consequences are a matter for empirical investigation. The adjustments involved may not always involve dramatic interest changes or dramatic changes in demand for PY. But sometimes they may and a credit boom could spell trouble.

NOTES

1. 'Endogeneity' is used throughout in Davidson's 'independence' rather than 'elasticity' sense. The money supply curve *shifts* in response to demand changes because the central bank supplies the necessary reserves (Davidson, 1988).
2. In this context, Moore (1991) is surely correct when he says that '...it is demonstrably the case that virtually *all* introductory and intermediate general economics, money and banking, and macroeconomic textbooks...develop the base-multiplier approach as the central pedagogical tool in the money supply chapters, and not just as a straw man to ridicule' (pp. 126–7). It is not that the exogeneity of money is *nowhere* questioned; it is that the question never features in macro texts which are hell-bent on exploring so-called Keynesian–monetarist differences within an *IS/LM* framework.

3. Interestingly, Hicks (1937) was much more aware of endogenous tendencies. In deriving the *LL* (later *LM*) curve he quite specifically says that it will '... slope upwards only gradually...' (p. 153) because the authorities will often prefer to create new money than see interest rates rise.
4. It would be interesting to know in just how many cases of empirical work where GDP appears as an explanatory variable, some measure of total transactions would make more theoretical sense.
5. The transactions data developed in this paper formed the basis of the *PT* series used in Howells and Biefang (1992).
6. The figures in this paragraph are taken from Bank of England, *Statistical Abstract, 1993*, Part 1, table 5.
7. The table referred to in note 6 shows that lending for house purchase rose from 32 per cent of total lending to the personal sector in 1978 to 69 per cent in 1992.
8. House prices rose by 300 per cent between 1976 and 1992 compared with 260 per cent for the consumers' price index. This comparison includes one year of absolute falls in house prices, 1991–92. House price data from *Housing Finance, 1994*, table 8; CPI data from MIDAS, series code FRAG.
9. We limit the discussion to the adult population.
10. The summary version here has benefited from a number of critical comments made on the longer versions by Lavoie (1995). While I do not think he will agree with all that is here, I am nonetheless grateful for observations which have helped clarify a number of points.

REFERENCES

Arestis, P. and P.G.A. Howells (1994), 'Theoretical Reflections on Endogenous Money', University of East London, *Department of Economics Working Paper* no. 1, November, forthcoming in *Cambridge Journal of Economics*.

Bain, K. and P.G.A. Howells (1991), 'The Income and Transactions Velocities of Money', *Review of Social Economy*, 49(3), 383–95.

Chick, V. (1973), *The Theory of Monetary Policy*, London: Gray-Mills.

Chick, V. (1983), *Macroeconomics after Keynes*, Oxford: Philip Allan.

Chick, V. (1986), 'The Evolution of the Banking System and the Theory of Investment, Saving and Interest', *Économies et Sociétés* (Money and Production Series) no.3.

Chrystal, K.A. (ed.) (1990), *Monetarism*, 2 vols, Aldershot, Hants: Edward Elgar.

Cottrell, A. (1986), 'The Endogeneity of Money and Money–Income Causality', *Scottish Journal of Political Economy*, 33(1), 2–27.

Cuthbertson, K. (1985), 'Sterling Bank Lending to UK Industrial and Commercial Companies', *Oxford Bulletin of Economics and Statistics*, 42(2).

Davidson, P. (1972), *Money and the Real World*, London: Macmillan.

Davidson, P. (1988), 'Endogenous Money, the Production Process and Inflation Analysis', *Économie Appliquée*, 41(1), 151–69.

Davidson, P. (1994), *Post Keynesian Macroeconomic Theory*, Aldershot, Hants: Edward Elgar.

Fisher, I. (1911), *The Purchasing Power of Money*, New York: Macmillan. Reprinted New York: Augustus M. Kelley, 1963.

Fisher, I. (1926), *The Purchasing Power of Money*, second edition, New York: Macmillan.

Goodhart, C.A.E. (1989), 'Has Moore become too Horizontal?', *Journal of Post Keynesian Economics*, 12(1), 29–34.

Goodhart, C.A.E. (1991), 'Is the Concept of an Equilibrium Demand for Money Meaningful?', *Journal of Post Keynesian Economics*, **14**(1), 134–6.

Graziani, A. (1990), 'The Theory of the Monetary Circuit', *Economies et Sociétés*, **24**(6).

Hicks, J.R. (1937), 'Mr Keynes and the "Classics"; A Suggested Interpretation', *Economica*, **5**, 147–59.

Housing Finance, 1994, London: Council of Mortgage Lenders.

Howells, P.G.A. (1995a), 'Endogenous Money', *International Papers in Political Economy*, **2**(2).

Howells, P.G.A. (1995b), 'The Demand for Endogenous Money', *Journal of Post Keynesian Economics*, **18**(1).

Howells, P.G.A. and I. Biefang-Frisancho Mariscal (1992), 'The Recent Behaviour of Income and Transactions Velocities in the UK', *Journal of Post Keynesian Economics*, **14**(2).

Kaldor, N. and J. Trevithick (1981), 'A Keynesian Perspective on Money', *Lloyds Bank Review*, January.

Keynes, J.M. (1971), *The General Theory of Employment, Interest and Money*; and *Treatise on Money*. Reprinted as Vols VII and V/VI respectively of *Collected Writings*, London: Macmillan for the Royal Economic Society.

Laidler, D. (1984) 'The Buffer Stock Notion in Monetary Economics', *Conference Proceedings: Supplement to the Economic Journal*, **94**, 17–34.

Lavoie, M. (1992), *Foundations of Post Keynesian Economic Analysis*, Aldershot, Hants: Edward Elgar.

Lavoie, M. (1995), 'The Demand for Loans Creates Deposits: What then has become of the demand for money?', mimeo.

Meulendyke, A.-M. (1988), 'Can the Federal Reserve Influence whether the Money Supply is Endogenous?: A Comment on Moore', *Journal of Post Keynesian Economics*, **10**.

Moore, B.J. (1988), *Horizontalists and Verticalists*, Cambridge: Cambridge University Press.

Moore, B.J. (1989), 'The endogeneity of credit money', *Review of Political Economy*, **1**(1), 65–92.

Moore, B.J. (1991), 'Has the demand for money been mislaid?', *Journal of Post Keynesian Economics*, **14**(1), 125–33.

Moore, B.J. and A.R. Threadgold (1985), 'Corporate Bank Borrowing in the UK, 1965–81' *Econometrica*, **52**, February.

Niggle, C.J. (1990), 'The Evolution of Money, Financial Institutions and Monetary Economics', *Journal of Economic Issues*, **24**(2), 443–50.

Palley, T.I. (1995), 'The Demand for Money and non-GDP Transactions', *Economics Letters*, **48**, 145–54.

Pollin, R. (1991), 'Two Theories of Money Supply', *Journal of Post Keynesian Economics*, **13**(3), 397–403.

Robinson, J. (1956), *The Accumulation of Capital*, London: Macmillan.

Visser, H. (1974), *The Quantity of Money*, London: Martin Robertson.

Weintraub, S. (1978), *Keynes, Keynesians and Monetarists*, Philadelphia, Pa.: University of Pennsylvania Press.

9. Davidson on the labour market in a monetary production economy

Johan Deprez

Paul Davidson's work has persistently and consistently emphasized that understanding the operations of modern entrepreneurial economies and their component parts can only be achieved by explicitly situating one's analysis in the context of a monetary production economy. This context leads to a rejection of the classical postulates of '(a) the axiom of the neutrality of money; (b) the gross substitution axiom; and (c) the ergodic axiom' (Davidson, 1994, p. 11). Such a foundation necessarily leads to a re-evaluation of all the different components of common macroeconomic models, including the labour market component. Building on the work of Sidney Weintraub, Davidson situates the labour market explicitly in a monetary context where the wage bargain is made in monetary terms, the demand for labour is derived from the monetary demand for output that firms face, and the supply of labour is influenced by liquidity preference and other monetary considerations.

This differs from the classical approach to the labour market where the wage bargain is made in real terms (or 'as if' in real terms), the demand for labour is technologically determined and doesn't change with differences in output demand, and the supply of labour is independent of monetary considerations except if workers suffer from money illusion. The Davidsonian view of the labour market is consistent with his overall aggregate supply and demand approach, offers an alternative view of equilibrium in the labour market, provides for an alternative definition of unemployment, and explains rigid wages as being an outcome of the way a capitalist economy works by helping to reduce the uncertainty that firms face – as opposed to being a cause of unemployment.

This chapter analyses Davidson's perspective on the workings of the market for labour and how it fits into his body of work as a whole. The paper also points to certain ways in which the Davidsonian approach can be strengthened and extended, without losing the central components that Davidson adheres to. This includes a careful distinction between the roles of expectations, forward contracts, and realized sales that results in the formation of the effective demand for labour. The distinctions between equilibrium, disequilibrium, and full employment are carefully made, as is the possible distinction between short-period and long-period equilibrium. Finally, the avenues by which money and liquidity preference can enter into the labour supply decision are enumerated. This chapter points out how the Davidsonian approach is a general one that can capture a variety of macroeconomic scenarios and can incorporate the classical analysis of the labour market as a special case. The special case is, however, the one that assumes away uncertainty, history, money, and liquidity preference. If we agree with Davidson that these components are fundamental to a proper understanding of the economy, then the classical special case is irrelevant for analysing the real world.

KEYNES AND THE LABOUR MARKET

Keynes, in *The General Theory of Employment, Interest, and Money*, argues that the classical theory of employment is based on two fundamental postulates. These are 'I. *The wage is equal to the marginal product of labour ...* [and] II. *The utility of the wage when a given volume of labour is employed is equal to the marginal disutility of that amount of employment* (Keynes, 1964, p. 5). As has been repeated many times since, this means that

> ... the volume of employed resources is duly determined, according to the classical theory, by the two postulates. The first gives us the demand schedule for employment, the second gives us the supply schedule; and the amount of employment is fixed at the point where the utility of the marginal product balances the disutility of the marginal employment. (Keynes, 1964, p. 6)

Keynes goes on to reject the classical approach initially on the grounds that it views the wage bargain between firms and workers as being done in real terms, while he argues that the bargain can only settle the money-wage rate (Keynes, 1964, p. 11). The real wage will only be determined on the basis of actual results in the markets for output. It is in this sense that equilibrium results can create a real wage equal to the marginal product of labour. This result, however, does not mean that the demand curve for labour is identical to the marginal product of labour curve. In fact, Keynes's demand for labour is derived from the demand for output as a whole, which in turn depends upon '...the propensity to consume, the schedule of the marginal efficiency of capital and the rate of interest ...' (Keynes, 1964, p. 245). The inclusion of liquidity preference and an economy that can perpetually have less than full employment in the utility maximization decision of households is sufficient to reject the second classical postulate and the classical supply of labour curve.

For Keynes (1964, pp. 289–91, 303) full employment occurs when increases in effective demand do not generate increases in employment. A situation of less than full employment lasts as long as increases in effective demand can generate increases in employment. If the demand for labour is defined as depending upon effective demand considerations for output as a whole – as opposed to being a physical and technological constant – and the supply of labour being variable depending upon liquidity preference, expectations of the future, and related considerations, then labour market equilibrium does not mean full employment. While in the classical model labour market equilibrium means full employment, in Keynes's model labour market equilibrium is only consistent with full employment if labour demand and supply functions are the special case that is consistent with full employment demand and expected future conditions. This special case Keynes believed was one that rarely, if ever, existed in reality.

THE PERSISTENT MISINTERPRETATION OF KEYNES

Despite the explicit evidence to the contrary,[1] the standard interpretation of Keynes's general theory is that it explains involuntary unemployment on the basis of the downward rigidity of wages (Abel and Bernanke, 1992, pp. 447–9). Simply put, the actual real wage, being higher than the equilibrium real wage, causes a labour surplus called 'involuntary unemployment'. Following from this real supply and demand analysis, the solution to such unemployment is reducing the real-wage rate independent of any effective demand changes.

There are essentially two components to this error. The first flawed part of the neoclassical interpretation is based on Keynes's acceptance of the first classical postulate. This acceptance leads to the belief that Keynes was accepting the marginal product of labour curve as identical to the demand for labour curve, though he may have favoured presenting it in monetary, as opposed to real terms.

In that Keynes rejected the second postulate and emphasized money and uncertainty, the problem with his supply of labour function is seen to be one that incorporates errors through something like money illusion. Such illusions are seen to be only temporary so that unemployment based on them will not persist. If the supply curve of labour comes to be free of such illusion, then, with the demand curve of labour being the marginal product of labour curve, 'involuntary unemployment' can only exist if the wage rate is 'too high'. Consequently, Keynes added nothing new to our understanding of unemployment.

THE DAVIDSONIAN APPROACH TO THE LABOUR MARKET

Davidson (1994, pp. 175–97) has persistently and consistently railed against the neoclassical interpretation of Keynes's general theory. This has involved critiques of Friedman (Davidson, 1990, pp. 136–40), Patinkin (Davidson, 1990, pp. 507–22), Meltzer (Davidson, 1990, pp. 547–54), and Maynard-Rose, Barro-Grossman and Lucas (Davidson, 1990, pp. 555–66). Davidson has repeatedly pointed out the error of asserting that the demand for labour can be represented by the marginal product of labour, of excluding monetary considerations in the analysis, and of confusing equilibrium with full employment.

The Davidsonian interpretation of Keynes's analysis of the labour market has its roots in the work of Weintraub (1956, 1958, pp. 86–148). While Davidson is not the only one that has repeated, extended, and applied this approach (see Kregel, 1985; Reynolds, 1987, pp. 130–34), very few significant extensions have been incorporated into this approach since its inception.

The Davidsonian approach to the labour demand function captures a key aspect left out of the orthodox approach. As the money-wage rate increases it increases the labour costs of firms at each and every level of employment. This is accepted by both Post Keynesian and orthodox economists. The increase in the cost of labour for firms means that there is an identical increase in the nominal income of wage earners. This must be true in that this cost and this income are the same magnitude examined from different perspectives. The increase in nominal income, in turn, increases the amount of nominal aggregate expenditures in that spending is directly related to income. In other words, money-wage rate changes have both a supply and a demand effect on output in general, so that to the extent labour demand is derived from the firm sector's output decisions, both demand and supply effects need to be taken into account in deriving the labour demand function. The flaw of the orthodox approach is that it only incorporates the supply considerations while leaving out the demand impact of wage changes. The strength of the Davidsonian approach to the demand for labour is that it focuses on this fundamental relationship.

There is, however, a common and key flaw in this Post Keynesian presentation of the demand for labour. The production decision and, consequently, the employment decision are usually presented as being made with respect to actual demand conditions. As was argued above, these decisions are, in fact, made with respect to expected market conditions. The formulation of the demand for labour should include this consideration explicitly. The discussion of actual market demand and how this is influenced by changing wage rates is part of what helps justify the 'sensibility' of particular expectations, but is not itself what generates the demand for labour. The emphasis on expectational magnitudes also makes it clear that the wage bargain and the employment decision logically predate production, the completion of production, and the sale of output. Consequently, different actual sales conditions have an impact only on employment decisions in so far as they modify future expectations of sales. There is no going back and re-making the current period's employment decisions should there be disequilibrium in the output markets. Just as Keynes rejected the second classical postulate as being an improper reflection of the supply of labour, Davidson has similarly rejected the modern variations on the classical idea as inconsistent with Keynes and the behaviour of the household in a monetary production economy.

Davidson's analysis of the aggregate supply function of labour is less detailed than his analysis of the corresponding demand function (1990, pp. 562–4; 1994, pp. 191–3). Nevertheless, the following ideas come to the forefront. First, Davidson makes it clear that he rejects the classical attempt '...to explain real world unemployment patterns except via an analysis of intertemporal substitutability of labour by optimizing households' (1990, p. 562). Similarly, Davidson states that it is inappropriate to explain unemployment by workers being off their labour supply curve. At the same time, workers make their decisions while realizing the costs of present and future unemployment. Davidson (1990, p. 563) also claims that household decisions need to incorporate the realization that savings can be put in non-reproducible assets and that income can come to rest in those assets, rather than be spent now or in the future. In combination, these considerations lead one to a different aggregate supply function for labour than is postulated by classical economists.

The limitation of Davidson's discussions of the supply of labour is that they present certain key ideas, but do not contain the same detail or formalism as the labour demand presentations. Weintraub (1958, pp. 117–22) and, more recently, Kregel (1985, pp. 549–54) have pushed this type of analysis further by constructing a 'labour offer curve' or 'labour supply path' explicitly in order to capture some of the above-mentioned considerations This chapter offers some ways of introducing these Davidsonian considerations into household decisions.

The conclusion that Davidson's analysis leads to is that equilibrium and unemployment are mutually consistent. The solution for unemployment does not lie with reductions in wages, but in increases in effective demand. In a monetary production economy there are no self-adjustment mechanisms that will solve the unemployment problem, which is the usual and persistent scenario for such an economy.

SHORT-TERM EXPECTATIONS AND THE DEMAND FOR LABOUR

In a monetary production economy, decisions of what and how much output to produce and, consequently, of how much labour to hire are based upon the expectations of firms as to how much can be sold in the market in the future.[2] In that 'production takes time', the formation and utilization of these short-term expectations (Keynes, 1964, p. 47) has to occur before actual market conditions are fulfilled or can be known.

When the firm is, hypothetically, faced with a higher money-wage rate, there are two types of effects that should be recognized. First, this higher money wage results in different cost curves measured in money terms. If the costs that change are only the labour costs, as is assumed in most models, then the cost curves would remain unchanged if measured in terms of the wage unit itself. Second, a higher money wage may affect the expectations that firms have with respect to future market conditions. It is this second part that tends to be left out of classical/neoclassical models, which tend to assume that these expectations will remain unchanged in the face of changing money wages. This is nothing but a special case out of the full range of possibilities that emerge from the Davidsonian perspective. Keynes himself dealt initially with the simplest case. Davidson, following Weintraub, looked at a broader range of cases. If one assumes that economic agents tend to focus on real results, as do classical/neoclassical economists, then it would logically follow that a higher money wage would be associated with higher expected prices for output in monetary terms. If both change by the same percentage, then the expected price in terms of the wage unit remains unchanged. This is the inverse of the expected real wage from the firm's point of view. Consequently, under these simple conditions, the quantity of employment offered by firms will remain unchanged.

A SIMPLE AND FORMAL EXAMPLE

To illustrate the above relationship, a simple, formal example is presented. This illustrative case is the standard short-period profit maximization of a firm with a constant returns to scale, Cobb–Douglas production function and a given capital stock. The only difference from the standard presentation is that the firm is maximizing expected gross profits, Π_g^e, using its expectation of the money price per unit of output, P^e. The remaining notation is Q for the quantity of output produced and sold, thereby implicitly assuming a perishable output and a flex-price system; W is the money-wage rate or wage unit; N is the quantity of labour units used in production; and K_0 is the given stock of capital available to be used in production. The technological parameter is α, and $0 < \alpha < 1$. If one assumes, as is common, that all firms are fully identical and there is only one output in the economy, then the analogous problem holds for the firm sector as a whole (see Casarosa, 1981).

The maximization problem is:

$$\max \Pi_g^e = P^e Q - WN$$

$$\text{s.t. } Q = N^\alpha K^{1-\alpha} \tag{1}$$

$$K = K_0$$

The reduced form of this problem is:

$$\max \Pi_g^e = P^e N^\alpha K_0^{1-\alpha} - WN \tag{2}$$

The first-order condition of this maximization problem is:

$$\frac{\partial \Pi_g^e}{\partial N} = P^e \alpha N^{\alpha-1} K_0^{1-\alpha} - W = 0 \tag{3}$$

This first-order condition solves for the profit maximizing quantity of labour required in production and which is usually taken to be the labour demand function:

$$N^d = N^{\max} = \alpha^{\frac{1}{1-\alpha}} \left(\frac{P^e}{W} \right)^{\frac{1}{1-\alpha}} K_0 \tag{4}$$

While there is nothing unusual about this result in a technical sense, a careful interpretation breathes some different life into this equation. The standard neoclassical textbook interpretation (McCafferty, 1990, p. 12) argues that the demand for labour is essentially a function of the real wage, given the quantity of capital and the technology of production. This interpretation arises out of the fact that the problem is usually posed in terms of an existing price level or directly in physical terms. In other words, the P^e/W term is seen as its inverse – the real wage – and is not interpreted to have any expectational content. If one were to recognize that this problem deals with expected profits, then a parallel interpretation would be that labour demand is a function of what firms expect the real wage to be.[3]

From the perspective of a monetary production economy, the proper interpretation of this equation is a bit simpler. Given the quantity of capital and the technology of production, the quantity of labour demanded depends upon the money-wage rate that the firm faces, as well as the price for which it expects to sell its output. Put more compactly, the quantity of labour demanded depends upon the expected money price of output relative to the money-wage rate. In Keynes's (1964, pp. 41–5) language, the quantity of employment offered by firms depends upon their expected price of output measured in terms of the wage unit. What is relevant for firms' production and employment decisions is not the money price *per se*, but the price in wage units. This captures the firm's expected demand under conditions of perfect competition,[4] relative to its direct labour costs.

For a given value of the technological coefficient α, the total differential of the labour demand function is:

$$dN^d = -\frac{1}{1-\alpha}(\alpha P^e)^{\frac{1}{1-\alpha}}(W)^{\frac{\alpha-2}{1-\alpha}}K_0 dW$$

$$+\frac{1}{1-\alpha}\left(\frac{\alpha}{W}\right)^{\frac{1}{1-\alpha}}(P^e)^{\frac{\alpha}{1-\alpha}}K_0 dP^e \qquad (5)$$

$$+\alpha^{\frac{1}{1-\alpha}}\left(\frac{P^e}{W}\right)^{\frac{1}{1-\alpha}}dK_0$$

Thus the change of the quantity of labour demanded with respect to changes in the money-wage rate, on the basis of no impact of changes in the money-wage rate on the given quantity of capital, is:

$$\frac{dN^d}{dW} = -\frac{1}{1-\alpha}(\alpha P^e)^{\frac{1}{1-\alpha}}(W)^{\frac{\alpha-2}{1-\alpha}}K_0$$

$$+\frac{1}{1-\alpha}\left(\frac{\alpha}{W}\right)^{\frac{1}{1-\alpha}}(P^e)^{\frac{\alpha}{1-\alpha}}K_0\left(\frac{dP^e}{dW}\right) \qquad (6)$$

In other words, the money-wage rate has both a direct impact on the quantity of labour demanded, the first term in Equation (6), and an indirect impact on the quantity of labour demanded through its impact on the expected price of output, the second term in Equation (6). The direct impact is negative with a higher money-wage rate being associated with a lower quantity of labour demanded. The increase in the direct cost of labour, *ceteris paribus*, leads to a reduction in the quantity of output supplied and a reduction in the need for direct labour. This is the key component that the neoclassical models emphasize.

The indirect impact of a change in the money wage is positive. If a higher money-wage rate is associated with a higher expected price of output, then this will in turn be associated with a higher quantity of labour demanded. If firms believe that an increase in the money-wage rate signals an increase in the nominal level of demand, then they will revise upward the unit price they think they can get for their output. It is this component that is the logical extension of Keynes's approach and the work of Weintraub and Davidson that this chapter points out as not having been explicitly stated before. This is the way that the Davidsonian approach can capture the impact of economy-wide effective demand on aggregate labour demand.

The importance of the indirect impact can be highlighted by a taxonomy of elasticities The previous equation can be rearranged to give the following elasticities relationship:

$$\frac{dN^d}{dW}\frac{W}{N^d} = -\frac{1}{1-\alpha}\left(1 - \frac{dP^e}{dW}\frac{W}{P^e}\right) \tag{7}$$

The elasticity of the quantity of labour demanded with respect to the money-wage rate is equal to a term that depends upon the elasticity of the price expectation of output held by firms with respect to the money-wage rate and a constant term independent of that consideration.

Consequently, the answer to the question of the impact of a different money-wage rate on the quantity of labour demanded by firms depends significantly on the impact that a different money-wage rate has on the short-term price expectation that firms have. This can be broken down into a taxonomy of four different cases. The four cases depend upon what one postulates about the elasticity of the short-term price expectation with respect to the money-wage rate. The four cases correspond – with a limited modification – to the typology that Davidson (1994, pp. 181–3) employs and was first presented by Weintraub (1956, p. 841–6; 1958, pp. 111–12) . This taxonomy also helps to introduce a distinction between a 'pure classical' case from a 'general classical' case.

1.   The 'pure Keynes' case:

$$\text{If } \frac{dP^e}{dW}\frac{W}{P^e} = 1$$

$$\tag{8}$$

$$\text{then } \frac{dN^d}{dW}\frac{W}{N^d} = 0$$

Here the elasticity of the quantity of labour demanded with respect to the money-wage rate is equal to unity. The changes in the money-wage rate are reflected in a proportional change in the expected price of output. In other words, the expected price in terms of the wage unit does not change as the money-wage unit changes. This is the basic case that Keynes employs.

2. The 'pure classical' case:

$$\text{If } \frac{dP^e}{dW} \frac{W}{P^e} = 0$$

$$\text{then } \frac{dN^d}{dW} \frac{W}{N^d} = -\frac{1}{1-\alpha}$$

(9)

In this case the elasticity of the quantity of labour demanded with respect to the money-wage rate is equal to zero. The changes in the money-wage rate do not have any effect at all on the expected price of output. This case is consistent with treating the expected price level as a constant determined independently of production and employment decisions and of demand. A common approach would be to see the price level as being determined by some version of the quantity theory of money.

3. The 'general classical' case:

$$\text{If } 1 > \frac{dP^e}{dW} \frac{W}{P^e} > 0$$

$$\text{then } 0 > \frac{dN^d}{dW} \frac{W}{N^d} > -\frac{1}{1-\alpha}$$

(10)

Once one allows for an interrelationship between the expected price of output and the money-wage rate, then a number of cases are possible. It is still possible that there is an inverse relationship between the quantity of labour demanded and the money-wage rate. That arises when the expected price of output changes proportionally less than the money-wage rate.

4. The 'underconsumptionist' case:

$$\text{If } \frac{dP^e}{dW} \frac{W}{P^e} > 1$$

$$\text{then } \frac{dN^d}{dW} \frac{W}{N^d} > 0$$

(11)

It is also possible that the firms' expectations of the price of output changes proportionally more that the money-wage rate. Such a situation could occur if firms believe that an increase in the money-wage rate signals some type of general prosperity. In this case, the increase in the money-wage rate results in an increase in the quantity of labour demanded.

This formal, but simple, example captures the point that once one deals with expected prices of output and money-wage rates, one must create room for the possible interrelationship between the two. The interrelationship is justified on the basis of the changes in demand that changes in the money-wage rate can bring about. This captures one fundamental idea of the Davidsonian approach. The example above is also able to keep the taxonomy that Davidson employs, even though expected aggregate demand – as opposed to actual aggregate demand – is employed.

AGGREGATE DEMAND AND THE VALIDATION OF SHORT-TERM EXPECTATIONS

If the labour demand curve is based on short-period expectations, then how does the interrelationship between the money-wage rate and the actual demand for output fit in? The answer is that the actual market results give feedback as to which expectations are realized and which are not. Examining this feedback information indicates which expectations are 'sensible' (see Davidson, 1990, p. 326) with respect to money-wage rate changes on effective demand.

As Davidson has pointed out repeatedly (Davidson, 1994, pp. 23–7), part of aggregate demand is directly related to the current level of output and part is not. Consequently, changes in the money wage must necessarily change the part of aggregate demand that is directly related to the level of employment. Changes in the money-wage rate can also affect demand related to other categories of current income – such as profits – or those demand categories independent of current employment via more indirect paths.

Davidson (1994, pp. 183–9) enumerates a non-exhaustive list of effects of changes in the money-wage rate on actual aggregate demand. He explores the impact of 'a once-for-all change in money wages' and contrasts it to the case of 'inflationary expectations'. Also explored are the 'real balance effect' and the 'Keynes interest rate effect', as well as the 'open economy effect'. Put together, Davidson explores the impact of money-wage rate changes on actual consumption spending, investment spending, imports and exports. Aggregate consumption spending is influenced not only through the direct changes in nominal wage income, but also any redistribution of income, the revaluation of savings, and modified expectations about future income and prices. Investment spending is influenced through changes in long-term expectations, the supply price of capital goods, and the rate of interest. Imports and exports are influenced by these same factors as well as changes in relative cost of products between countries brought about by the money-wage rate changes. Davidson concludes that the predominant effect coming out of these considerations is that actual aggregate demand will tend to move roughly in step with aggregate supply as money-wage rates change, though there may be periods where the actual demand changes may either be noticeably larger or smaller than the supply effect. This leads to the conclusion that reductions in money wages cannot be an effective means of generating sufficient aggregate spending to support full employment.

Consequently, part of the equilibrium in the labour market occurs if the expected price of output from the point of view of firms, which forms part of the labour demand equation, turns out to be the actual price of output. Then the key expectational part of the labour demand function is validated. In a flex-price model the amount of output produced in what is sold. As such, 'too much' or 'not enough' labour being hired does not show up in terms of output not sold or in terms of queues of potential buyers that didn't get the goods they wanted. Disequilibrium in the goods market shows up as the actual price of output being different from the price that was expected. In terms of labour demand this disequilibrium means that the actual quantity of labour demanded, based on the firms' expected price of output, is different from the quantity of labour that would have been demanded had it been based on the actual price.[5] Equilibrium in the goods market means that these two labour quantities, the actual and the hypothetical, are identical.

What does equilibrium in the labour market mean from this perspective? If it means, as it usually does, that the quantity of labour supplied is equal to the quantity of labour demanded, then equilibrium in the labour market says nothing about equilibrium in the goods market. There can be equilibrium in both or in one but not the other.

UNEMPLOYMENT, LIQUIDITY PREFERENCE, UNCERTAINTY AND THE SUPPLY OF LABOUR

Davidson has repeatedly pointed out that Keynes's general theory rejected the classical approach to the aggregate supply of labour and that it needs to be replaced by a more general approach. Specifically, he argued that the supply of labour needs to be more than just a function of the real wage. The following four extensions are necessary in order to arrive at a formulation of the aggregate supply of labour consistent with Davidson's approach.

First, the aggregate household labour supply decision must deal directly with the money wage that households face. As Keynes emphasized, the wage bargain is made directly in terms of the money wage, not a real wage. Under free market conditions, neither the firm sector as a whole nor the household sector as a whole can guarantee what the real wage will turn out to be. The real wage depends on what the price of consumer goods will be in the future. It follows from this point that the individual must form an expectation of the price of consumer goods. Hence, the money-wage bargain is also a bargain for an expected real wage. As with all expected magnitudes in Davidson's approach, the expected price of wage goods may turn out to be wrong. In equilibrium conditions, however, this expectation will be exactly met. The model must, however, be able to deal with both the disappointment of this magnitude and the real wage turning out as expected. Contrary to the view held by many economists, Keynes's result of involuntary unemployment occurs without workers 'being fooled'.

Second, Davidson always emphasizes the temporal nature of his analysis. Consequently, the intertemporal elements that are introduced in some neo-classical approaches to the labour supply decision would be quite appropriate from his perspective. It also brings in the possibility of discussing time preference considerations of households, a topic that Keynes (1964, p. 166) was not averse to raising. Time preference, of course, does not have the same central role for Keynes as it does for the classical economists.

The introduction of the intertemporal elements has, however, a key difference in approach. The classical/neoclassical approach tends to treat the current and future periods on an equal footing. In the Davidsonian approach the future period(s) should be put in expectational terms. Hence, a Davidsonian model would not have present and future equilibria being determined in the present or some simultaneous fashion. Current-period equilibria are determined in the light of specific values of these expectations.

Third, there ought to be some type of recognition on the part of households that they are living in an economy that experiences unemployment, today and in the future. The future element may be included on the basis of expected future employment levels.

The fourth consideration, and the one that most clearly drives a wedge between the classical approach and that of Davidson, is households' desire for liquidity. The way in which households carry purchasing power over time should have at least two alternatives – an interest-earning asset and non-interest-earning money. The approach should recognize that there is a liquidity benefit to households of holding money. This, in and of itself, is sufficient to reject the classical approach to the aggregate supply of labour and requires a more general approach.

A SIMPLE AND FORMAL EXAMPLE

Some of the points made above with respect to the supply of labour can – just as was done for the demand of labour – be illustrated using a formal example. A standard two-period utility maximization problem is presented. Utility is derived, in each period, from consumer goods, $Q_{c,t}$ and $Q_{c,t+1}$ and from leisure, L_t and L_{t-1}. Liquidity preference is captured by the utility that the holding of money in the first period, M_t, provides for the representative household/individual. An additive and separable utility function is used. Capturing time preference is done by directly including the discount factor δ. In keeping with the Davidsonian emphasis on an economy set in time, the economic agent makes decisions on the basis of expectations formed on the amount of time they will work in the next period, N_{t+1}^e, which results in an expectation of the leisure time in the next period that will be consumed, L_{t+1}^e. In that the money-wage bargain is made before wages are paid and, consequently, before consumer goods are available to be bought and are bought, expectations are included about the price of current-period consumer goods, $P_{c,t}^e$. Similarly, current-period expectations of the price of placements are included $P_{p,t}^e$. The agent carries from the past a stock of money, M_{t-1}, and a stock of placements, $Q_{p,t-1}$. Income is earned on the basis of a market-determined money-wage rate, W_t. Expectations of the second-period price of consumer goods, $P_{c,t+1}^e$, the second-period price of placements, $P_{p,t+1}^e$, and the money-wage rate, W_{t+1}^e, are included. The quantities of time available in each period are T_t and T_{t+1}.

The basic problem facing the representative household/individual or the economy's household is:

$$\max V = \max[U(Q_{c,t}; L_t; M_t) + \frac{1}{1+\delta} U(Q_{c,t+1}; L_{t+1}^e)]$$

$$= \max[\sigma lnQ_{c,t} + \psi lnL_t + \theta lnM_t + \frac{\sigma}{1+\delta} lnQ_{c,t+1} + \frac{\psi}{1+\delta} lnL_{t+1}^e]$$

$$\text{s.t. } L_t = T_t - N_t \tag{12}$$

$$L_{t+1}^e = T_{t+1} - N_{t+1}^e$$

$$P_{c,t+1}^e Q_{c,t+1} = P_{p,t+1}^e Q_{p,t} + M_t + N_{t+1}^e W_{t+1}^e$$

$$P_{p,t}^e Q_{p,t} + M_t + P_{c,t}^e Q_{c,t} = P_{p,t}^e Q_{p,t-1} + M_{t-1} + N_t W_t$$

The Lagrangian that is maximized is:

$$\ell = \sigma \ln Q_{c,t} + \psi \ln(T_t - N_t) + \theta \ln M_t$$

$$+ \frac{\sigma}{1+\delta} \ln Q_{c,t+1} + \frac{\psi}{1+\delta} \ln(T_{t+1} - N_{t+1}^e)$$

$$+ \lambda [P_{p,t}^e (1+i_p^e) Q_{p,t-1} + (1+i_p^e) M_{t-1} + (1+i_p^e) N_t W_t -$$

$$(1+i_p^e) P_{c,t}^e Q_{c,t} - i_p^e M_t + N_{t+1}^e W_{t+1}^e - P_{c,t+1}^e Q_{c,t+1} = 0]$$

$$\text{where } i_p^e \doteq \frac{P_{p,t+1}^e}{P_{p,t}^e} - 1$$

The first-order conditions of this maximization problem are:

$$\frac{\partial \ell}{\partial Q_{c,t}} = \frac{\sigma}{Q_{c,t}} - \lambda(1+i_p^e) P_{c,t}^e = 0$$

$$\frac{\partial \ell}{\partial N_t} = \frac{\psi}{T_t - N_t} + \lambda(1+i_p^e) W_t = 0$$

$$\frac{\partial \ell}{\partial M_t} = \frac{\theta}{M_t} - \lambda i_p^e = 0$$

$$\frac{\partial \ell}{\partial Q_{c,t+1}} = \frac{\sigma}{(1+\delta) Q_{c,t+1}} - \lambda P_{c,t+1}^e = 0$$

$$\frac{\partial \ell}{\partial \lambda} = P_{p,t}^e (1+i_p^e) Q_{p,t-1} + (1+i_p^e) M_{t-1} + (1+i_p^e) N_t W_t -$$

$$(1+i_p^e) P_{c,t}^e Q_{c,t} - i_p^e M_t + N_{t+1}^e W_{t+1}^e - P_{c,t+1}^e Q_{c,t+1} = 0$$

The utility-maximizing quantity of labour time supplied is:

$$N_t^s = N_t^{max} = T_t - \frac{\psi T_t}{\left[\psi + \sigma + \theta + \dfrac{\sigma}{(1+\sigma)} \right]}$$

$$- \frac{\psi(1+i_p^e)[P_{p,t}^e Q_{p,t-1} + M_{t-1}] + \psi N_{t+1}^e W_{t+1}^e}{(1+i_p^e) W_t \left[\psi + \sigma + \theta + \dfrac{\sigma}{(1+\sigma)} \right]}$$

(13)

(14)

(15)

A few things are worthy of note in this labour supply function. The quantity of labour time supplied depends positively upon the money-wage rate, but is independent of the price of consumer goods. Thus, even using this rather neoclassical formulation of the labour supply problem, the quantity of labour supplied doesn't depend upon the expected real wage. The past enters via the money stock brought from the past and the expected value of the stock of placements brought from the past. The future enters via the expectations of the rate of return on placements, the future level of employment, and the future money-wage rate. The parameters from the utility function also enter, including the degree of liquidity preference. The labour supply function will shift if preferences are different with respect to consumer goods, leisure, time and liquidity. It will also be different if what is carried from the past is different and what is expected of the future is different. Hence, given a certain structure of preferences, a labour supply function corresponds to a past and future of full employment only if those relevant variables take on the appropriate values. If there is a past and/or an expected future at less than full employment, then the labour supply function will differ from the full employment one.

The relationship between the quantity of labour supplied and the money-wage rate can be illustrated by the partial differential with respect to the money-wage rate of this function, which is:

$$\frac{dN_t^{\max}}{dW_t} = \frac{dN_t^s}{dW_t} =$$

$$\left[\frac{\psi(1+i_p^e)[P_{p,t}^e Q_{p,t-1} + M_{t-1}] + \psi N_{t+1}^e W_{t+1}^e}{(1+i_p^e)W_t^2\left[\psi + \sigma + \theta + \dfrac{\sigma}{(1+\sigma)}\right]} \right]$$

$$-\left[\frac{\psi Q_{p,t-1}}{W_t\left[\psi + \sigma + \theta + \dfrac{\sigma}{(1+\sigma)}\right]} \right]\frac{dP_{p,t}^e}{dW_t}$$

$$-\left[\frac{\psi N_{t+1}}{(1+i_p^e)W_t\left[\psi + \sigma + \theta + \dfrac{\sigma}{(1+\sigma)}\right]} \right]\frac{dW_{t+1}^e}{dW_t} \qquad (16)$$

$$-\left[\frac{\psi W_{t+1}^e}{(1+i_p^e)W_t\left[\psi+\sigma+\theta+\dfrac{\sigma}{(1+\sigma)}\right]}\right]\frac{dN_{t+1}^e}{dW_t}$$

$$+\left[\frac{\psi N_{t+1}^e W_{t+1}^e}{(1+i_p^e)^2 W_t\left[\psi+\sigma+\theta+\dfrac{\sigma}{(1+\sigma)}\right]}\right]\frac{di_p^e}{dW_t}$$

Just as was pointed out with respect to the demand for labour, there may well be an interrelationship between the money-wage rate and the expected values included in the labour supply function. Key is the expectation of the current period price of consumer goods (Kregel, 1985, pp. 549–54), though this variable is not included in this specific example. But one can also see that changes in the money-wage rate can modify other expectations. Depending upon the nature of those effects, they may dampen or heighten the positive relationship between the money-wage rate and the quantity of labour supplied.

EQUILIBRIUM IN THE LABOUR MARKET AND UNEMPLOYMENT

From the simple examples above can be constructed the functions for the determination of the money-wage rate and employment level. If it is assumed, as is usual, that market forces create an equality of the quantities of labour demanded and supplied and/or the demand and supply prices of labour, then the market-clearing values of the above two variables jointly depend upon the variables included in the labour demand and supply functions. Formally:

$$N^{mc} = f(\alpha; P^e; K_0; \psi; \sigma; \theta; \delta; T_t; i_p^e; P_{p,t}^e; Q_{p,t-1}; M_{t-1}; N_{t+1}^e; W_{t+1}^e) \qquad (17)$$

$$W^{mc} = g(\alpha; P^e; K_0; \psi; \sigma; \theta; \delta; T_t; i_p^e; P_{p,t}^e; Q_{p,t-1}; M_{t-1}; N_{t+1}^e; W_{t+1}^e) \qquad (18)$$

A number of observations are important with respect to these two functions. First, these market-clearing values depend upon the expected value of a number of variables from both the firm and the household perspective. Key among these is the expected value of the price of output from the perspective of the producers. Consequently, for different expectations related to any of these variables the market-clearing money-wage rate and employment level will be different, even if the underlying physical productivity of labour and the utility preferences of households remain constant. In other words, there is no unique set of market-clearing values of the money-wage rate and the employment level in a given structure of productivity and utility considerations.

A second central observation is that the determining variables of the money-wage rate and the employment level are the same ones that determine the overall level of production. If the production question is asked when the money-wage rate is allowed to vary, the output level will change with the same considerations that determine the money-wage rate and the level of employment. An increase in the expected price of output from the perspective of the producers, *ceteris paribus*, generally leads to increased production and employment. These market-clearing values are influenced by the degree of liquidity preference, expectations of the price and the rate of return of placements, inherited financial assets, and expectations of future labour market conditions – factors not always acknowledged as playing a role.

It is important to recognize that the term 'equilibrium' is not used above when discussing the intersection of the labour demand and supply curves. The concept of equilibrium is, for Davidson (1994, p. 178), as it was for Keynes, not equivalent to the intersection of supply and demand.[6] For Davidson (1994), 'equilibrium is a state where no forces are at work to alter the position of the economy as long as the specified conditions remain unchanged' (p. 178). This means that equilibrium occurs when different expectational values turn out exactly as expected. From this perspective, equilibrium can be consistent with any market-clearing outcome in the labour market. But, market clearing doesn't mean that equilibrium exists.

The diagrammatic presentation of Davidson, Weintraub, Kregel and a few others are representations of alternative equilibrium situations. As is made clear by them, such equilibria are consistent with a wide range of employment levels, even given the same technical conditions of production and utility considerations. The current analysis has explicitly added the important role of expectations, independent of whether or not they are realized. This means the analysis can now deal with the market determination of the employment level and the money-wage rate that end up not being consistent with equilibrium. This includes results when the supply and demand of labour are equal, as well as when they are not.

But what is the relationship of full employment with equilibrium? For the classical economist these two concepts are identical. Within the Davidsonian approach they are not. Keynes (1964) argued that:

Men are involuntarily unemployed if in the event of a small rise in the price of wage-goods relatively to the money-wage, both the aggregate supply of labour willing to work for the current money-wage and the aggregate demand for it at that wage would be greater than the existing volume of employment'. (p. 15)

In other words, if the expected price of output were to increase, then involuntary unemployment exists as long as the market-clearing level of employment also increases. Full employment occurs when there is no increase in market-clearing employment. Formally, involuntary unemployment exists if the market-clearing level of employment, N^{mc}, is such that:

$$\frac{dN^{mc}}{dP^e} \frac{P^e}{N^{mc}} > 0 \qquad (19)$$

Full employment exists if the market-clearing level of employment is such that:

$$\frac{dN^{mc}}{dP^e} \frac{P^e}{N^m} = 0 \qquad (20)$$

Equilibrium at full employment occurs when full employment exists in a situation where all expectations are being met. Hence, full employment is only one specific equilibrium. The general case of equilibrium is not consistent with the special requirements of full employment.

SUMMARY AND CONCLUSIONS

The Davidsonian approach to the labour market is one true to Keynes's method of building with Marshallian tools and of giving the classicals as much as possible and still end up with unemployment equilibrium conclusions. As such, it is not – nor is it meant to be – a fully positive, descriptive approach to what actually happens in the labour market.[7] Even so, the Davidsonian approach incorporates key elements habitually left out of classical approaches and that are necessary components of any Post Keynesian theory. To recapitulate, these elements are:

1. The macrofoundations of the labour market;
2. The wage bargain is made in monetary terms;
3. The demand for labour function is not identical to the marginal product of labour.
4. The supply of labour is influenced by liquidity preference and expectations of future unemployment.

5.　Labour market equilibrium can exist at less than full employment.

Building on these elements of the Davidsonian approach one can (a) more clearly articulate Keynes's own work; (b) point out the limitations of the classical approach; and (c) push further away from current orthodox articulations in a logically consistent manner.

NOTES

1. Keynes (1964, pp. 15–17) makes it clear that he is not arguing that the problem comes from wages that are 'too high'.
2. Davidson (1978, p. 39) also examines the implications of producing 'to order' as opposed 'to market'.
3. Once one starts dealing with an economy producing multiple goods, like a capital good and a consumer good, there are particular problems that arise to challenge this interpretation. The monetary interpretation does not bring about such problems and can be extended more easily to a multi-good framework.
4. Davidson and Smolensky (1964, pp. 128–31) explicitly extend Keynes's model to conditions of imperfect competition.
5. Care must be exercised, however. If the actual price, when different from the equilibrium price of output, is the expected one, this does not automatically mean that it will be an equilibrium price. This is because the equilibrium conditions change with expectations. The demand for output will be different if expectations are different.
6. Kregel (1976) is another great discussion of these concepts.
7. Post Keynesian approaches that primarily focus on descriptive content are discussed by Eichner (1979), Appelbaum (1979), Arestis (1992, pp. 163–78), and Lavoie (1992, pp. 217–25).

REFERENCES

Abel, Andrew B. and Ben S. Bernanke (1992), *Macroeconomics*, Reading, Mass.: Addison-Wesley.

Appelbaum, Eileen (1979), 'The Labor Market' in Alfred S. Eichner (ed.), *A Guide to Post-Keynesian Economics*, White Plains, NY: M.E. Sharpe, pp. 100–119.

Arestis, Philip (1992), *The Post-Keynesian Approach to Economics: An Alternative Analysis of Economic Theory and Policy*, Aldershot, Hants: Edward Elgar.

Casarosa, Carlo (1981), 'The microfoundations of Keynes's aggregate supply and expected demand analysis', *Economic Journal*, **91**(361), March, 188–94.

Davidson, Paul (1978), *Money and the Real World*, second edition, London: Macmillan.

Davidson, Paul (1990), *Money and Employment: The Collected Writings of Paul Davidson,* 1, edited by Louise Davidson, New York: New York University Press.

Davidson, Paul (1991), *Inflation, Open Economies and Resources: The Collected Writings of Paul Davidson*, 2, edited by Louise Davidson, New York: New York University Press.

Davidson, Paul (1994), *Post Keynesian Macroeconomic Theory: A Foundation for Successful Economic Policies for the Twenty-First Century*, Aldershot, Hants: Edward Elgar.

Davidson, Paul and Eugene Smolensky (1964), *Aggregate Supply and Demand Analysis*, New York: Harper & Row.

Eichner, Alfred S. (1979), 'An anthropogenic approach to labor economics', *Eastern Economic Journal*, **5**(4), October, 349–66.

Keynes, John M. [1936] (1964), *The General Theory of Employment, Interest and Money*, New York: Harcourt Brace Jovanovich.

Kregel, J.A. (1976), 'Economic methodology in the face of uncertainty: the modelling methods of Keynes and the Post-Keynesians', *Economic Journal*, **86**(2), June, 209–25.

Kregel, J.A. (1985), 'Sidney Weintraub's macrofoundations of microeconomics and the theory of distribution', *Journal of Post Keynesian Economics*, **7**(4), Summer, 540–58.

Lavoie, Marc (1992), *Foundations of Post-Keynesian Economic Analysis*, Aldershot, Hants: Edward Elgar.

McCafferty, Stephen (1990), *Macroeconomic Theory*, New York: Harper & Row.

Reynolds, Peter J. (1987), *Political Economy: A Synthesis of Kaleckian and Post Keynesian Economics*, Brighton, Sussex: Wheatsheaf and New York: St Martin's Press.

Wells, Paul (1960). 'Keynes' aggregate supply function: A suggested interpretation', *Economic Journal*, **70**(279), September, 536–42.

Weintraub, Sidney (1956), 'A macroeconomic approach to the theory of wages', *American Economic Review*, **46**(5), December, 835–56.

Weintraub, Sidney (1958), *An Approach to the Theory of Income Distribution*, Philadelphia, Pa.: Chilton.

10. European monetary integration: a post Keynesian critique and some proposals

Philip Arestis and Malcolm Sawyer

INTRODUCTION

The underlying Keynesian themes for this chapter are not only the importance of the level of effective demand for the levels of economic activity and employment but also the creation of the institutional arrangements which will be supportive of high levels of effective demand. Within that broad theme, the chapter has two objectives. The first is to scrutinize the case for an independent European system of central banks (hereafter IESCB), which is rejected on the grounds that it would worsen the performance of the real economy. The second objective is to propose an alternative institutional arrangement more conducive to the achievement of high levels of employment. The origin of this can be found firmly in Keynes's scheme for an international clearing union. Our approach relates to the work of Paul Davidson in at least two respects. First, we view the real and monetary sides of the economy as intimately related such that they cannot be separated as they are in the classical dichotomy. Second, the achievement of high levels of economic activity and full employment requires the construction of suitable national and international financial systems: Paul has made proposals at the international level (Davidson, 1992–93) and argued for the creation of an international money clearing unit, a proposal which is in the spirit of Keynes but without the requirement of an international central bank. Our proposal relates to the European level, and comparable to Paul's suggestions, also involves a clearing unit without an IESCB.

We proceed by discussing some theoretical aspects of the application of Keynesian policies. This theoretical framework also enables us to pursue two interrelated themes: the institutional aspects of an IESCB and a critique of the proposals for one. Our own proposal is discussed in a later section, before we summarize and conclude.

THEORETICAL CONSIDERATIONS

The two major objections which non-Keynesians raise against the effectiveness of expansionary demand policies to secure full employment relate to the existence of a supply-side-determined equilibrium level of employment or output (often summarized by the term NAIRU: non-accelerating inflation rate of unemployment) and to problems of funding any resulting budget deficits, including the reactions of financial markets. In this section we address these objections and argue that they do not present insurmountable difficulties. We should, though, make clear that our view is that a high level of aggregate demand (however generated) is a *necessary but not sufficient* condition for the achievement of high levels of economic activity (including employment).[1]

The NAIRU concept generally implies three related ideas. It is, first, a supply-side equilibrium position. Second, the NAIRU supports a classical dichotomy with the level of output set by supply-side considerations alone, leaving demand-side considerations to set the level of prices. Third, there is the strong suggestion that the equilibrium position is unique: the term itself refers to a single rate of unemployment (and this is more clear-cut with the related concept of the natural rate of unemployment).

The unique equilibrium and the complete separation of the supply and demand sides are *not* an inevitable feature of the type of models from which the NAIRU is generated. Manning (1992), for example, provides a model of price and wage setting which has two equilibrium positions for which he provides some empirical support. Sawyer (1982) provides a model which involves not only multiple equilibria but also a less than clear separation between demand and supply sides. However, these models are very much in the minority, and the popular representation does involve unique equilibrium and the separation of the demand and supply-side considerations. It is, of course, the case that if indeed the economy is characterized by either multiple equilibria or the influence of aggregate demand on the level of economic activity, then a role for Keynesian-style demand management policies re-emerges.

The NAIRU is a construct of economic theorizing which may (or may not) be helpful in thinking about the economy. But there is no way in which it can be demonstrated to actually exist in the real world and hence using estimates of the NAIRU involves a leap of faith in the existence of some (unique) NAIRU. Estimates of the NAIRU are typically derived from price and wage setting equations and the theoretical construct is imposed on the estimation of those equations. The concept is only of use if observations about the real world are consistent with predictions derived from a theory which makes significant use of the concept. It can be further observed that the price and wage relationships which interact to determine the NAIRU have proved unstable and subject to shifts, which makes any estimate of the NAIRU also unstable. It is argued here that the estimates of the NAIRU (or related concepts) which have been produced have shown a strong tendency to move in sympathy with actual levels of unemployment. Further the estimates are sensitive to the precise form of equations estimated. Both of these features, which we now illustrate, must cast severe doubt on the existence of any unique and stable NAIRU.

Nickell (1990, table 1) provides estimates of the equilibrium rate of unemployment (equivalent to the NAIRU) in the UK alongside the actual rate of unemployment. The figures for the equilibrium rate are (with actual rates of unemployment given in parentheses): 1956–59: 2.2 per cent (2.24 per cent) 1960–68: 2.5 per cent (2.62 per cent) 1969–73: 3.6 per cent (3.39 per cent) 1974–80: 7.3 per cent (5.23 per cent) 1981–87: 8.7 per cent (11.11 per cent) 1988–90: 8.7 per cent (7.27 per cent).

Lombard (1995) reports three estimates for the NAIRU in France for the early 1980s (when the actual unemployment rate averaged 8.3 per cent) of 9.0 per cent, 7.7 per cent and 6.9 per cent, which suggest a high level of NAIRU and some sensitivity to methods of estimation. Some further estimates covering a wide range of countries are given in Table 10.1, where the NAWRU is the non-accelerating wage inflation rate of unemployment which

Table 10.1   Unemployment rates and NAWRU averages

	1970–79	1980–89	1990–93	1994
Non-European countries				
unemployment rates	4.6	5.9	5.6	5.7
NAWRU	4.8	5.8	5.4	5.5
Four major European countries				
unemployment rates	4.3	8.7	8.8	10.2
NAWRU	4.3	8.4	9.0	9.4
Small EC countries				
unemployment rates	4.7	13.4	12.9	16.7
NAWRU	4.6	12.5	14.1	15.0
Other European countries				
unemployment rates	1.3	2.1	3.8	5.8
NAWRU	1.3	2.1	3.5	5.1

Note: NAWRU is non-accelerating wage inflation rate of unemployment.

Source: OECD (1994), p. 22.

is clearly closely related to the NAIRU. The tendency of the NAWRU to mimic the actual level of unemployment over time is clear from that table. A similar picture is given in figures reported in ECE (1992, Table 5.7, and summarized in UNCTAD, 1995, p. 170).

Setterfield, Gordon and Osberg (1992) 'suggest that estimates of the NAIRU [for Canada] are extremely sensitive to model specification, the definition of variables and the sample period used. [Further] ... the final range of all NAIRU estimates ... is about 5.5 percentage points. Indeed, the size of this range is so great that it covers virtually the entire range of male unemployment rates in Canada since 1956' (p. 134). The Directorate-General for Economic and Financial Affairs of the European Commission concluded that the concept of the NAIRU is 'unusable operationally' because

> empirical studies on both sides of the Atlantic have shown that large variations in NAIRU may be caused by apparently small differences in sample, retained explanatory variables and analytical formulation. Furthermore, the confidence interval around these estimates is so large that it generally contains the whole historical range of unemployment rates observed in the last 15 to 20 years.[2]

But as UNCTAD (1995) observes, 'natural rate estimates are still used to assess and guide macroeconomic policy, thereby contributing to rising unemployment' (p. 172). Theoretical constructs in economics are unlikely to be neutral in their policy implications or more generally in guiding the way in which economists think about policy issues.

Keynesian demand management is often associated with the use of fiscal policy to guide aggregate demand and in particular the use of budget deficits to sustain aggregate demand. Keynesian demand policies are broader than that, and specifically can involve the stimulation of investment through, for example, seeking to reduce uncertainty or to lower the cost of finance.[3] However, here we focus on the narrower issue of the limits on the use of budget deficits for the creation of sufficient aggregate demand to underpin full employment.

There are two possible (though to some degree related) limits on the ability of governments to run a budget deficit sufficient to underpin full employment. The first arises from the argument that continuing budget deficits are unsustainable, and the second from the reaction of the financial markets. A budget deficit is seen as unsustainable if it leads to a spiralling national debt to GDP ratio (and hence to rising interest payments on the debt relative to GDP) or if the level of interest payments, whilst not rising (relative to GDP), may nevertheless constitute what is seen as too heavy a burden on taxpayers (through adverse incentives from the tax rates and from the general transfer from the relatively poor to the relatively rich which the interest payments on national debt often represent).

The algebra relating to the budget deficit can be readily laid out. Define D as the outstanding public debt, B the primary budget deficit (that is excluding interest payments on debt and taxation paid on any such interest payments), g the growth rate of the economy and r the (post tax) rate of interest; then it is well known that the debt to GDP ratio will not rise provided that $(g - r).D = B$ (which can also be written as $g.D = r.D + B$) (with the primary deficit to GDP ratio being held constant). Any size of primary deficit (relative to GDP) will not lead to the overall deficit rising (relative to GDP) provided that the growth rate exceeds the post tax rate of interest (either both expressed in nominal terms or in real terms).[4] The difficulty for budget deficits which has arisen in recent years is simply that real rates of interest have been at historically unprecedentedly high levels whilst economic growth has been sluggish.[5] We would attribute these higher interest rates to the pursuit of tight monetary policies in the belief that tight money and high interest rates will (eventually) dampen down inflation.[6]

In so far as governments, like individuals, face the 'principle of increasing risk' (Kalecki, 1937) then higher deficits (relative to GDP) would entail higher interest rates: if we knew the relationship between the interest rate which had to be paid by government and the size of its budget deficit we could calculate the nature of the barrier presented by the condition $g - r \geq 0$. Since if $(g - r)$ is positive it is likely to be rather small, i.e. of the order of 0.01 or 0.02, the debt to GDP ratio will stabilize at a large multiple of the primary budget deficit to GDP ratio (clearly with numbers given previously at multiples of 100 or 50). But perhaps more significantly, the interest payments would stabilize at $(r/g - r)$ B/Y. This would mean that the overall budget deficit (including interest payments) would be much larger than the primary deficit and that those payments would appear to constitute a large transfer of income to the holders of government debt. The transfer may be an apparent one in so far as the financing of those interest payments comes from further borrowing and in that way it is a transfer within the rentier class. Further, it should be noted that the government is in effect permitting the savings to occur by running a deficit and absorbing those savings. If investment were higher, thereby reducing the need for public expenditure, savings would again occur and profits flow to the wealthy.

The national accounts identity provides $S = I + (G - T) + (X - M)$, where S is savings, I investment, G government expenditure, T taxation, X exports and M imports. Applying the identity at full employment makes the obvious point that a budget deficit corresponds to some combination of excess of private savings over investment and foreign trade deficit. In so far as the budget deficit is in effect mopping up the excess of private savings over investment (net private savings), then the Keynesian alternative to running a deficit would be the stimulus of investment and the discouragement of savings. But the Keynesian position is clear: budget deficits are the counterpart of net private savings. If it is considered politically or otherwise infeasible to run budget deficits, action should be taken on net private savings (i.e. reduce them).

The financial markets are often viewed as placing limits on the use of fiscal policy (notably budget deficits) and to do so through two channels. First, interest rates (particularly on bonds) rise with a budget deficit, thereby limiting the government's ability to borrow. It can here first be noted that in the international financial markets any government is still a relatively small borrower. Thus the bidding up of price against oneself, which can arise when there is a dominant buyer, may not arise here. But the operation of the 'principle of increasing risk' may still arise (though as indicated in note 6 there is little evidence to suggest a higher budget deficit leads to higher interest rates faced by government).

Second, adverse reactions (or the threat of such) by the foreign exchange markets to particular policies may lead to a fall in the value of the currency. The distinction which is utilized by Sayer (1992) in his discussion of the power of the City of London as to 'whether market prices are based on economic fundamentals or bubbles, fads and herd behaviour...' is useful here.[7] Clearly, if it is the former, then the financial markets may perform a useful service by providing early signals that an economic policy is unsustainable in the longer term. As Sayer (1992) argues, fundamentally unsustainable

> policy strategies [include those] that give rise to accelerating inflation, a worsening balance of trade or rapidly growing public sector deficit. Sooner or later such policy strategies would have to be abandoned in response to underlying fundamental constraints such as the disruption caused by hyperinflation, balance of payments constraints and the 'fiscal crisis of the state'. (p. 141)[8]

In such a case, the financial markets do not pose any threat to the range of policies (Keynesian or otherwise) which we would wish to advocate (but no one is going to admit to advocating unsustainable policies).

However, even when financial asset prices reflect fundamentals, the operation of financial markets may still pose a constraint on the economic policies pursued. The 'fundamentals' of interest to the financial markets may be quite different from the 'fundamentals' of concern to others: for example, the financial markets may focus more on the rate of inflation whilst others may feel that unemployment is of more importance. Market participants will be concerned over the rate of inflation (in foreign exchange markets specifically expectations on the differential inflation rates between countries, in domestic financial markets expectations over domestic inflation relative to the nominal rate of interest). Inflation affects the returns which participants in financial markets receive. Unemployment and the level of economic activity are of no immediate concern.

The financial markets pose a different type of constraint on the pursuit of sustainable fiscal policies when the 'bubbles, fads and herd behaviour' come to determine movements in prices (notably interest rates and exchange rates). There is now an extensive literature which indicates that financial market prices are excessively volatile (and casual observation of the movements in the exchange rates in the past 25 years would be supportive of that view).[9] Further, there are theoretical literatures (surveyed by, for example, Camerer, 1989) which show that behaviour which could be termed as rational at the level of the individual can generate 'bubbles'. In a world of uncertainty where knowledge of the economic fundamentals is given to few it is perhaps inevitable that asset prices will fluctuate and follow fads and fashions. The significant question here is whether the adoption of policies of reflation of demand (especially if pursued by a left-of-centre government) would set off adverse reactions in the financial markets. These reactions may be individually rational in the sense that if most individuals believe that others believe that such a reflection would be harmful and mark down prices, then doing so themselves may be rational. There is no need to evoke conspiracy theories but if there are sufficient perceptions that others think that some policy or event will lead to a deterioration in 'fundamentals', whether or not it would actually do so, then the exchange rate falls and interest rates rise. Expectations and beliefs are important driving forces behind price movements in financial markets, and expectations have a self-fulfilling element to them. Expectations that the price of a particular currency is going to fall set up forces which lead to a fall in that currency's price.

We would draw three conclusions from this discussion. First, there is no evidence of a unique equilibrium supply-side-determined level of employment (or of unemployment or of output) which prevents the achievement of full employment. It follows that the classical dichotomy is also rejected. Second, a necessary though not sufficient condition for the achievement of full employment is the creation of an appropriate level of aggregate demand whether through expansionary fiscal policy or through the stimulus of investment and the discouragement of savings. Third, the operation of financial markets may be a major obstacle to the creation of sufficient aggregate demand and hence policies are required to control financial markets.

The prevalence of unemployment is an unfortunate stylized fact of most peacetime industrialized economies during most of this century. We do not propose a monocausal explanation of unemployment but rather see an inadequacy of aggregate demand, a financial system which has deflationary tendencies and effects, lack of productive capacity to employ the available labour, balance of trade and inflationary constraints, unemployment itself as a disciplining device as amongst the more significant causes (some of which are more important at a particular time and country than others). We also see forces of cumulative causation operating in market economies to generate disparities between regions and countries, so that even if full employment can be achieved in the more prosperous regions the less prosperous regions are still left with substantial unemployment.

We judge the financial institutional arrangements by their contribution to the achievement of full employment. Specifically, we would look to these arrangements to be structured to limit or avoid deflationary tendencies, to enable correction of trade imbalance without deflationary biases and to underpin an adequate level of aggregate demand. Further, there must be mechanisms within the financial system to offset the forces of cumulative causation, thereby helping to spreading prosperity to the peripheral areas which would otherwise tend to decline. We believe that the proposals we put forward below can deliver such results. Before we discuss them, however, we look at the institutional arrangements surrounding the creation of the IESCB and the problems it may entail; we suggest that these arrangements fall short of satisfying the theoretical criteria just referred to.

INSTITUTIONAL DETAILS

The IESCB comprises two important institutions: the national central banks and the European central bank. The latter will thus be the single focus of IESCB, which will be formed from the voluntary union of national central banks and the European central bank itself. National central banks will not be abolished; they will merely become operating arms of the IESCB and expect themselves to be independent from the national governments. The IESCB is part of the attempt at European monetary union (EMU). There are three stages on the road to EMU.[10] The third stage is scheduled to start at some time between January 1997 and January 1999, when exchange rates will be irrevocably fixed, and national currencies will eventually be replaced by a single Union currency. The IESCB will take over from the European Monetary Institute (EMI), and will assume responsibility for monetary policies. But it will be the Council of Ministers, and not the IESCB, which is empowered to conclude agreements on the exchange rate system in relation to non-EU currencies and to change the central rates tor the single currency within the system.[11]

The primary objective of the IESCB will be to maintain price stability, using whatever monetary policy will be necessary regardless of the costs involved in unemployment and lost output, and to support the Union's objectives within the framework of free market principles. It is argued that such an institution would be accountable to the European Parliament through regular monitoring of performance, and in that way democratic accountability would be retained.

This view of the common monetary policy entails two aspects designed to give it extra credibility. The first is the proposition in the Maastricht agreement that IESCB should operate within 'a framework of free market principles'. The second is that in pursuing this objective the IESCB is intended to be completely independent of the institutions of the community and member state governments. This independence is consistent with the view that the main danger to financial stability is not the activities of market agents but the workings of elected governments, which make necessary an independent check on public spending. The central bank is thus given the responsibility for avoiding the 'inflationary' finance of government deficits, thereby becoming an instrument for the control of government actions rather than the agent of economic policy.

A country's membership of the IESCB system will require the fulfilment of four criteria:

1. A high degree of price stability close to that of the three best-performing member states;
2. 'Healthy' government finance, defined as a maximum ratio of 3 per cent government deficit to GDP at market prices, and a maximum ratio of 60 per cent of government debt to GDP at market prices.
3. Observance of the normal ERM fluctuation margins for at least two years without any devaluation among the member state currencies.
4. Long-term interest rate levels which do not exceed two percentage points from the nominal long-term government bond rates of the three best-performing member states in terms of price stability.

The figures of a maximum deficit equal to 3 per cent of GDP and national debt equal to 60 per cent of GDP are essentially described as 'reference values', rather than as binding constraints. A justification (EC, 1992) for these figures appears to be that they are mutually consistent with some plausible interest and growth rates. Specifically, if the budget deficit is treated as including interest payments, then a nominal growth rate of 5 per cent would be required to reconcile a 3 per cent deficit ratio with a 60 per cent debt to GDP ratio.[12] It should be noted that this condition is being applied across all countries which would appear to assume common nominal growth rates, and since there is the presumption of common inflation rates that would mean common real growth rates. There is, though, an infinite number of pairs of deficit ratio and debt ratio which are mutually consistent with one another, and of course, a nominal growth rate of 5 per cent can originate from an infinite combination of real growth rates and inflation rates.

Buiter et al. (1993) suggest that the choice of the 3 per cent figure for the deficit to GDP ratio may have arisen from a combination of advocacy of the so-called 'golden rule' (that current expenditure should be covered by current revenue) and that 'EC public investment averaged almost exactly 3 per cent of EC GDP during 1974–91' (p. 63). They then argue that 'such a derivation of the fiscal guidelines is illegitimate unless inflation is literally zero. Otherwise, inflation accounting must be properly done; it is the *inflation-adjusted* deficit that must not exceed public investment' (italics in original). With a 2 per cent rate of inflation, a 60 per cent debt to GDP ratio declines in real value by the equivalent of 1.2 per cent of GDP per annum, so that public investment equivalent to 3 per cent of GDP would be compatible with an inflation-adjusted deficit of 4.2 per cent (p. 63).

In handing over part of economic policy to an unelected body, there is clearly a need to consider in whose interests that body will operate. Any central bank, independent or otherwise, is likely to be strongly influenced by the interests of the financial markets, and these interests are unlikely to coincide with the interests of the population as a whole.

IMPLICATIONS FOR UNEMPLOYMENT

The criteria referred to above are very stringent and will have severe implications for the European Union's unemployment prospects. Most countries, especially those in the periphery (for example Greece, Portugal) will find them extremely difficult, if not impossible, to meet. Not that other countries will be in a better position. It is now expected by some that by 1999 'even Germany runs the risk of no longer being able to meet the total debt criterion of 60 per cent [of GDP]' (Alexander Lamfalussy, President of the EMI, reported in the *Guardian*, 28 October 1995). The glaring omission from the convergence conditions is any mention of output or employment considerations. They suggest that price stability is to be pursued through the free market mechanism rather than through positive interventionist measures to encourage economies to absorb rising costs by productivity increases and not by higher prices. There is no allowance for the clear differences in inflationary tendencies in the member countries. A common level of inflation would be associated with quite different experiences on the real side of the economy, and notably in terms of unemployment. There are numerous reasons for these differences, including the wage and price setting arrangements, the nature of the financial system, past experience of inflation, none of which will change rapidly just because of monetary union. Thus the imposition of an external requirement for a common inflation rate will generate economic disruption rather than changes in those institutional and other arrangements.

Neither the announcement of an inflation target nor the imposition of an apparent constraint on the rate of inflation in themselves lead to lower inflation. Specifically, the British experience of inflation and monetary targets in the early 1980s and with membership of the exchange rate mechanism (ERM) in the early 1990s (with the notion that British inflation would have to come into line with German inflation) deny any painless way through which inflation rates come down or converge with others. The creation of a single currency zone may ensure that there is a common inflation rate across the countries participating in the single currency but clearly cannot ensure that this convergence will not have adverse effects in many countries.

The impact on countries that strive to meet the conditions will inevitably be asymmetrical, given the differential tendencies to inflation among them. Different levels of unemployment and output growth in different countries will ensue. Bean (1992), for example, finds the fiscal convergence conditions in particular 'positively harmful ... and ... Since the rules are asymmetric ... the consequence will be a contractionary bias to fiscal policy for some time to come' (p. 48), and this is especially so if the cause of budget deficits is a private sector surplus of savings over investment. This bias will limit any boost to output and growth in the Union which might emanate from the completion of the monetary union (this boost, however, is expected to be negligible; see De Grauwe, 1992a, p. 81).

For the peripheral countries, the cost is likely to be high, in view of their inefficient public sectors and tax evasions due to their underground economies (generating public sector deficits) and their higher inflationary tendencies. To the extent that they try to meet the criteria despite the high cost, they will find their economies plunging into deep economic crises and diverging even more from those of the core countries (Arestis and Paliginis, 1993; Bain, 1995). Attempts to control inflation through deflation suppress growth, which tends to worsen the government budget position, which in turn under the Maastricht conditions would lead to further deflation in an attempt to restrain the budget deficit (Hutton, 1994). Some countries, if not most, will be left out of the European monetary system. Once outside the system, the credibility of any promises to achieve convergence in future will be low, making the cost of convergence even higher and the chances of subsequently joining EMU substantially lower. Equally serious for these countries is the immense pressure they will face not to restructure their economies (with appropriate help from the Community), but to reform their economic policies to adhere to the convergence criteria. Resultant policies of fiscal stringency and high interest rates (aiming at propping up their currencies) will weaken these economies further.

The case for an IESCB is based on the view that inflations are monetary in origin and as such they should be tackled by monetary policy alone. In contrast, we view inflation as essentially non-monetary in origin (though money is and has to be created to sustain inflation), and using monetary policy to fight inflation will be ineffectual and will have detrimental effects on output and employment; unemployment will inevitably deteriorate. We view inflations as the result of imbalances and conflicts on the real side of the economy (for example, capacity shortages in the face of demand expansion and conflict over income shares can both generate inflationary pressures). The monetary sector virtually automatically validates the inflation, but the source of the inflation is on the real side of the economy (Arestis and Skuse, 1991; Sawyer, 1983).

The proposition that IESCB should operate according to 'free market principles' in the conduct of monetary policy means that the control of the money stock is to be achieved via central bank influence on market interest rates (Bain, 1995). It is pointless demanding that the IESCB should attempt to control the money stock when this is essentially endogenous and not controllable. This raises the question of how price stability is to be achieved in the absence of any other policy instrument, other than using unemployment deliberately to achieve lower inflation rates (and that may well be ineffectual and/or costly). Central bankers, with their heavy emphasis on 'sound' money, are prone to pursuing deflationary policies without giving sufficient attention, if any, to full employment and growth targets. This will heighten, rather than mitigate, financial fragility, since interference with the credit system in the fight against inflation causes frequent interruptions to the production process. Another difficulty arises from the crucial assumption that appointed central bankers are to be trusted more than elected governments. But since central bankers see themselves as the custodians of international capital, the formation of monetary policy will be geared more to the interests of international financial capital rather than to those of the EU (see also Coakley and Harris, 1983). Full employment is never one of their targets. In practice, the focus on the role of an independent central bank in the control of inflation is likely to have two unwelcome side effects. First, the search for control over the growth of the stock of money will generally lead to higher (than otherwise) rates of interest. Second, it draws attention away from the need to construct institutional arrangements which are consistent with low inflation and high levels of employment.

Within any individual country, there is not only a single currency but also fiscal and other mechanisms for transferring funds from the relatively rich regions to the relatively poor. These mechanisms include progressive taxation and social security systems which act to automatically transfer funds to poorly performing regions through lower taxation revenues and higher transfer payments in those regions. In addition, most countries engage in explicit discretionary regional transfers through government grants, taxation

allowances and subventions to local government. Clearly, the EU does not
have an overall taxation and social security system to transfer funds to the
less prosperous regions. Transfers resulting from the operation of automatic
stabilization do not occur at EU level. Thus the check on the decline of weak
areas which emanates from this economic mechanism is absent, with a real
danger that depressed areas in particular will fall into a spiral of decline.
Also, given the lower degree of labour mobility across national borders rather
than within them, the full and final loss of the exchange rate instrument
requires an adequate policy of regional transfers through a Union fiscal
policy to accompany the proposed common monetary policy. The absence of
quasi-automatic transfers along with the effects of 'circular and cumulative
causation' are likely to damage the periphery and benefit the core of the EU.
The pattern of the EU experience in the 1980s and 1990s is consistent with
this view (MacKay, 1994, p. 582). This would be highly detrimental to monetary union which would not function well without automatic fiscal transfers,
as the experience of the re-unification of Germany has demonstrated (De
Grauwe, 1992b) .

This raises the question of the relationship of monetary policy to fiscal
policy. Under the IESCB proposals, coordination between monetary policy
and fiscal policy will be very difficult. This is so since the independent
central bank would be responsible for monetary policy whilst fiscal policy
would remain in the hands of national governments (though with severe
constraints placed on the pursuit of any independent fiscal policy). It would
be realistic to assume, though, that within a monetary union the fiscal budget
is bound to be set up at Community level, precisely because of the enormous
problems that lack of coordination of these policies would entail. However,
once the fiscal budget is set at the Community level, national governments
will not be able to monetize their deficits. There are already two major rules
in this context: first, there should be no monetary financing of public sector
deficits under any circumstances; and second, there should be no responsibility to bail out any member state which gets into budgetary difficulty. Community lending to states viewed as profligate that run into trouble should be
on extremely tough and restrictive terms. Since the option of monetization of
public deficits will not be open to national governments, a considerable
element of 'discipline' is introduced.

This issue is even more serious given the limitations on the fiscal deficits
of individual members and the controls over methods of financing them
imposed as part of the movement to EMU. However, the EU allows for
transfers of funds for convergence purposes, although their size is entwined
with the general issue of the size of the EU budget and very little attempt has
been made to relate them to the increased imbalance likely to result with
EMU or attempts to achieve it. These funds were neither quantitatively

sufficient, nor qualitatively appropriate to deal with the problems of the periph-eral countries and regions (Arestis and Paliginis, 1993). In 1992 only 24 per cent of the EU budget was directed to the Structural Funds, while 53.3 per cent went to the European Agricultural Guidance and Guarantee Funds (EAGGF).

The bulk of Structural Funds is directed towards the building of the infra-structure of the EU periphery. But since these countries lack the necessary expertise for undertaking large infrastructure projects, a substantial part of the budget for Structural Funds finishes back in the developed countries as payments for capital goods and technical services provided. The periphery thus benefits as consumers of the infrastructure and contributes at the level of unskilled and semiskilled labour in its production. The EAGGF part of the budget is utilized for agricultural price guarantee. This is a payment to farmers mostly in the core countries. Any benefits that may accrue to farmers in the periphery are likely to be spent on consumption goods, mostly im-ported from the core countries. In this way the EAGGF is regressive as it benefits mostly the rich farmers of the developed countries and introduces fundamental distortions in the distribution of funds.

The arguments advanced in this section against the IESCB are consistent with notions of liquidity preference and pervasive uncertainty. The IESCB will not provide a stable monetary system. Lack of such a system means that liquidity preference is high in view of uncertainty, which keeps interest rates higher than they would otherwise be, thus adversely affecting investment, employment and income. What is needed, therefore, is a system to provide stability which will reduce or eliminate excess supplies or demands for currencies, thus enabling the volume of European trade to expand. This will contain uncertainty and reduce liquidity preference. With lower interest rates, economic activity should be stimulated across countries. Clearly, the IESCB is not such a system.

A KEYNESIAN ALTERNATIVE TO THE IESCB

The purpose of this section is to sketch an alternative to the IESCB.[13] The development of such an alternative is based on the general idea that institu-tional arrangements supportive of high levels of aggregate demand are re-quired to underpin full employment, but that at the same time the supply side of the economy must be developed to provide sufficient capacity to employ the workforce.

First, the alternative is firmly based on the objective of achieving and maintaining full employment in all EU economies. This entails symmetric and reciprocal rights and responsibilities between surplus and deficit coun-tries, both of which should be responsible for balance of payments imbalances, so that there is not a deflationary bias in the correction of imbalances. It also entails that any payments system should avoid built-in deflationary tendencies. In this sense it is vital to recognize the importance of a fixed exchange rate system with sufficient flexibility to guarantee that any imbalances are not translated into policies which always result in unemployment. There should be, therefore, a minimal agreement over paths of unemployment and employment, growth and inflation for all member states to achieve full employment. But, whilst employment and growth should be recognized as explicit policy objectives, realistic inflation rate paths are also important, given that increases in money wages above productivity normally lead to higher prices. This proposal stops short of a single currency since although based on fixed (albeit adjustable) exchange rates it is recognized that the economies of Europe are not currently (and in our view will not be for the next few decades) sufficiently integrated to permit a single currency without significant and unwelcome economic disruption. The economies are not similar enough to be able to forego completely the occasional realignment of exchange rates.

Second, we envisage the establishment of a European clearing agency (ECA), with personnel appointed by national governments reporting to a democratically elected body. The ECA would issue a European clearing unit (ECU) to serve as a medium of exchange and reserve assets. The ECA would issue ECUs in return for gold, dollar and other reserves of member central banks. ECUs should be held only by central banks, and in more general terms the ECA would operate as an institution which would periodically settle outstanding balances between central banks. The ECA would, therefore, be a 'double-entry bookkeeping clearing institution', providing overdraft facilities so that unused credit balances could be mobilized effectively. It would be committed, along with its member central banks, to guaranteeing one-way convertibility from ECU deposits to domestic money.

Third, alongside and under the aegis of the ECA there should be a European investment agency (EIA), armed with two specific aims: to provide finance for long-term investment, especially to the peripheral countries which need to industrialize in a way that does not increase dependency on the core economies; and to provide long-term lending facilities to enable countries to avoid foreign exchange difficulties. This aspect of the proposal relies on the notion that European countries are at different stages of banking and economic development and as such they do not run continuously balanced current and capital accounts. The EIA attached to the ECA would provide the necessary long-term lending to enhance the real sector of the borrowing economy, and in the case of peripheral countries such lending should be linked to industrialization. If these conditions are not met, changes in exchange rates may be required. Creditor countries would be expected to introduce appropriate policies to reduce their surpluses (which could include reflation and revaluation). In extending loans to countries the EIA should have the power to direct borrowers to use the loans to increase their imports from countries which have deficits in their balance of payments but are not themselves in the process of industrialization.

Fourth, a fixed but adjustable exchange rate system will be needed with sufficient flexibility to guarantee that any imbalances are not always translated into policies which result in unemployment. Changes in parities can take place when money wages and profit margins relative to productivity are permanently out of line, or when countries experience chronic difficulties in their balance of payments for other reasons. In the case of the peripheral countries, transfer of credit balances from surplus countries should be a requirement, but only to the extent that peripheral countries are prepared to undertake positive steps at developing their economies, raising capacity and skill levels etc.

Fifth, anti-speculation measures to mitigate the instabilities and fragilities of the financial system would allow exchange rate policies to be determined by forces other than erratic capital movements and 'market confidence'. Two such measures suggest themselves: the imposition of capital controls; and the taxing of transactions in the foreign exchange market. Under an adjustable exchange rate system speculative pressures are inevitable at times and, as is well known, those pressures sometimes become uncontainable, forcing changes in exchange rates. Capital controls could contain if not eliminate speculative pressures so long as there is cooperation and coordination of economic policies among the ECA members. It would be desirable to have cooperation amongst the world's nations on this front but such an arrangement may have to wait until the establishment of a monetary system at the international level more akin to the proposals for the European level discussed in this section. One form of capital controls which may rely less on coordination is the imposition of high reserve requirements on banks and other financial institutions against their foreign exchange transactions, including transactions in financial derivatives (these are innovations in foreign exchange markets, such as futures, swaps and options). Since these reserve requirements would be at zero interest rate, they would impose a cost on foreign exchange speculation which would increase as interest rates rise, and would thus be expected to dampen speculation. Here again, banks could evade these types of control, in view of the internationalization of their operations. However, high reserve requirements, which discriminate against evaders, may very well discourage banks from attempts of this type.

The other possibility referred to above is the tax on foreign exchange transactions designed to contain speculative capital movements (see, for example, Tobin, 1994; Eichengreen, Tobin and Wyplosz, 1995). Without any financial costs in the transfer from one currency to another, even a minimal risk of devaluation can precipitate a crisis by causing a large-scale shift out of the troubled currency. A transaction tax increases the required interest rate differential necessary to cause speculation, and as such it is expected to help contain it. It must be recognized, though, that the possibility always exists that such a tax could be passed on by speculators. A multinational company, for example, could raise the price of its product, and commercial banks could raise their 'profit margins' by spreading the cost around. A further problem is that a tax on spot transactions could lead to foreign exchange transactions driven offshore. The offshore problem would have to be tackled by developing a transaction tax in collaboration with other countries as part of a policy coordination strategy.

A disadvantage of a transaction tax identified by Davidson (1995) is that it also operates as a tax on trade especially when, as he argues, on average a final trade of a good or service is preceded by five transactions in intermediate goods each of which would attract the tax. Hence, he argues, a $1/2$ per cent tax on financial transactions effectively translates into a $2^1/2$ per cent tax on trade. In our view this impact on trade is overstated (for example much of the trade in intermediate goods occurs within transnational corporations), and the possible negative impact on trade from a transaction tax may be partially offset by the positive impact of less volatile exchange rates which should come about as a result of the tax.

These problems notwithstanding, beyond the obvious advantage of being a source of government revenue, the transaction tax should contribute to an orderly realignment of currencies when this becomes necessary. But just as in the case of controls on capital movement, effective imposition of such a tax may have to cover not just the EU but all the countries in the world under the aegis of a revamped international monetary system. Some go even further and suggest that since it is speculation in all asset markets that is responsible for the observed market instability, a moderate worldwide tax on all financial transactions would produce 'stabilizing speculation'. The success of such an endeavour, though, would require cooperation and policy coordination amongst countries.

Sixth, the industrialization of the EU periphery is an important ingredient of this proposal. In addition to the EIA, it would require the creation of more localized institutions charged with the objective to produce an economic order to help finance economic growth and development. Regional banking, where regions would in some cases encompass countries, is most relevant. The argument for regional banking is based on the premise that financial institutions, banking in particular, play a vital role in regional growth and development. More concretely, peripheral countries in the EU are characterized by volatile credit creation, which is absorbed by the centre especially in periods of high liquidity preference, since this is satisfied by holding assets issued in the core (Arestis and Paliginis, 1993). The financial centre acts as a magnet, especially for large corporate investors who possess market power and thus better access to credit. As credit creation is increasingly centralized, concentration of production becomes concomitant with financial concentration. This remoteness of financial markets from the business of the periphery discriminates against firms and projects there, with the added implication that the periphery experiences tight financial constraints. An asymmetry in regional credit creation and thus in regional development ensues. Regional banking should be expected to alleviate this problem, and also enhance regional growth and development. One envisages, for example, a network of regional public investment banks which would have close ties with local industry and the EIA. Since they would have knowledge of the credit, collateral and character of all major borrowers in the regions, they would be in a better position than European-wide institutions, to boost the capacity for local industrial initiative.

Such a scenario, which emphasizes full employment and requires economic policy coordination amongst member countries, will avoid most, if not all, of the problems enumerated above. It will thus be in a better position to tackle the unemployment problem than the IESCB.

SUMMARY AND CONCLUSIONS

Our theoretical position on the relationship between the monetary and real sectors leads us to the conclusion that an IESCB is marred with difficulties. We summarized these problems and concluded that the prospects of such an institution within the European Union are rather bleak.

This conclusion inevitably calls for an alternative scenario for the European Union. This should begin with the clear recognition that monetary and real phenomena are organically linked, and with a full-employment target clearly stated. These two elements are firmly embedded in our own proposal, the details of which we summarized in this chapter.

NOTES

1. For discussion of the constraints on the achievement of full employment in a capitalist economy see Sawyer (1995a).
2. Quote is from *European Economy*, Supplement A, January 1995, p. 2 as reported in UNCTAD (1995, p. 172).
3. For illustration on this point see papers in the special issue of *International Review of Applied Economics*, vol. 10.

4. Pasinetti (1996) also discusses the conditions for a sustainable budget deficit.
5. 'Since modern capital markets came into existence, there have never been such high long-term rates as we recently have had all over the world' (Homer and Sylla, 1983, p. 1, quoted in Pasinetti, 1996). The recent high levels of real interest rates are indicated by the estimates of Tease, Dean, Elmeskov and Hoeller (1991). They estimate the long-term real rate of interest for the UK as 2.86 per cent in the 1960s, –1.34 per cent in the 1970s and 5.00 per cent in the 1980s: corresponding figures for France were 1.72, –3.79 and 4.07; for Germany 3.85, 3.16 and 5.00 and for the United States 2.60, 1.31 and 6.20.
6. It could, of course, be argued that the high interest rates arose from high levels of government borrowing. But the evidence linking budget deficits and interest rates is weak. For example, in a paper which is generally hostile to Keynesian macroeconomic policies (in effect answering 'no' to the question posed in the title of their paper), Cunningham and Vilasuso (1994–95) have to concede that '[u]nfortunately, empirical studies examining the relationship between interest rates and fiscal deficits are far from conclusive' (p. 190) and that 'whether fiscal deficits are associated with higher interest rates has yet to be resolved in the economics literature' (p. 191).
7. There is the complication here that even if the actions of the financial markets are based on bubbles, fads etc. they may nevertheless influence the economic fundamentals. Clearly, if the fad raises interest rates, investment may be thereby affected and hence the fundamentals of the economy changed. Similarly, a falling exchange rate would stimulate domestic inflation which would change the fundamental value of the (nominal) exchange rate.
8. A further difficulty arises here: any fiscal expansion of the economy is likely to involve some elements of rising inflation, worsening balance of trade and growing budget deficit. The advocates of fiscal expansion would argue that such effects may be short-lived or 'a price worth paying' and do not lead to hyperinflation etc.
9. The work of Shiller (e.g. Shiller, 1981, 1984, 1990, and the papers collected together in Shiller, 1989) has strongly suggested that there is excessive volatility in the stock and bond markets.
10. See Coakley (1995) for an outline of the stages.
11. It is now the case that a meeting planned for 1996 will decide the fate of stage three and indeed the future of European monetary union and, of course, of the IESCB.
12. From the condition given previously in the text stability of the debt ratio would require $g.D = r.D + B$. In conventional accounting terms this would require interpretation in nominal terms. Hence the Maastricht figures of 60 per cent of GDP for D and 3 per cent for $r.D + B$ would require a nominal growth rate of 5 per cent.
13. In Arestis (1993) the possibility of other alternatives is explored, and a new proposal for the EU which draws on Keynes (1980), Kalecki (1946), Kalecki and Schumacher (1943) and Davidson (1992–93), is put forward.

REFERENCES

Arestis, P. (1993), 'An Independent European Central Bank: A Post-Keynesian Perspective', paper delivered at the 11th Keynes Conference, University of Kent, 19 November 1993.

Arestis, P. and F.E. Skuse (1991), 'Wage and Price Setting in a Post-Keynesian Theory of Inflation', *Économies et Sociétés*, 11–12 November/December, 91–106.

Arestis, P. and E. Paliginis (1993), 'Divergence and peripheral Fordism in the European Economy', *Journal of Economic Issues*, **27**(2), June, 657-65.

Arestis, P. and M.C. Sawyer (1996), 'The Problematic Nature of Independent Central Banks' in A. Cohen, H. Hagemann and J. Smithin (eds), *Money, Financial Institutions and Macroeconomics*, Boston, Mass. and London: Kluwer, forthcoming

Bain, K. (1995), 'European Monetary Integration and Unemployment in the Periphery' in P. Arestis and M. Marshall (eds) *The Political Economy of Full Employment: Conservatism, Corporatism and Institutional Change*, Aldershot, Hants: Edward Elgar.

Bean, C.R. (1992), 'Economic and Monetary Union in Europe', *Journal of Economic Perspectives*, **6**(4), Fall, 31–52.

Buiter, W., G. Corsetti and N. Roubini (1993), 'Excessive Deficits: Sense and Nonsense in the Treaty of Maastricht', *Economic Policy*, 16, 58–90.

Camerer, C. (1989), 'Bubbles and Fads in Asset Prices', *Journal of Economic Surveys*, **3**, 3–43.

Coakley, J. (1995), 'The ERM Crises and Maastricht', *Review of International Political Economy*, **2**.

Coakley, J. and L. Harris (1983), *The City of Capital*, Oxford: Basil Blackwell.

Cunningham, S.R. and J. Vilasuso (1994–95), 'Is Keynesian Demand Management Policy Still Viable?', *Journal of Post Keynesian Economics*, **17**(2), Winter, 187–210.

Davidson, P. (1992–93), 'Reforming the World's Money', *Journal of Post Keynesian Economics*, **15**(2), Winter, 153–79.

Davidson, P. (1995), 'Are Grains of Sand in the Wheels of International Finance Sufficient to do the Job when Boulders are often Required?', mimeo, University of Tennessee.

De Grauwe, P. (1992a), *The Economics of Monetary Integration*, Oxford: Oxford University Press.

De Grauwe, P. (1992b), 'German Monetary Unification', *European Economic Review*, **36**(2/3), April, 445–53.

Delors, J. (1989), *Report on Economic and Monetary Union in the European Community*, Luxembourg: Office for Official Publications of the EC.

ECE (1992), *Economic Survey of Europe in 1990–1991*, United Nations publications, sales no. E.92.II.E.1.

Eichengreen, B., J. Tobin and G. Wyplosz (1995), 'Two Cases for Sand in the Wheels of International Finance', *Economic Journal*, **105**, 162–72.

European Community (EC) (1992), *The Unseen Treaty: Treaty on European Union, Maastricht*, Oxford: David Pollard.

Homer, S. and R. Sylla (1983), *A History of Interest Rates*, third edition, New Brunswick: Rutgers University Press.

Hutton, W. (1994), 'Reviving Bretton Woods', *New Economy*, **1**(4), Winter, 207–12.

Kalecki, M. (1946), 'Multilateralism and Full Employment', *Canadian Journal of Economics and Political Science*, **12**, February/November, 322–7.

Kalecki, M. and E.F. Schumacher (1943), 'International Clearing and Long-Term Lending', *Bulletin of the Oxford Institute of Statistics*, **5**, Supplement, August, 29–33.

Keynes, J.M. (1980), *The Collected Writings of John Maynard Keynes*, XXV, London: Macmillan.

Kregel, J. (1993), 'Bank Supervision: The Real Hurdle to European Monetary Union', *Journal of Economic Issues*, **27**(2), June, 667–76.

Lombard, M. (1995), 'A Re-examination of the Reasons for the Failure of Keynesian Expansionary Policies in France, 1981–1983', *Cambridge Journal of Economics*, **19**(2), 359–72.

MacKay, R.R. (1994), 'Automatic Stabilisers, European Union and National Unity', *Cambridge Journal of Economics*, **18**, 571–85.

Manning, A . (1992), 'Multiple Equilibria in the British Labour Market: Some Empirical Evidence', *European Economic Review*, **36**(7), 1333–65.

Nickell, S. (1990), 'Inflation and the UK Labour Market', *Oxford Review of Economic Policy*, **6**(4), 26–35.

OECD (1994a), *Employment Outlook, 1994.*

OECD (1994b), *Economic Outlook*, no. 58, December.

Pasinetti, L. (1996), 'The Social "Burden" of High Interest Rates' in P. Arestis, G. Palma and M. Sawyer (eds), *Capital Controversy, Post Keynesian Economics and the History of Economic Theory*, London: Routledge, forthcoming

Sawyer, M. (1982), 'Collective Bargaining, Oligopoly and Macro Economics', *Oxford Economic Papers*, **34**.

Sawyer, M. (1983), *Business Pricing and Inflation*, London: Macmillan.

Sawyer, M. (1994), 'The Case against an Independent Central Bank', *Centre for Industrial Policy and Performance Bulletin*, Summer.

Sawyer, M. (1995a), 'Obstacles to the Achievement of Full Employment in Capitalist Economies' in P. Arestis and M. Marshall (eds), *The Political Economy of Full Employment: Conservatism, Corporatism and Institutional Change*, Aldershot, Hants: Edward Elgar.

Sawyer, M. (1995b), *Unemployment, Imperfect Competition and Macroeconomics*, Aldershot, Hants: Edward Elgar.

Sawyer, M . (1995c), 'Overcoming the Barriers to Full Employment in Capitalist Economies', *Économie Appliquée*, **38**, 183–216.

Sayer, S. (1992), 'The City, Power and Economic Policy in Britain', *International Review of Applied Economics*, **6**(2), 125–51.

Setterfield, M.A., D.V. Gordon and L. Osberg (1992), 'Searching for a will o'wisp: an empirical study of the Nairu in Canada', *European Economic Review*, **36**(1), 119–36.

Shiller, R.J. (1981), 'Do Stock Prices Move too Much to be Justified by Subsequent Changes in Dividends', *American Economic Review*, **71**, 421–35.

Shiller, R.J. (1984), 'Stock Prices and Social Dynamics', *Brookings Papers on Economic Activity*, no. 2, 457–98.

Shiller, R.J. (1989), *Market Volatility*, Cambridge, Mass.: MIT Press.

Shiller, R.J. (1990), 'Speculative Prices and Popular Models', *Journal of Economic Perspectives*, **4**(2), 55–66.

Tease, W., P. Dean, J. Elmeskov and P. Hoeller (1991), 'Real Interest Rate Trends: The Influence of Saving, Investment and Other Factors, *OECD Economic Studies*, no . 17, Autumn.

Thirlwall, A.P. (1979), 'The Balance of Payments Constraint as an Explanation of International Growth Rate Differences', *Banca Nazionale del Lavoro Quarterly Review*, **128**, 45–53.

Tobin, J. (1994), 'Speculators' Tax', *New Economy*, **1**(2), 104–9.

UNCTAD (1995), *Trade and Development Report, 1995*, New York and Geneva: UN.

11. International trade and the real world

Robert A. Blecker

INTRODUCTION

In *International Money and the Real World*, Paul Davidson extended his post Keynesian theoretical paradigm to the analysis of open economies. In this and later writings, Davidson has expressed his opposition to flexible exchange rates and monetarist macroeconomic policies on the ground that they exacerbate, rather than minimize, the degree of instability in international financial markets and in real productive activity. Rather than allow an essentially unregulated international payments mechanism with independent national monetary policies, Davidson (1991, 1996) has proposed a revival of Keynes's original scheme for an international clearing union based on fixed exchange rates combined with mechanisms to compel surplus nations to bear most of the international adjustment burden by 'living up to their means' through increased expenditures.

Davidson and most other post Keynesians who have studied the international economy have focused mainly on the macroeconomic and monetary dimensions of international transactions. In addition to Davidson, some of the most important contributors to this tradition include Kaldor (1981), who focused on feedback mechanisms from trade imbalances to domestic productivity growth, and Thirlwall (1979), who developed a model of 'balance-of-payments-constrained growth'. While these analyses differ in their details, they share a common view that the international demand for a nation's products can affect its long-run growth prospects. Post Keynesians have paid less attention to the 'micro' aspects of international trade, such as explaining the pattern of international specialization and analysing the distributional effects of trade.[1] In a sense, there never can be a post Keynesian 'pure' trade theory, if the latter is understood in the traditional sense of a pure barter model of trade based on the twin assumptions of balanced trade and full employment. Milberg (1993, 1994) points out that Keynes himself rejected comparative advantage theories of trade because they assumed full employment and argues that a post Keynesian approach to trade should be based instead on a concept of absolute competitive advantage.

In challenging the foundations of free trade theory, post Keynesians enter an area in which mainstream neoclassical economists have shown a more religious devotion to orthodox principles than in almost any other field of economics. Since the time of Adam Smith's first assertion of the virtues of free trade, and certainly since David Ricardo's enunciation of the law of comparative advantage, support for the purest of free trade policies has been a virtual litmus test for respectability in the mainstream of the economics profession. Paul Krugman – probably the most creative of the younger generation of neoclassical trade theorists – has acknowledged that support for free trade policies is 'as close to a sacred tenet as any idea in economics' (1987, p. 131).

Although Davidson has never focused on trade theory *per se*, his critical approach to economics certainly suggests that there should be no such sacred cows in economics that are above rational criticism. This chapter explores some recent controversies in the field of international trade in the spirit of Davidson's characteristic concern over the 'real world' effects of theoretically motivated economic policies and over the types of policies that 'civilized' societies ought to adopt. In particular, this chapter will focus on three outstanding issues in current debates about trade policy: the effects of trade liberalization on income distribution; the existence of absolute competitive advantages; and the desirability of increased global integration. The last of these topics will lead into a reconsideration of the relevance of some of Keynes's famous objections to free trade policies in the 1930s.

INCOME DISTRIBUTION EFFECTS OF TRADE

Davidson has repeatedly criticized orthodox macroeconomic policies that unnecessarily redistribute income away from the less affluent members of society. For example, in criticizing 'the Monetarists' depressing medicine for limiting money income claims', Davidson (1982) argues that 'Governments should not permit the terrorism of slack markets to force "voluntary" cooperation with any indirect incomes policy...' (pp. 264–5). In the same vein, it is legitimate to question the desirability of promoting trade policies that are known, or at least reasonably expected, to generate a regressive upward redistribution of income, while causing widespread social dislocations, in the absence of any compensatory public policies.

Since the work of Ricardo (1821), it has been recognized that international trade can have strong effects on the internal distribution of income within a country. Although Ricardo's model is often presented in textbooks as a 'single-factor' model, in which labour is the only input and wages comprise all income, his complete trade model emphasized the effects of trade liberalization on the distribution of income between the three great social classes: the landlords, capitalists and workers.[2] Writing from the English perspective, Ricardo thought that the abolition of the protectionist Corn Laws would lower rents and raise the rate of profit, thus postponing England's descent into the 'stationary state' due to diminishing marginal productivity in agriculture. Moreover, in so far as profits were accumulated and the real wage depended positively on the rate of accumulation, free trade in corn would permit real wages to be higher in relation to the minimum subsistence level than if the Corn Laws remained in effect and accumulation slowed down (Maneschi, 1983).

Thus, the effect of free trade in a country that imported basic food commodities was to redistribute income from landlords to both capitalists and workers. Ricardo was not bothered by this predicted outcome, of course, since he had little sympathy for the landlord class, which in his view spent most of its rental income on unproductive luxury consumption.[3] Indeed, the fact that income would be redistributed to the thrifty capitalists, whose extra savings would boost the rate of capital accumulation, was Ricardo's strongest argument for free trade (not the law of comparative advantage *per se*, which occupies a mere two pages in his chapter on trade). Modern welfare theorists would also be little bothered by a redistributive policy that benefits those in the middle and at the bottom of the income distribution at the expense of those at the top.

Later theories of international trade also imply strong redistributive effects of trade liberalization. The Heckscher–Ohlin model incorporates the Stolper–Samuelson theorem, according to which (in its 'strong version') owners of the relatively scarce factor of production lose absolutely from reductions in import tariffs. The specific factors model generalizes Ricardo by predicting that any immobile factor of production (e.g. labour with sector-specific skills) gains from free trade if it is employed in an export sector and loses from free trade if it is employed in an import-competing sector. The logic of these theories, applied to contemporary industrialized nations such as the United States and the United Kingdom, clearly implies that so-called 'unskilled' workers (i.e. those without advanced technical or professional training),[4] who are concentrated in import-competing manufacturing industries, should be victimized by trade liberalization – especially with low-wage, labour-abundant developing countries (see, for example, Wood, 1994). The fact that real wages of such workers have been falling in the United States since the 1970s, while unemployment of such workers has reached catastrophic proportions in Europe (where real wages are purported to be more rigid), at a time when international markets have become more open and trade with developing countries has mushroomed, is at least casual evidence in favour of this implication of traditional trade models (see Batra, 1993). If such a view

is correct, then anyone concerned about inequality in society would have to
be very cautious about a policy orientation that would be likely to redistribute
income upward.

What has been the reaction of most mainstream trade economists to this
dilemma? One might think that trade economists would be happy to see some
of their most cherished models proved in practice, and would focus on
promoting domestic policies to offset the distributional consequences of free
trade (as well as any adjustment costs) before endorsing further trade liberalization. But the opposite has been the case. Remaining faithful to the religion
of free trade, and fearing that any admission of negative distributional consequences of free trade would give aid and comfort to 'protectionists', many
orthodox trade economists have sought to downplay or even deny the existence of adverse effects of free trade on workers' wages or employment in the
real world. Economists such as Bhagwati and Dehejia (1994) and Krugman
and Lawrence (1994) have argued that: (1) since there are other trade models
(e.g. scale economies with monopolistic competition[5]) in which free trade
'lifts all boats', Stolper–Samuelson and specific factors effects are just theoretical curiosities that can safely be ignored;[6] (2) the empirical evidence at
least in the US case shows that trade variables explain at most a very small
part of the increased inequality in the distribution of income (especially the
rising gap between the wages of 'skilled' and 'unskilled' labour); and (3)
technological change, rather than international trade, accounts for almost all
of the shift in income distribution against unskilled workers.

Although empirical studies initially appeared to support the view that trade
had little effect on US income distribution, and all contributors to the debate
acknowledge a need for more empirical research, there is now an emerging
consensus that trade (at least with labour-abundant, low-wage countries) is at
least one of the factors (along with biased technical change) that accounts for
a significant part of the growing inequality between skilled and unskilled
workers and stagnant or falling real hourly earnings.[7] Burtless (1995, p. 815)
points out that certain new studies 'imply that liberal trade can affect
adversely the real earnings of a wide class of workers, and not just those
workers employed in a handful of hard-hit industries'. At the same time,
Burtless notes that most professional economists 'reject protectionism, whether
or not they believe [free trade] is an important source of increased inequality'
(p. 815). What is the basis for this rejection of trade policy remedies, even if
trade is admitted to be part of the problem?

The answer lies, of course, in the trade economists' traditional view that
any adverse distributional consequences of trade can be offset by appropriate
domestic redistributions. This view derives principally from Samuelson's
(1962) famous compensation principle, which says that free trade is *potentially* Pareto-optimal if the aggregate gains from trade *could* be redistributed

in such a way that no one is made worse off while others still benefit. The problem, however, as Bhagwati (1994) candidly admits, is that 'while free trade is Pareto-better in the potential compensation sense, its adverse impact on income distribution *in the absence of actual compensation* makes it an unattractive policy' (p. 232, emphasis added). Moreover, the recent discussions have added another potential domestic policy response: policies to change factor supplies in such a way as to counteract adverse distributional consequences of trade. Leamer (1993) and Wood (1994) among others advocate improving the education and training of workers in the industrialized countries, so as to reduce the supply of 'unskilled' labour. But the problem with this argument is the same as the one noted by Bhagwati in regard to the compensation principle: what if education and training are not actually improved (or attempted improvements do not work as intended)? On what basis does one then support free trade policies? Or rather, why do so many economists not make their support for free trade *conditional* on the enactment of actual compensation schemes and/or effective educational enhancements?

To clarify the issues at stake, it may be helpful to borrow a page from the neoclassical welfare theorists who have studied economic development. Suppose that there is a social welfare function W of the form:

$$W = W(y, g, i, n), \quad W_y > 0, W_g > 0, W_i < 0, W_n > 0, \quad (1)$$

where y is per capita income, g is the growth rate of per capita income, i is an index of inequality (say, the ratio of skilled to unskilled wages, or a more standard Gini coefficient) and n is a measure of real hourly earnings by the median worker (thus representing the absolute income earning potential of a typical non-professional, non-technical labourer). Now let us stipulate (setting aside for the moment any criticisms of standard trade theory) that trade liberalization raises y and g, but (assuming for the sake of discussion the critics' view) that trade liberalization also raises i and lowers n. In this situation, any economist who admits the adverse distributional effects but still supports trade liberalization – in the absence of any *actual* compensatory distributional policies or effective educational remedies – is making an *implicit welfare judgement* that the aggregate income and growth benefits of trade are more important than the negative distributional consequences. Or, in other words, support for free trade in this situation is tacitly support for a policy of fostering income gains that are captured primarily if not exclusively by upper-income groups (capital owners and professional or technical workers).

Weber (1949) taught that the purpose of the social sciences is to find the most efficient means to achieve given social ends – and to illuminate the trade-offs that are implied by any particular policy objective. Neoclassical economists have long proclaimed their fealty to this principle of value-free social science – that their only objective is to find the most economically efficient allocations of scarce resources to satisfy exogenously given individual preferences or social welfare objectives. By this criterion, many contemporary free trade advocates are clearly stepping over the line in terms of their own scientific methodology. Rather than determining how a country can best achieve its stated objectives (as defined, for example, through democratic political processes), these economists are implicitly *advocating the objectives of economic policy*. In effect, today's free traders are arguing that industrial countries like the US and the UK should elevate aggregate income and growth gains over distributional consequences, and should be willing to tolerate lower incomes for substantial groups of middle- and lower-income workers in order to create higher incomes for upper-income groups.

There is, of course, another argument for trade liberalization in the industrialized countries today, which is that relatively small losses to unskilled workers in those countries are less important than relatively large gains to workers in export industries in less developed countries whose incomes are much lower to begin with. In this vein (but with a genuine concern over workers' welfare in the 'Northern' or industrialized countries), Wood urges 'Northern governments to adopt policies which would lessen the political pressure for protection against imports from the South, and so help to remove a major obstacle to the efforts of hundreds of millions of people in the South to work their way out of poverty through trade' (1994, p. 327). An unstated (and unproved) assumption of this argument is that industrialization in the South can only be achieved by taking advantage of export markets in the North, rather than by expanding the demand for manufactures in the South through widening of the internal market or South–South economic integration. And whether all the export markets in the developed countries could provide enough demand to lift 'hundreds of millions of people' out of poverty in the developing countries remains to be demonstrated.

At any rate, as Steedman (1979) has warned, 'Policies can only be chosen in the light of given aims and it should not be the business of the international trade theorist to engage in the covert recommendation of aims of economic policy' (p. 93). If we are to give up the pretence of value-free social science, at least we should be honest about the value judgements we are making.

ABSOLUTE COMPETITIVE ADVANTAGES

Concern over competitiveness arose in the United States in the 1980s in response to the persistent large trade deficits of that decade, similar to the concern that arose in the United Kingdom in the 1960s and 1970s. In the US case, sensible economists of all persuasions realized that the trade deficit itself was not an adequate measure of competitive problems, since it also reflected the macroeconomic policies that had resulted in an overvalued dollar and relatively rapid growth (compared with Europe and Japan) in the first half of that decade. Rather, competitiveness became widely defined as the ability of a country to balance its trade while achieving 'acceptable' growth in living standards (see, for example, Hatsopoulos, Krugman and Summers, 1988). Neoclassicals (at least those who are willing to discuss 'competitiveness' at all) have tended to view this as a question of exchange rate adjustment: a country is uncompetitive if it cannot balance its trade without continuous currency depreciation that lowers real income. Post Keynesians have tended to see the issue more in the terms of Thirlwall's model of 'balance-of-payments-constrained growth': a country is uncompetitive if it must keep growing more slowly than its trading partners in order to keep its trade balanced (at a given real exchange rate).[8]

For neoclassicals, even the admission that equilibrium exchange rates could be affected by micro-level competitiveness was a major departure from the standard emphasis on comparative advantage trade (albeit a departure that followed directly and logically from conventional open economy macro models). Some authors were quite explicit about this connection. For example, Dornbusch, Krugman and Park (1989) wrote that

> The macroeconomic adjustment that the United States faces over the years ahead is *linked to the microeconomic issues of competitiveness* in particular products and the general performance of U.S. exports and import-competing industries. How well we compete will determine how far the dollar needs to fall, which in turn makes a major difference to the costs in terms of our standard of living of bringing our trade deficit down. (p. 9, emphasis added)

The same point has been conceded in regard to the US–Japanese bilateral trade imbalance by Bergsten and Noland (1993), who conclude that 'the sizable and ongoing trade imbalance between the [two] countries is caused by microeconomic as well as macroeconomic factors' (p. 202).

Although these points may seem obvious, their admission raised enormous fears among the faithful that the concerns over competitiveness could be illegitimately used by 'protectionists' to advocate interventionist trade and industrial policies or 'aggressive' bilateral confrontations over market-opening measures (e.g. with Japan or China). As a result, the usual suspects once again circled the wagons and launched a volley of attacks on all those who dared to assert that competitiveness problems warranted serious policy action. Even some of those who had originally acknowledged the existence of a competitiveness problem suddenly backed away from their own conclusions, like reformed sinners recanting their previous heresies.

A notable case in this regard is Paul Krugman, co-author of the previously cited statement about competitiveness. In the early 1990s, Krugman published a series of blistering attacks on the 'pop internationalists' who were allegedly pandering to public prejudices by emphasizing competitiveness as a concern of economic policy making. Krugman (1993) asserted that undergraduate economics teaching should stick to 'the insights of Hume and Ricardo... that trade deficits are self-correcting and that the benefits of trade do not depend on a country having an absolute competitive advantage over its rivals' (p. 26). Sounding more like a high priest than an open-minded scholar, Krugman announced that 'our primary mission should be to vaccinate the minds of our undergraduates against the misconceptions' foisted upon them by the 'pop internationalists' (p. 23). Undergraduates should not be exposed to the new trade theories (many of which were developed by Krugman himself), which admit cases in which appropriate government intervention can improve on free trade outcomes, because unsuspecting students (who clearly cannot be trusted to make rational decisions!) would be likely to misinterpret these new theories and think that they might actually have practical applications.

Krugman (1994) continued his campaign by claiming that 'the obsession with competitiveness is not only wrong but dangerous' (p. 30). While admitting that 'competitive problems could arise in principle', Krugman asserted that trade is so unimportant in the US and other leading industrialized countries that 'as a practical, empirical matter the major nations of the world are not to any significant degree in economic competition with each other' (pp. 34–5). In Krugman's view, the stagnation of living standards in the US is due entirely to the slowdown in productivity growth; the possibility that the latter might be influenced by international competitive forces (including the movement of manufacturing capacity offshore) is not considered.[9] While confessing that he had formerly yielded to the temptation 'to pander to popular prejudices' by using competitiveness arguments to justify good policies (such as improving education or raising the saving rate), Krugman proclaimed that he was now 'courageous' enough to say that 'competitiveness is a meaningless word when applied to national economies' (p. 44).

There is no question that the term 'competitiveness' is often used loosely, and that some public policy analysts who have addressed themselves to this problem have ignored basic economic principles such as the national income identity which links the trade balance to the excess of national saving over domestic investment. There is also no question, however, that some neoclassical economists, in their zeal to stamp out heretical thinking, have falsely claimed that this identity necessarily implies causality flowing from saving rates to trade balances. For this reason, the disengagement of economists like Krugman from reasonable discourse over competitiveness problems represents a genuine intellectual loss.

Economic theory *is* needed to formulate competitiveness hypotheses in ways that do not violate basic accounting identities or theoretical principles (see Blecker, 1992). Critics of free trade often *do* need reminding that trade is not a zero-sum game, and that the benefits (dynamic, distributional, or macroeconomic) of any sort of intervention to redirect trade flows must be balanced against the losses in static efficiency. There are probably more cases of ill-conceived and disastrous trade policies in world history than there are of carefully crafted and successful interventions of the sort found in some East Asian nations – although there are also unheralded examples of successful industrial policies (e.g. the US government in aviation equipment). Krugman (1987) and others have been right to stress the possibility of 'government failures' in efforts to correct 'market failures' in the trade arena, even if these economists have often exaggerated the predominance of the former based on scanty evidence and casual assertions (or empirical tests designed in such a way as to make government interventions seem excessively costly).

By retreating into blanket denials of competitiveness problems and personal attacks on those who believe in them, economists like Krugman have only made it more difficult to inform popular discussions of competitiveness with rigorous economic reasoning. Yet, in a sense, the inability of neo-classical trade economists to deal forthrightly with the issue of competitiveness is not surprising. Although the concept of competitiveness can clearly be framed in terms of conventional neo-Keynesian open economy macro models, it does not easily coexist with the micro-level theory of comparative advantage. Nevertheless, theoretically rigorous ways of defining competitiveness already exist in the trade literature. Perhaps the simplest and clearest framework in which this concept can be given a rigorous foundation is that of Ricardian trade theory which, paradoxically, is most often used to deny the possibility of absolute competitive advantages. Yet a simple extension of the Ricardian trade model, proposed by Brewer (1985), shows how the standard interpretation of Ricardian trade theory in which trade always follows comparative advantages is really a restrictive case.

In the textbook version, Ricardian trade theory assumes that wages are perfectly flexible and adjust freely to clear the labour market with full employment. Both labour and capital are assumed to be immobile internationally, but perfectly mobile between sectors domestically. Trade is always balanced by the adjustment of relative wages measured in a common currency. Under these assumptions, trade always follows comparative advantage. In a two-country, many-commodity model, the relative wages of the two countries must settle at an equilibrium ratio which is between the relative productivities of the two goods at the furthest ends of the comparative advantage spectrum (the good in which the home country has the relatively greatest productivity advantage and the one in which the home country has the relatively smallest such advantage). If the home country happens to have an absolute productivity advantage in all commodities, then *a fortiori* that country *must* have a higher wage, and the foreign country must have a lower wage. In this case, the lower wage in the foreign (less developed) country does not imply any overall competitive advantage, but merely compensates for lower productivity of labour and thereby enables the country to export those goods in which it has a comparative advantage.

This model is often invoked (e.g. by Krugman and Obstfeld, 1994, pp. 20–22) to claim that the popular fear of low-wage competition is simply an unfounded myth, based on logical fallacies. But even this model admits that international productivity differentials – surely a relevant aspect of competitiveness – are reflected in international wage differentials. Thus, semantic quibbling aside, the argument still admits that competitiveness affects living standards (even when trade follows comparative advantages). Indeed, the notion that relative wages reflect relative productivity levels across countries is just another way of putting the neoclassical argument stated previously, that competitiveness affects the equilibrium real exchange rate (with the nominal exchange rate deflated by relative nominal wages in domestic currencies).

Put another way, this interpretation of the Ricardian trade model says that relative wages are always equal to appropriately weighted relative productivities, or in other words trade-weighted average unit labour costs (measured in a common currency) must always be equal across countries. Stated this way, however, it is clear that it is a demonstrably false empirical proposition, as average unit labour costs vary widely even among the industrial countries, and especially between developed and less developed countries, in terms of tradable manufactured goods. The problem with this application of the Ricardian model is that it is a characterization of an equilibrium situation (assuming balanced trade with full employment) in an extremely simplified model, which does not generally hold in more complex models. In short, the argument that competitiveness does not matter because wage (or exchange rate) adjustments offset productivity differentials is a case of what Schumpeter called the 'Ricardian vice' with a vengeance.

Brewer (1985) showed that some simple modifications of the assumptions of the textbook Ricardian model, moving it in the direction of greater realism, highlight the reasons why absolute competitive advantages may sometimes determine the pattern of trade. If the assumptions of flexible wages and immobile capital are both dropped and replaced with the assumptions of rigid wages and mobile capital, then the location of production in each industry depends (in a simple model with only labour inputs) on which country has the absolutely lowest unit labour costs. If one country has absolutely lower unit labour costs in a wide range of industries, capital in those industries will move to that country in order to locate production where unit labour costs are lowest, thus giving the country a substantial trade surplus. This logic by no means implies that low wages *per se* are always a competitive threat (which *is* a logical fallacy), but rather that the *combination* of low wages with high productivity (implicitly aided by technology transfers, either via capital mobility or through trade in capital goods) can confer absolute competitive advantages in unit labour costs – which may be particularly significant in labour-intensive sectors or activities.

This outcome assumes that the wages (and exchange rates) are rigid, or at least not so flexible as to bring about balanced trade with full employment, and that capital and technology are mobile. But who could deny that these conditions are often met in today's world, and that they can explain situations such as the large US trade deficit with China, which reached nearly \$30 billion in 1994? Chinese wages are suppressed by a combination of surplus labour supply and government repression of independent labour organizations, while the Chinese exchange rate *vis-à-vis* the US dollar is tightly managed and US wages are unlikely to fall to Chinese levels (although they have been moving slowly downward since the mid-1970s). China now welcomes foreign investment, which generally brings with it up-to-date technology. These are the precise conditions under which the Brewer model of absolute competitive advantage applies.

Of course, low wages in countries like China may be correlated with low average productivity in all sectors of the economy, including those producing non-tradable goods and services. Thus, low productivity in Chinese rice production can help to explain low wages in Chinese manufacturing. But precisely because those goods in which productivity is relatively lowest are non-tradable, a country like China is able to achieve an overall competitive advantage in unit labour costs in tradable manufactures as long as it can prevent the exchange rate adjustments that would offset that advantage – and so far China (like Taiwan before it) has been able to achieve this by purchasing large quantities of dollars in order to keep its own currency undervalued. This is just the latest version of what Robinson (1937) once referred to as the modern form of 'beggar-my-neighbour' trade.

However, the Brewer model is not a complete conceptualization of competitiveness. For one thing, it is cast in purely 'real' or physical terms, e.g. wages are measured in baskets of workers' necessities. Without a monetary dimension, the model cannot fully take account of the balance of payments implications of absolute competitive advantages or the exchange rate policies required to maintain them. This is why it is vitally important to develop the type of trade theory suggested by Milberg (1994), which builds on the idea of a monetary production economy to construct a theory of industry-level competitive advantages in trade due to international differences in monetary unit labour costs and absolute gaps in technological capabilities in a world with mobile capital and path-dependent technological innovation. In addition, Brewer's argument only applies to what Vernon (1966) called 'standardized products', in which labour costs are paramount in determining the location of production and the direction of trade. For innovative products at the front end of the 'product cycle', it is essential to focus on absolute technological advantages among the industrialized countries in developing a more complete approach to competitiveness (see Dosi, Pavitt and Soete, 1990).

THE INEVITABILITY OF GLOBALIZATION RECONSIDERED

In response to the preceding concerns about competitiveness and living standards, it is often argued that, even if these problems are genuine, nothing can be done about them because of an inevitable tendency for the global economy to become more integrated. Revolutions in communications and transportation, along with the spread of market institutions to every corner of the globe, are said to make it impossible to retreat into a world of closed economies. As a result, we are powerless to stop whatever depressing effects global trade is having on living standards, and the best we can do is to try to become more competitive (through improved education, greater institutional flexibility, corporate downsizing and intensified research and development efforts) in an ever more integrated global economy. If this requires lower wages for industrial workers, we are told, it is unfortunate but unavoidable in the new competitive environment. Similarly, the requisites of satisfying international financial investors are often cited as precluding the use of expansionary domestic macroeconomic policies, not only in relatively small economies such as Mexico, but even in the United States. Nations which, only a generation ago, could guarantee something close to full employment with a decent standard of living to their middle classes and industrial workers, thus find themselves faced with the appearance of an unavoidable choice between American-style declining real wages and European-style chronic unemployment.

The insidious notion that all these trends are made inevitable by something called 'globalization' stems from a conflation of three distinct concepts into this one term. These three concepts are: globalization, integration and liberalization. Let us examine each of these briefly in turn.

Globalization in the strict sense refers to the increasing closeness of formerly separate societies around the world made possible principally by modern communication and transportation technologies. This process is nothing new, of course, but it has accelerated in the late twentieth century as a result of such factors as jet air travel and the microelectronics revolution. While this acceleration of globalization is certainly real and palpable, it by no means necessarily implies a particular form of economic organization or a specific set of economic policies.

Integration refers to the deliberate combination of separate and distinct political units into a larger federation for some purpose, economic or otherwise. Economic integration takes well known forms such as free trade areas, customs unions, common markets and economic unions. But nations may integrate in other ways as well, for political, social, security, or environmental purposes, for example. Globalization, in the strict sense defined above, does lead to greater interest in integration efforts, but it does not necessarily favour any one form of integration over another. For example, whether the world will integrate by weakening environmental protection in the interest of free trade, or by restricting trade in the interest of environmental protection, is not determined simply by the existence of facsimile machines and electronic mail. The 'global village' may either protect or destroy the 'global commons'.

Finally, *liberalization* refers to the removal of public policy constraints on the operation of private agents in a market economy. Liberalization is, in effect, the imposition of a particular model of political economy, based on faith in 'free markets' and distrust of the public sector. There has been a worldwide trend toward liberalization since the 1980s, including the dismantling of planned economies in the former Soviet bloc, the abandonment of import substitution policies in developing countries and the deregulation of markets in many industrialized countries. In part, this trend has been a response to genuine failures of some past interventionist systems, but to a large extent the trend has been imposed on countries by the Bretton Woods institutions (International Monetary Fund and World Bank) as part of the 'Washington policy consensus' regardless of whether it makes sense in particular national circumstances (see Taylor, 1996). Recent economic integration schemes such as the North American Free Trade Agreement (NAFTA) have had a pronounced liberalizing bias, as they have made the relaxation of constraints on private capital and property rights a necessary condition for the opening up of markets for goods and services.

But aside from the removal of trade barriers between the nations forming a unified market area, there is nothing in economic integration *per se* that is inherently liberalizing. An integrated market area could adopt harmonized social policies and economic regulations in numerous fields, ranging from political democracy and human rights to environmental protection, consumer protection and labour rights, as many opponents of the NAFTA advocated before its adoption. These provisions could involve greater restrictions on 'free markets' in many areas, while permitting freer trade within the confines of a more harmonized set of social regulations. The fact that this path was not chosen reflects the political power of the interests that stand to benefit from liberalizing forms of integration (see Blecker, 1996), not any intrinsic necessities in the process of globalization alluded to earlier.

Thus, what the world economy faces today is the promotion of a particular form of liberalizing integration under the guise of an 'inevitable' process of globalization. In effect, the world is being made safe for international investment, both direct and financial, by the suppression of all social and political barriers to the fullest mobility of capital. This is a deliberate policy of governments, enacted at the behest of powerful interests that seek to throw off the shackles of national social regulations. Economists, often oblivious to the real interests involved, support the process through allegiance to models of free trade that are increasingly irrelevant to the actual way in which economic integration is taking place. Adam Smith believed that free trade was the best policy for eliminating powerful monopoly interests, which in his day existed largely through state protection. How ironic it is that the promotion of free trade today effectively serves the interests of the largest transnational corporations, often at the expense of the public interest. But the problem today is not free trade *per se*; rather, it is the whole package of domestic deregulation and contractionary macro policies that is sold along with the elimination of trade barriers.

These considerations lead us to reexamine the famous objections to free trade policies raised by Keynes in the 1930s. There were essentially two parts to Keynes's critique of free trade, one political and one economic. In his 1933 essay on 'National Self-Sufficiency', Keynes (1982, pp. 233–46) argued that free trade may be incompatible with national 'experiments' in social policies, and that the costs of trade barriers in foregone efficiency (which he did not deny, but considered relatively small) may be offset by the gains in the achievement of other social objectives such as distributional equity, full employment and the fullest achievement of the material prosperity made possible by modern technology. In Keynes's words, 'increased national self-sufficiency is to be considered not as an ideal in itself but as directed to the creation of an environment in which other ideals can be safely and conveniently pursued' (p. 240). Elsewhere, in various writings cited by Milberg (1993), Keynes argued that the economic benefits of free trade depend on the assumption of full employment. In the absence of full employment of resources, trade liberalization is likely to increase the idleness of resources rather than promote their most efficient utilization. Under conditions of unemployment, Keynes argued, protection of the home market could increase production and not merely divert it to less 'efficient' uses.

Of these two arguments, the political one is really the most salient in regard to present efforts at economic integration *cum* liberalization. What is happening is that powerful private interests are using international 'trade' agreements as levers to overturn domestic regulations, restrictions and policies in individual countries. This process is effectively eliminating the space for national 'experiments' of the type that Keynes sought to encourage. Thus, for example, if Mexico were to seek to imitate the types of interventionist industrial and trade policies that were used so successfully in South Korea and Taiwan, it would be prohibited from doing so by virtue of its international commitments under the NAFTA. Underneath the rhetoric of 'globalization' is thus an agenda of promoting a uniform model of deregulated markets with strong protections for property rights and disregard for the interests of workers, communities and the environment throughout the world.

Keynes's other point, about the full employment assumption in free trade theory, also remains valid and relevant today. Keynes was particularly prophetic in warning of how the liberalization of international financial markets could place a straitjacket on the adoption of more expansionist macro policies. 'Advisable domestic policies might often be easier to compass', Keynes (1982) wrote, 'if ... the phenomenon known as "the flight of capital" could be ruled out' (p. 236). Ironically, then, the liberalization of financial markets helps to hinder the conditions under which the liberalization of commodity trade can best achieve its theoretical purpose of enhancing the efficiency with which a given set of resources are allocated. The world would certainly be safer for trade liberalization, in the narrow sense of the removal of tariff and non-tariff barriers to commodity movements, if governments remained free to pursue full employment objectives without fear of capital flight and currency runs.

CONCLUSIONS

The basic message of this chapter is that trade policy should be the servant of domestic policy objectives, and not the other way around. Too many economists today, enamoured of their theoretical models of the blessings of free trade, have turned a blind eye to the real-world consequences of promoting trade liberalization and ignoring competitiveness problems. It has been suggested here that the criteria for determining desirable levels of openness to (or regulation of) international trade and investment flows should emphasize objectives of equitable income distribution, adequate employment provision and rising living standards. To suggest this is to make a set of value judgements; those who disagree should be willing to state clearly what their own value judgements are and to defend them, rather than hide behind deceptively neutral-sounding theorems about the optimality of free trade in a hypothetical, idealized world.

The international trade economists are undoubtedly correct that the best solutions to distributional and competitive problems lie at home. But this does not mean that international competitive pressures cannot exacerbate domestic problems such as unequal distribution of income and sluggish growth of productivity and wages. The question, then, is whether it makes sense to liberalize trade first and worry about the consequences for income distribution and living standards later, as so many trade economists implicitly assume, or whether it may sometimes be necessary to alleviate international competitive pressures in order to create space for needed domestic reforms and adjustments.

At the same time, it is important not to let the criticism of free trade policies, as they are currently practised, lead to a nationalistic reaction. It is the current structure of international trade and investment, and the lack of mechanisms to maintain global full employment, that forces workers in different countries to compete with each other for jobs and incomes. The point is to transform this structure so as to allow workers and citizens everywhere to share in the potential gains from increased trade and efficiency – *not* to restore the jobs and incomes of, say, US workers at the expense of their foreign counterparts. The real issue for the next century, then, is how to reconcile the drive for greater economic integration with the legitimate pursuit of other social and economic objectives.

NOTES

1. Neo-Ricardian economists have done more in this regard, albeit in models where trade is barter. Some of these efforts are discussed further below.
2. See Maneschi (1983) for a complete Ricardian trade model, including dynamic distributional effects, and Maneschi (1992) for a thorough discussion of alternative interpretations of Ricardo's trade theory.
3. Ricardo does not seem to have noticed the implication, pointed out by Maneschi (1983), that free trade would redistribute income to the landlord class in the countries exporting corn, thus lowering their profit rates and slowing their economic growth.
4. It should be noted that, by most currently accepted definitions, the vast majority of the labour force in the US and other industrialized countries is 'unskilled'.
5. This type of trade model, originally developed by Krugman (1979), typically assumes free entry of firms (thus guaranteeing zero profits and prices equal to average costs) and full employment with balanced trade, as well as symmetrical cost and demand functions in all countries. See Kaldor (1981) for an implicit critique of this way of modelling trade with scale economies.
6. These economists are of course right that the factor price equalization (FPE) theorem makes such strong assumptions that it was never regarded as a predictive tool. Nevertheless, the Stolper–Samuelson theorem rests on much weaker assumptions and at least one key assumption of FPE – identical technology in all countries – is now much closer to reality than ever before thanks to international technological diffusion.
7. See, for example, the surveys by Belman and Lee (1996) and Burtless (1995), as well as the

studies by Leamer (1993) and Wood (1994) and the conference volume edited by Collins (1996).

8. As one would expect, the neoclassicals focused on the price adjustments to a loss of competitiveness while the post Keynesians focused on the income adjustments. For further discussion of these two views see Blecker (1994).

9. Krugman's assertion that there is no gap between the rate of productivity growth and the rate of real wage increase has also been challenged on empirical grounds. See Belman and Lee (1996), who show that by many measures real wages did lag behind productivity growth in the US in the 1970s and 1980s.

REFERENCES

Batra, R.N. (1993), *The Myth of Free Trade*, New York: Scribner's.

Belman, D. and T.L. Lee (1996), 'International Trade and the Performance of U.S. Labor Markets' in R.A. Blecker (ed.), *U.S. Trade Policy and Global Growth: New Directions in the International Economy*, Armonk, NY: M.E. Sharpe.

Bergsten, C.F. and M. Noland (1993), *Reconcilable Differences? United States–Japan Economic Conflict*, Washington, DC: Institute for International Economics.

Bhagwati, J. (1994), 'Free Trade: Old and New Challenges', *Economic Journal*, **104**, March, 231–46.

Bhagwati, J. and V.H. Dehejia (1994), 'Freer Trade and Wages of the Unskilled – Is Marx Striking Again?' in J. Bhagwati and M.H. Kosters (eds), *Trade and Wages: Leveling Wages Down?*, Washington, DC: American Enterprise Institute Press, pp. 36–75.

Blecker, R.A. (1992), *Beyond the Twin Deficits: A Trade Strategy for the 1990s*, Armonk, NY: M.E. Sharpe.

Blecker, R.A. (1994), 'Relative Wages and the Balance of Payments Constraint', paper presented at Eastern Economics Association meetings, Boston, Mass., March.

Blecker, R.A. (1996), 'The Political Economy of the North American Free Trade Agreement' in R.A. Blecker (ed.), *U.S. Trade Policy and Global Growth: New Directions in the International Economy*, Armonk, NY: M.E. Sharpe.

Brewer, A. (1985), 'Trade with Fixed Real Wages and Mobile Capital', *Journal of International Economics*, **18**, 177–86.

Burtless, G. (1995), 'International Trade and the Rise in Earnings Inequality', *Journal of Economic Literature*, **33**(2), June, 800–16.

Collins, S.M. (ed.) (1996), *Imports, Exports, and the American Worker*, Washington, DC: Brookings Institution, forthcoming.

Davidson, P. (1982), *International Money and the Real World*, London: Macmillan, and New York: John Wiley.

Davidson, P. (1991), 'What International Payments Scheme Would Keynes Have Suggested for the Twenty-first Century?' in P. Davidson and J.A. Kregel (eds), *Economic Problems of the 1990s: Europe, the Developing Countries and the United States*, Aldershot, Hants, and Brookfield, VT: Edward Elgar.

Davidson, P. (1996), 'Reforming the International Payments System', in R.A. Blecker (ed.), *U.S. Trade Policy and Global Growth: New Directions in the International Economy*, Armonk, NY: M.E. Sharpe.

Dornbusch, R., P. Krugman and Y.C. Park (1989), *Meeting World Challenges: U.S. Manufacturing in the 1990s*, Rochester, NY: Eastman Kodak Corporation.

Dosi, G., K. Pavitt and L. Soete (1990), *The Economics of Technical Change and International Trade*, London: Pinter, and New York: New York University Press.

Hatsopoulos, G.N., P.R. Krugman and L.H. Summers (1988), 'U.S. Competitiveness: Beyond the Trade Deficit', *Science*, **241**, 15 July, 299–307.

Kaldor, N. (1981), 'The Foundations of Free Trade Theory and their Implications for the Current World Recession' in J. Los et al. (eds), *Studies in Economic Theory and Practice: Essays in Honor of Edward Lipinski*, Amsterdam: North-Holland.

Keynes, J.M. (1982), *The Collected Writings of John Maynard Keynes*, XXI, *Activities 1931–1939*, edited by D. Moggridge, London: Macmillan.

Krugman, P. R. (1979), 'Increasing Returns, Monopolistic Competition, and International Trade', *Journal of International Economics*, **9**(4), November, 469–79.

Krugman, P. R. (1987), 'Is Free Trade Passé?', *Journal of Economic Perspectives*, **1**(2), Fall, 131–44.

Krugman, P. R. (1993), 'What Do Undergrads Need to Know about Trade?', *American Economic Review, Papers and Proceedings*, **83**(2), May, 23–6.

Krugman, P. R. (1994), 'Competitiveness: A Dangerous Obsession', *Foreign Affairs*, **73**(2), March/April, 28–44.

Krugman, P.R. and R.Z. Lawrence (1994), 'Trade, Jobs, and Wages', *Scientific American*, **270**(4), April, 44–9.

Krugman, P.R. and M. Obstfeld (1994), *International Economics: Theory and Policy*, third edition, New York: HarperCollins.

Leamer, E.E. (1993), 'Wage Effects of a U.S.–Mexican Free Trade Agreement' in P.M. Garber (ed.), *The Mexico–U.S. Free Trade Agreement*, Cambridge, MA., and London: MIT Press, pp. 57–125.

Maneschi, A. (1983), 'Dynamic Aspects of Ricardo's International Trade Theory', *Oxford Economic Papers*, **35**(1), March, 67–80.

Maneschi, A. (1992), 'Ricardo's International Trade Theory: Beyond the Comparative Cost Example', *Cambridge Journal of Economics*, **16**(4), December, 421–37.

Milberg, W. (1993), 'The Rejection of Comparative Advantage in Keynes and Marx', unpublished, New School for Social Research, New York.

Milberg, W. (1994), 'Is Absolute Advantage Passé? Towards a Post-Keynesian/Marxian Theory of International Trade' in M. Glick (ed.), *Competition. Technology and Money: Classical and Post-Keynesian Perspectives*, Aldershot, Hants, and Brookfield, VT: Edward Elgar.

Ricardo, D. (1821), *Principles of Political Economy and Taxation*, vol. I in *The Works and Correspondence of David Ricardo*, edited by P. Sraffa, Cambridge: Cambridge University Press, 1951.

Robinson, J. (1937), 'Beggar-My-Neighbour Remedies for Unemployment' reprinted in J. Robinson, *Contributions to Modern Economics*, New York: Academic Press, 1978.

Samuelson, P. A. (1962), 'The Gains from International Trade Once Again', *Economic Journal*, **72**, 820–29.

Steedman, I. (1979), *Trade Amongst Growing Economies*, Cambridge and New York: Cambridge University Press.

Taylor, L. (1996), 'Income Distribution, Trade, and Growth', in R.A. Blecker (ed.), *U.S. Trade Policy and Global Growth: New Directions in the International Economy*, Armonk, NY: M.E. Sharpe.

Thirlwall, A.P. (1979), 'The Balance of Payments Constraint as an Explanation of International Growth Rate Differences', *Banca Nazionale del Lavoro Quarterly Review*, (128), March, 45–53.

Vernon, R. (1966), 'International Trade and International Investment in the Product Cycle', *Quarterly Journal of Economics*, **80**, 190–207.

Weber, M. (1949), *The Methodology of the Social Sciences*, New York: Free Press.

Wood, A. (1994), *North–South Trade, Employment, and Inequality: Changing Fortunes in a Skill-driven World*, Oxford and New York: Oxford University Press.

Paul Davidson: A bibliography

BOOKS

Theories of Aggregate Income Distribution, New Brunswick: Rutgers University Press, 1960.

Aggregate Supply and Demand Analysis (with E. Smolensky), New York: Harper & Row, 1964.

The Demand and Supply of Outdoor Recreation (with C.J. Cicchetti and J.J. Seneca), Bureau of Economics Research–Rutgers University, reprinted by Bureau of Outdoor Recreation, US Department of Interior, 1969.

Money and the Real World, second edition, London: Macmillan, 1978; New York: Halsted Press, John Wiley, 1978; Japanese edition, 1980.

Milton Friedman's Monetary Theory: A Debate with his Critics (with M. Friedman, J. Tobin, D. Patinkin, K. Brunner, A. Meltzer), Chicago: University of Chicago Press, 1974; Japanese edition, 1978.

International Money and the Real World, London: Macmillan; New York: Halsted Press, John Wiley.

International Money and the Real World, revised edition, London: Macmillan, 1992; New York: St Martin's Press, 1992.

Economics for a Civilized Society (with G. Davidson), London: Macmillan; New York: W.W. Norton, 1988.

The Struggle over the Keynesian Heritage (a script for an audiotape narrated by Louis Rukeyser), Knowledge Products, 1989.

Macroeconomic Problems and Policies of Income Distribution: Functional, Personal, International (co-edited with J.A. Kregel), Aldershot, Hants: Edward Elgar, 1989.

Money and Employment, The Collected Writings of Paul Davidson, Volume 1, edited by Louise Davidson, London: Macmillan, 1990; New York: New York University Press, 1991.

Inflation, Open Economies and Resources, The Collected Writings of Paul Davidson, Volume 2, edited by Louise Davidson, London: Macmillan, 1991; New York: New York University Press, 1991.

Controversies in Post Keynesian Economics, Aldershot, Hants: Edward Elgar, 1991.

Economic Problems of the 1990s: Europe, the Developing Countries and the United States (co-edited with J.A. Kregel), Aldershot, Hants: Edward Elgar, 1991.

Can the Free Market Pick Winners? Editor, and author of 'Introduction', Armonk, NY: M.E. Sharpe, 1993.

Post Keynesian Macroeconomic Theory: A Foundation for Successful Economic Policies in the Twenty-First Century, Aldershot, Hants: Edward Elgar, 1994.

Employment, Growth and Finance: Economic Reality and Economic Growth (co-edited with J.A. Kregel), Aldershot, Hants: Edward Elgar, 1994.

ARTICLES

'A Clarification of the Ricardian Rent Share', *Canadian Journal of Economics and Political Science*, May 1959.

'Increasing Employment, Diminishing Returns, Relative Shares, and Ricardo', *Canadian Journal of Economics and Political Science*, February 1960.

'Rolph on the Aggregate Effects of a General Excise Tax', *Southern Economic Journal*, July 1960.

'Wells on Excise Tax Incidence in an Imperfectly Competitive Economy', *Public Finance*, 1961.

'More on the Aggregate Supply Function', *Economic Journal*, June 1962.

'Employment and Income Multipliers and the Price Level', *American Economic Review*, September 1962.

'Public Policy Problems of the Domestic Crude Oil Industry', *American Economic Review*, March 1963; reprinted in *Economics of Natural and Environmental Resources*, edited by V.L. Smith, New York: Gordon and Breach 1977.

'Public Policy Problems of the Domestic Crude Oil Industry: A Rejoinder', *American Economic Review*, March 1964.

'Modigliani on the Interaction of Real and Monetary Phenomena' (with E. Smolensky), *Review of Economics and Statistics*, November 1964.

'Keynes's Finance Motive', *Oxford Economic Papers*, March 1965; reprinted in Japanese in *Reappraisal of Keynesian Economics*, edited by Toyo Keizai Shinpo Sha.

'The Social Value of Water Recreational Facilities Resulting from an Improvement in Water Quality in an Estuary: The Delaware – A Case Study' (with F.G. Adams and J.J. Seneca), in *Water Research*, edited by A.V. Kneese and S.C. Smith, Baltimore, Md., Johns Hopkins University Press, 1966.

'The Importance of the Demand for Finance', *Oxford Economic Papers*, July 1967.

'A Keynesian View of Patinkin's Theory of Employment', *Economic Journal*, September 1967; reprinted in *Disequilibrio, Infacion y Desempleo*, edited by Vicens-Vives, Madrid, 1978; reprinted in *The Keynesian Heritage*, edited by G.K. Shaw, Cheltenham, Glos: Edward Elgar, forthcoming.

'An Exploratory Study to Identify and Measure the Benefits Derived from the Scenic Enhancement of Federal-Aid Highways', *Highway Research Record*, no. 182, 1967.

'The Valuation of Public Goods', in *Social Sciences and the Environment*, edited by M.G. Garnsey and J. Hibbs, Boulder: University of Colorado Press, 1968; reprinted in *Economics of the Environment*, edited by R. Dorfman and N.S. Dorfman New York: W.W. Norton, 1972.

'Money, Portfolio Balance, Capital Accumulation, and Economic Growth', *Econometrica*, April 1968; reprinted in *Post Keynesian Theory of Growth and Distribution*, edited by C. Panico and N. Salvadori, Aldershot, Hants: Edward Elgar, 1993.

'The Demand and Supply of Securities and Economic Growth and Its Implications for the Kaldor–Pasinetti vs. Samuelson–Modigliani Controversy', *American Economic Review*, May 1968; reprinted in *Post Keynesian Theory of Growth and Distribution*, edited by C. Panico and N. Salvadori, Aldershot, Hants: Edward Elgar, 1993.

'An Analysis of Recreation Use of TVA Lakes' (with J.J. Seneca and F.G. Adams), *Land Economics*, November 1968.

'The Role of Monetary Policy in Overall Economic Policy', *Compendium on Monetary Policy Guidelines and Federal Structure*, US Congress, December 1968.

'A Keynesian View of Patinkin's Theory of Employment: Comment', *Economic Journal*, March 1969.

'A Keynesian View of the Relationship Between Accumulation, Money and the Money Wage Rate', *Economic Journal*, June 1969.

'The Economic Benefits Accruing from the Scenic Enhancement of Highways' (with J. Tomer and A. Waldman), *Highway Research Record*, no. 285,1969.

'The Depletion Allowance Revisited', *Natural Resources Journal*, January 1970; reprinted in *Towards a National Petroleum Policy*, edited by A. Utton, Albuquerque, NM: University of New Mexico Press, 1970.

'Discussion Paper' in *Money in Britain 1959–69*, edited by D.R. Croome and H.G. Johnson, Oxford: Oxford University Press, 1970.

'Money and the Real World', *The Economic Journal*, March 1972.

'A Keynesian View of Friedman's Theoretical Framework for Monetary Analysis', *Journal of Political Economy*, September/October 1972.

'Income Distribution, Inequality, and the Double Bluff', *The Annals*, September 1973; reprinted in *Mercurio*, April 1974.

'Money as Cause and Effect' (with S. Weintraub), *The Economic Journal*, December 1973; reprinted in *Keynes, Keynesians and Monetarists*, edited by S. Weintraub, Philadelphia, University of Pennsylvania Press, 1978; reprinted in *The Money Supply in the Economic Process*, edited by M. Musella and C. Panico, Aldershot, Hants: Edward Elgar, 1995.

'Market Disequilibrium Adjustments: Marshall Revisited', *Economic Inquiry*, June 1974.

'Oil: Its Time Allocation and Project Independence' (with L.H. Falk and H. Lee), *Brookings Papers on Economic Activity*, 1974:2.

'The Relations of Economic Rent and Price Incentives to Oil and Gas Supplies' (with L.H. Falk and H. Lee), in *Studies in Energy Tax Policy*, edited by G.M. Brannon, Cambridge, Mass.: Ballinger Publishing, 1975.

'Disequilibrium Market Adjustment: A Rejoinder', *Economic Inquiry*, April 1977.

'Post-Keynesian Monetary Theory and Inflation' in *Modern Economic Thought*, edited by S. Weintraub, Philadelphia: University of Pennsylvania Press, 1977.

'The Case for Divestiture', *Chemical Engineering Process 73*, 1977.

'A Discussion of Leijonhufvud's Social Consequences of Inflation' in *Microfoundations of Macroeconomics*, edited by G. Harcourt, Cambridge: Cambridge University Press, 1977.

'Divestiture and the Economics of Energy Supplies' in *R & D in Energy: Implications of Petroleum Industry Reorganization*, edited by D.J. Teece, Stanford, Calif.: Institute for Energy Studies, 1977.

'The Carter Energy Proposal', *Challenge*, September/October 1977.

'Money and General Equilibrium', *Economie Appliquée*, 4–77, 1977.

'Why Money Matters: Some Lessons of the Past Half Century of Monetary Theory', *Journal of Post Keynesian Economics*, **1**, Fall 1978; reprinted in *Keynes: La Macroeconomia de Desequilibrio*, edited by C.F. Obregon Diaz, Mexico City: Editorial Trillas, 1983.

'The United States Internal Revenue Service: The Fourteenth Member of OPEC?', *Journal of Post Keynesian Economics*, **1**, Winter 1979.

'Post Keynesian Approach to the Theory of Natural Resources', *Challenge*, March/April 1979; reprinted in *A Guide to Post-Keynesian Economics*, edited by A.S. Eichner, Armonk, NY: M.E. Sharpe, 1979.

'Monetary Policy, Regulation and International Adjustments' (with Marc A. Miles), *Économies et Sociétés*, no. 1, 1979.

'Is Monetary Collapse in the Eighties in the Cards?', *Nebraska Journal of Economics and Business*, **18**, Spring 1979.

'Oil Conservation: Theory vs. Policy', *Journal of Post Keynesian Economics*, **2**, Fall, 1979.

'What Is the Energy Crisis?', *Challenge*, July/August 1979.

'Keynes Paradigm: A Theoretical Framework for Monetary Analysis' (with J.A. Kregel), in *Growth, Property and Profits*, edited by E.J. Nell, Cambridge: Cambridge University Press, 1980.

'Money as a Factor of Production: A Reply', *Journal of Post Keynesian Economics*, **2**, Winter 1979–80.

'The Dual Faceted Nature of the Keynesian Revolution: The Role of Money and Money Wages in Determining Unemployment and Production Flow Prices', *Journal of Post Keynesian Economics*, **2**, Spring 1980.

'On Bronfenbrenner and Mainstream Views of the Essential Properties of Money: A Rejoinder', *Journal of Post Keynesian Economics*, **2**, Spring 1980.

'Keynes's Theory of Employment, Expectations and Indexing', *Revista de Economia Latinoamericana*, no. 57/58.

'Causality in Economics: A Review Article', *Journal of Post Keynesian Economics*, **2**, Summer 1980.

'Post Keynesian Economics: Solving the Crisis in Economic Theory', *Public Interest*, special issue 1980; reprinted in *The Crisis in Economic Theory*, edited by D. Bell and I. Kristol, New York: Basic Books, 1981.

'Is There a Shortage of Savings in the United States? The Role of Financial Institutions, Monetary and Fiscal Policy in Capital Accumulation During Periods of Stagflation' in *Special Study on Economic Change, Vol. 4 Stagflation: The Causes, Effects and Solutions*, Washington, DC: Joint Economic Committee, 1980.

'Can VAT Resolve the Shortage of Savings (SOS) Distress?', *Journal of Post Keynesian Economics*, **4**, Fall 1981.

'Alfred Marshall is Alive and Well in Post Keynesian Economics', *IHS Journal* (Journal of the Institute for Advanced Studies, Vienna), **5**, 1981.

'A Critical Analysis of the Monetarist–Rational Expectations Supply Side (Incentive) Economics Approach to Accumulation During a Period of Inflationary Expectations', *Kredit und Kapital*, 1981.

'Expectations and Economic Decision Making', *Compendium on Expectations in Economics*, Joint Economic Committee, US Congress, 1981.

'Post Keynesian Economics' in *Encyclopedia of Economics*, edited by D. Greenwald, New York: McGraw-Hill, 1982.

'Rational Expectations: A Fallacious Foundation for Studying Crucial Decision-Making Processes', *Journal of Post Keynesian Economics*, **5**, Winter 1982–83.

'Monetarism and Reagonomics', in *Reagonomics in the Stagflation Economy*, edited by S. Weintraub and M. Goodstein, Philadelphia: University of Pennsylvania Press, 1983.

'The Dubious Labor Market Analysis in Meltzer's Restatement of Keynes's Theory', *Journal of Economic Literature*, **21**, March 1983; reprinted in *John Maynard Keynes*, **1**, edited by M. Blaug, Aldershot, Hants: Edward Elgar, 1991.

'International Money and International Economic Development', *Proceedings of the Conference on Distribution, Effective Demand and Economic Development at Villa Manin, Italy, 1981*, London: Macmillan, 1983.

'The Marginal Product Curve Is Not The Demand Curve For Labor and Lucas' Labor Supply Function Is Not the Supply Curve for Labor', *Journal of Post Keynesian Economics*, **6**, Fall 1983.

'An Appraisal of Weintraub's Work', *Eastern Economic Journal*, **2**, 1983.

'Reviving Keynes's Revolution', *Journal of Post Keynesian Economics*, **6**, 1984; reprinted in *John Maynard Keynes*, **1**, edited by M. Blaug, Aldershot, Hants: Edward Elgar, 1991.

'Why Deficits Hardly Matter', *The New Leader*, August 1984.

'The Conventional Wisdom on Deficits Is Wrong', *Challenge*, November/December 1984.

'Incomes Policy as a Social Institution', in *Macroeconomic Conflict and Social Institutions*, edited by S. Maital and I. Lipnowski, Cambridge, Mass.: Ballinger Publishing, 1985.

'Policies For Prices And Incomes', *Keynes Today: Theories and Politics*, edited by A. Barrere, Paris: Economica, 1985; reprinted in *Money, Credit and Prices in a Keynesian Perspective*, edited by A. Barrere, London: Macmillan, 1988.

'Financial Markets and Williamson's Theory of Governance: Efficiency vs. Concentration vs. Power' (with Greg S. Davidson), *Quarterly Review of Economics and Business*, 1984.

'Liquidity and Not Increasing Returns Is The Ultimate Source of Unemployment Equilibrium', *Journal of Post Keynesian Economics*, **7**, 1985.

'Can Effective Demand and the Movement Towards Income Equality Be Maintained in the Face of Robotics?', *Journal of Post Keynesian Economics*, **7**, 1985.

'Sidney Weintraub – An Economist of the Real World', *Journal of Post Keynesian Economics*, **7**, 1985.

'Can We Afford To Balance The Budget?', *The New Leader*, January 1986.

'A Post Keynesian View of Theories and Causes of High Real Interest Rates', *Thames Papers in Political Economy*, Spring 1986: reprinted in *Post Keynesian Monetary Economics: New Approaches to Financial Modelling*, edited by P. Arestis, Aldershot, Hants: Edward Elgar, 1988.

'Finance, Funding, Savings, and Investment', *Journal of Post Keynesian Economics*, **9**, Fall 1986.

'The Simple Macroeconomics of a Nonergodic Monetary Economy vs. A Share Economy: Is Weitzman's Macroeconomics Too Simple?', *Journal of Post Keynesian Economics*, **9**, Winter 1986–87.

'Aggregate Supply' in *The New Palgrave: A Dictionary of Economic Theory and Doctrine*, edited by J. Eatwell, M. Milgate and P. Newman, London: Macmillan, 1987.

'User Cost' in *The New Palgrave: A Dictionary of Economic Theory and Doctrine*, edited by J. Eatwell, M. Milgate and P. Newman London: Macmillan, 1987.

'Financial Markets, Investment, and Employment' in *Barriers to Full Employment*, edited by E. Matzner, J.A. Kregel, and S. Roncoglia, London: Macmillan, 1988; also German language edition *Arbeit Für Alle Ist Möglich*, Berlin: Edition Sigma, 1987.

'Sensible Expectations and the Long-Run Non-Neutrality of Money', *Journal of Post Keynesian Economics*, **10**, Fall 1987.

'Whose Debt Crisis is it Anyway?', *New Leader*, August 1987.

'A Modest Set of Proposals for Remedying The International Debt Problem', *Journal of Post Keynesian Economics*, **10**, Winter 1987–88; reprinted in *Research in International Business and Finance: The Modern International Environment*, edited by H. P. Gray, Connecticut: JAI Press, 1989; reprinted in *Ensayos de Economia*, **1**, 1990 (Columbia).

'Weitzman's Share Economy And The Aggregate Supply Function' in *Keynes and Public Policy After Fifty Years*, edited by O.E. Hamouda and J.N. Smithin, Aldershot, Hants: Edward Elgar, 1988.

'Endogenous Money, The Production Process, And Inflation Analysis', *Économie Apliquée*, **XLI**, no.1, 1988; reprinted in *The Money Supply in the Economic Process: A Post Keynesian Perspective*, edited by Marco Musella and Carlo Panico, Cheltenham, Glos: Edward Elgar, 1995.

'A Technical Definition of Uncertainty and the Long Run Non-Neutrality of Money', *Cambridge Journal of Economics*, September 1988.

'Achieving a Civilized Society', *Challenge*, September/October 1989; reprinted in *Economics 90/91*, edited by D. Cole, Guilford, Conn.: Dushkin Publishing, 1990.

'Keynes and Money' in *Keynes, Money, and Monetarism*, edited by R. Hill, London: Macmillan, 1989.

'Prices and Income Policy: An Essay in Honor of Sidney Weintraub', in *Money, Credit, and Prices in Keynesian Perspective*, edited by A. Barrere, London: Macmillan, 1989.

'Patinkin's Interpretation of Keynes and the Keynesian Cross', *History of Political Economy*, **21**, 1989; reprinted in *John Maynard Keynes (1883–1946)*, Volume 2, edited by Mark Blaug, Aldershot, Hants: Edward Elgar, 1991.

'Only in America: Neither The Homeless Nor The Yachtless Are Economic Problems', *Journal of Post Keynesian Economics*, **12**, Fall 1989.

'The Economics of Ignorance Or Ignorance of Economics?', *Critical Review*, **3**, nos 3 & 4, Summer/Fall 1989.

'Shackle and Keynes vs. Rational Expectations Theory on the Role of Time, Liquidity, and Financial Markets' in *Unknowledge and Choice in Economics*, edited by S. Frowen, London: Macmillan, 1990.

'Liquidity Proposals for a New Bretton Woods Plan' in *Keynesian Economic Policies*, edited by A. Barrere, London: Macmillan, 1990).

'On Thirlwall's Law', *Revista de Economia Politica*, **10**, October–December 1990.

'Is Probability Theory Relevant For Choice Under Uncertainty?: A Post Keynesian Perspective', *Journal of Economic Perspectives*, **5**, Winter 1991.

'A Post Keynesian Positive Contribution To "Theory"', *Journal of Post Keynesian Economics*, **13**, Winter 1990–91.

'What Kind of International Payments System Would Keynes Have Recommended for the Twenty-First Century?' in *Economic Problems of the 1990s: Europe, the Developing Countries and the United States*, edited by P. Davidson and J. A. Kregel, Aldershot, Hants: Edward Elgar, 1991.

'Money: Cause or Effect? Exogenous or Endogenous?', *Nicholas Kaldor and Mainstream Economics*, edited by E.J. Nell and W. Semmler, London: Macmillan, 1992.

'How To Avoid Another Great Depression?, *The New Leader*, 10–24 February 1992.

'Eichner's Approach to Money and Macroeconomics' in *The Megacorp and Macrodynamics*, edited by W. Milberg, Armonk, NY: M.E. Sharpe, 1992.

'Reforming The World's Money', *Journal of Post Keynesian Economics*, Winter 1992–93.

'Its Still The Economy Mr. President', *The New Leader*, 11 January 1993.

'Clinton's Economic Plan – Putting Caution First', *The Nation*, 1 March 1993.

'The Elephant and the Butterfly; or Hysteresis and Post Keynesian Economics', *Journal of Post Keynesian Economics*, 1993.

'Would Keynes Be a New Keynesian?', *Eastern Economic Journal*, October 1992.

'Asset Deflation and Financial Fragility' in *Money and Banking – Issues For The Twenty-First Century*, edited by P. Arestis, London: Macmillan, 1993.

'Post Keynesian Economics' in *The McGraw-Hill Encyclopedia of Economics*, edited by D. Greenwald, New York: McGraw-Hill, 1993.

'Monetary Theory and Policy In A Global Context With A Large International Debt' in *Monetary Theory and Monetary Policy: New Tracks For The 1990s*, edited by S.F. Frowen, London: Macmillan, 1993.

'Austrians and Post Keynesianson Economic Reality: A Response to the Critics', *Critical Review*, 7, 1993.

'Tampering With The American Dream', *The New Leader*, 11–25 April, 1994.

'Do Informational Frictions Justify Federal Credit Programs?: A Discussion of S.D. Williamson's Paper', *Journal of Money, Credit, and Banking*, 1994.

'The Asimakopulos View of Keynes's General Theory' in *Investment and Employment in Theory and Practice*, edited by G.C. Harcourt and A. Roncoglia, London: Macmillan, 1994.

'Uncertainty in Economics' in *Keynes, Knowledge and Uncertainty*, edited by Sheila Dow and John Hillard, Cheltenham, Glos: Edward Elgar, 1995.

Index